2

VICTORIAN INTERPRETATION

VICTORIAN INTERPRETATION

SUZY ANGER

CORNELL UNIVERSITY PRESS
ITHACA AND LONDON

First published 2005 by Cornell University Press

Printed in the United States of America

Library of Congress Cataloging-in-Publication Data

Anger, Suzy.
    Victorian interpretation / Suzy Anger.
        p. cm.
    Includes bibliographical references and index.
    ISBN-13: 978-0-8014-4201-8 (cloth : alk. paper)
    ISBN-10: 0-8014-4201-X (cloth : alk. paper)
        1. Interpretation (Philosophy)—History—19th century.   2. Hermeneutics—
History—19th century.   3. English literature—19th century—History and criticism.
4. Philosophy, English—19th century.   5. Great Britain—Intellectual life—19th
century.   I. Title.
B824.17.A54 2005
121'.686'094209034—dc22   2005025035

Cornell University Press strives to use environmentally responsible suppliers
and materials to the fullest extent possible in the publishing of its books.
Such materials include vegetable-based, low-VOC inks and acid-free papers
that are recycled, totally chlorine-free, or partly composed of nonwood fibers.
For further information, visit our website at www.cornellpress.cornell.edu.

Cloth printing   10 9 8 7 6 5 4 3 2 1

For Tom

If there's no meaning in it, that saves a world of trouble, you know, as we needn't try to find any.

—Lewis Carroll

Contents

Acknowledgments

This project was supported in its early stages by a fellowship at the University of Washington. I am also grateful to the American Council of Learned Societies for a fellowship grant, to the University of Maryland for a faculty research fellowship, and to the National Endowment for the Humanities for a Summer Stipend.

An earlier version of Chapter 2 was published in *Texas Studies in Literature and Language* 40.1 (March 1998): 78–96. A version of Intertext 3 appeared as "Literary Meaning and the Question of Value: Victorian Literary Interpretation" in *Pedagogy* 4.1 (2004): 27–41. Excerpts from Chapter 3 were published in "George Eliot and Philosophy" in *The Cambridge Companion to George Eliot*, ed. George Levine (Cambridge: Cambridge University Press, 2001): 76–97. (Reprinted by permission.)

Many have contributed to this book. I am indebted to George Levine, John McGowan, and Carolyn Williams, whose advice and encouragement have been invaluable. I owe much to Gary Handwerk, who encouraged my initial efforts from which this book developed. I also thank Charles Altieri, Kathleen Blake, and Richard Dunn, as well as the late Ernst Behler, whose seminar on hermeneutics helped shape my early thinking on this project. This book has benefited from the help of many other colleagues and friends in a variety of ways, and I would particularly like to thank Becca Bennett, Terri Hasseler, Jennifer Holberg, Gerhard Joseph, Jonathan Loesberg, and Andrew Miller. I am also grateful to Bernhard Kendler at Cornell University Press for his support of this project. Finally, my deepest thanks go to Elizabeth and David Anger, for their unflagging support, and, most of all, to Tom Bittner, for many discussions, and for his incisive thought and generous encouragement.

S.A.

2

VICTORIAN INTERPRETATION

An Overview

It is one of the characteristics of recent thought that it distrusts its own activity," wrote Henry Jones, a professor of philosophy at University College, in 1891. "Thought," he continued, "has become aware of its own activity; men realize more clearly than they did in former times that the apparent constitution of things depends directly on the character of the intelligence which apprehends them."[1] We might almost take his words to be a description of current intellectual and cultural discourse rather than an account of Victorian thought. In contemporary debate, self-reflexivity about the processes of understanding is pervasive: knowledge is historically and culturally situated, facts are theory dependent, subjectivity is involved in all representation; in short, interpretation is always at work. What is not so often noticed is that the Victorians were equally concerned with the general character of human knowledge and understanding. They were, after all, post-Kantians, and many of those who considered such questions believed that knowledge was not an unmediated perception of things, but rather that the mind partly constitutes what we know. It is commonly acknowledged that the Victorian period saw the rise of historical consciousness. Knowledge, it might be said, became aware of its historical and cultural constitution. An important consequence of the recognition of the influence of the knower on the known was a growing concern with the processes and role of interpretation in every discipline. As Jones put it, the philosopher, the scientist, the poet—"All alike endeavor to interpret experience" (35).

This study examines the importance of the concept of interpretation in Victorian culture and traces the emergence of a general hermeneutics in Britain. It argues that hermeneutics, or the theory of interpretation, is far more central to Victorian thought than has been recognized, and that Victorian speculation on interpretation has important resonance in contemporary debate, where its presence has been misperceived or altogether missed. The Victorians, as this book will demonstrate, contributed significantly to the development of a secular hermeneutic tradition.

Historical overviews of hermeneutics have focused on Germany, where the major systematic accounts of a universal linguistic hermeneutics were produced in the early nineteenth century, and an established hermeneutic tradition followed. That focus is not surprising, since hermeneutics underwent significant changes at the start of the nineteenth century when German Romantic hermeneutics shifted the study of interpretation from the attempt to establish specific interpretive rules for particular disciplines to a general concern with textual interpretation and understanding. This study seeks to show that an equally strong concern with interpretation—although less systematic than that which manifested itself in German nineteenth-century hermeneutics—emerged in Victorian England. The interest arose in part through the influence of German thought, but largely because cultural and historical factors similar to those that led to the development of a general hermeneutics in Germany were also present in Britain.

This book does not so much offer a history of influence as a parallel story of a preoccupation with interpretation that takes its own particular form in Victorian England. My argument is built on a study of Victorian speculation on interpretation and meaning, its connection to broader ethical, epistemological, and linguistic questions, and the ways in which that speculation is embodied in Victorian literary texts. While there have been studies of the intersections between Victorian scriptural exegesis and literary texts, there has until now been no sustained account of the pervasive concern with interpretation in the period, nor has there been an attempt to represent Victorian views on interpretation in the context of current hermeneutic controversies.

This book offers such a representation. My initial task is to consider how hermeneutics entered Victorian debates on religion and secularism. As a consequence of the weakening of religious authority, scriptural hermeneutics attempted to establish new grounds of authority and new principles of interpretive constraint by revising traditional modes of exegesis. I will be following the development and transformation of hermeneutics from a religious to a secular (and particularly literary) context. The narrative I

construct is twofold. First I trace the transition from scriptural to secular
hermeneutics. With the spread of theories of biblical exegesis that
regarded the Bible as a historical document, scriptural interpretation
moved out from the church to become more humanistic, and the boundaries between biblical and other texts began to dissolve. Another transformation was to come at the end of the century with what I mark as the
reinstitutionalizing of textual hermeneutics, but in a secularized form that
we can now recognize as the study of literature. Second, I trace a concur-
rent movement away from a hermeneutics based on the belief that a text
has a determinate meaning guaranteed in authoritative interpretations to a
hermeneutics that had to construct new principles of interpretation and
new grounds of authority for itself.

The development of hermeneutics in the Victorian age reveals much
about current interpretive practices. Although the turn to secular
hermeneutics initiates a movement toward our contemporary views on
interpretation, the Victorian achievement was distinctive. The recent
critical tendency to regard Victorian speculation on interpretation as
largely a precursor of postmodern hermeneutics is insufficient. A fuller
understanding of the Victorians instead requires attention to the shaping forces of their particular historical circumstances and traditions.
Such a reading not only changes our understanding of Victorian perspectives but may also encourage us to rethink aspects of contemporary
interpretive theory.

In explicating these views, I focus on the ways Victorian writers such as
John Henry Newman, Thomas Carlyle, George Eliot, and Oscar Wilde
comment on and deploy hermeneutics in their work. We better understand these writers if we recognize that their writing is preoccupied with
hermeneutics. Their narratives test the theoretical statements that they
have made in essays and reviews, and the trajectory of these works allows
me both to trace the transition from the religious to the secular and to
demonstrate the complexities of the Victorian hermeneutic project as it
engages large epistemological, ontological, and ethical issues. Each of the
four chapters in the book marks a stage in the narrative I am describing.
In three shorter "intertexts," I consider legal, scientific, and literary interpretation in the period; these brief chapters demonstrate the pervasiveness of the hermeneutic mode throughout Victorian culture.

Although the dominant focus is the interpretation of texts, the book also
emphasizes the ways in which hermeneutics became central to a wide range
of intellectual activities. The concept of interpretation was crucial not only
to Victorian theologians and literary critics, but it also came to play an
important role in disciplines such as history and anthropology. An epilogue

extends my discussion into the new discipline of psychology. That section, along with the intertext on the natural sciences, demonstrates that even in areas where the presumption has long been that objective method and a strong empiricism reigned, some investigators conceived of their methods in ways that borrowed from textual hermeneutics. It is from this broad concern with interpretation in the nineteenth century that the widespread twentieth-century preoccupation with interpretation in all areas of intellectual activity develops.

The examination of biblical hermeneutics with which this study begins sets up one of the chief arguments of the book: that secular interpretation in both the Victorian age and today is far more indebted to the strategies and conceptual models of sacred hermeneutics than has been acknowledged. Literary criticism in particular continues to reveal its roots in the biblical exegesis from which the concern with linguistic interpretation originally grew in modern European culture. Methods developed for biblical exegesis have left their mark on *all* current theoretical approaches to literature.

Victorian controversies over scriptural exegesis also serve to introduce the conflict between two broad theories of textual interpretation. The first holds that meaning is found in the past, either in the original meaning of the text itself or in the intentions of the author. The second maintains that meaning is always found in the present; it changes in history. All of the theories considered in this study are variants of these two views. In nineteenth-century scriptural hermeneutics, diachronic modes of interpretation began to supplant synchronic methods such as typology, as history and science began to challenge the Church's authoritative interpretations. The notion that interpretations would inevitably alter over time raised concerns about the subjective nature of meaning, concerns that became prominent in later considerations of literary interpretation.

It is often assumed that a conscious interest in the theory of literary interpretation is a twentieth-century phenomenon. Critics in earlier periods did not reflect on the problems of interpretation; they simply took meaning for granted and pushed on straightaway to make evaluative or ethical judgments on a text's literary merits or content. Discussing eighteenth- and nineteenth-century British criticism, for instance, K. M. Newton writes: "No distinction would have been made between reading and understanding and interpretation. . . . A major difference, then, between modern literary criticism and literary criticism of earlier eras is that in most criticism of the past interpreting the text is not seen as being different from reading and understanding it."[2] While it is certainly true that a great deal of literary criticism written in the eighteenth and nineteenth centuries concerns itself with evaluative questions, many Victorian writers, as this study will demonstrate, were increasingly aware of the problems of interpretation. While recent theory has seen itself as largely indebted to developments in German thought, it has overlooked the ways in which the Victorians—often working within the British empirical tradition, though often themselves influenced by German thought—have contributed to and shaped the current discussion. James Engell, commenting on Carlyle, Arnold, and Ruskin, makes a claim similar to Newton's: "The hermeneutical inquiries of Schleiermacher, Dilthey, and others failed to alter the mainstream of English criticism."[3] This book shows the opposite to be true; not only did German hermeneutics influence Victorian criticism, but the Victorians themselves provided their own significant contributions to interpretive theory and practice, and it is these that often directly influenced subsequent Anglo-American criticism.

An explanation is in order about how I use the word *hermeneutics* in this book, as it reflects a number of the ways it is used in current discourse. In general terms, hermeneutics refers to the theory of textual interpretation that emerges from the work of Schleiermacher and the Romantics. I also use it to designate something closer to what is currently known as philosophical hermeneutics, the idea that human experience is fundamentally interpretive. I often refer to any theory of interpretation in literary studies as a hermeneutic theory—whether it be the New Criticism, the intentionalist theory of E. D. Hirsch, or Derridean theory. The latter use means that I sometimes apply the term to schools of theory that have expressly designated themselves as antihermeneutic. My contention, as I've said, is that all theories of interpretation (literary and cultural) are deeply indebted to the strategies devised for sacred hermeneutics.

I

Examining Victorian thought on interpretation in relation to the more systematic approaches presented in nineteenth-century German hermeneutics helps foreground the methodological aspects of Victorian hermeneutical inquiry. As background to this book's investigation of Victorian hermeneutics, then, a very brief history of the hermeneutic tradition is necessary; further details about specific theorists will emerge in subsequent chapters.[4] The following overview focuses primarily on Schleiermacher's contributions to hermeneutics, given that intentionalist theories of meaning comparable to his were frequently advanced in nineteenth-century British thought.

In a general way, as I've suggested above, hermeneutics can be seen as a radicalization of Immanuel Kant's transcendental idealism. Kant's *Critique of Pure Reason* (1781) led to a broad interest in the operations of the mind and its processes of understanding. If, as Kant asserted, we know things only through the categories we bring to bear, then all knowledge might be understood as a form of interpretation. (This, of course, was not Kant's view; but later thinkers pushed his philosophy in that direction.) Textual interpretation was obviously a concern in earlier eras as well. Pre-nineteenth-century discourse on interpretation, however, tended towards the philological, and aimed to provide rules for interpretation in particular disciplines such as law, theology, and classics. One of its assumptions was that those principles were needed only in the case of obscure passages whose meaning was not immediately apparent. Some Enlightenment works on hermeneutics, notably the writings of Johann Martin Chladenius and Christian Wolff, moved toward a broader conception of hermeneutics in their presentations of general theories of interpretation. The Enlightenment theorist Georg Friedrich Meier was concerned with the theory of signs, in ways that would later find resonance in Carlyle's writing, as the ideas came through Novalis and Johann Gottlieb Fichte. For Enlightenment theorists, however, correct interpretation was not yet the general problem that it would become for Romantic theorists; reason provided strategies for perfect understanding of any part of a text that caused hermeneutic difficulties.

The turning point in the development of hermeneutics came with Romantic hermeneutics and particularly with Friedrich Schleiermacher's theories.[5] With Schleiermacher and the Romantics, hermeneutics became a theory of human understanding. It was no longer a term used for philology's attempts to explain obscure passages in a text. Schleiermacher's contribution was to regard understanding as always at work and always in question. Hermeneutics broadened to a general theory of interpretation concerned with all forms of linguistic understanding, including conversation. Even more significantly it turned toward an interest in the processes of interpretation themselves.

As a theologian Schleiermacher's recognition of the problems involved in textual understanding originally grew from biblical exegesis. Schleiermacher regards meaning as fixed in an author's intentions (both conscious and unconscious). The goal of interpretation is to overcome differences (often historical) between the text and the reader so as to understand the true meaning of the text. But for Schleiermacher that goal is never fully attainable: "The task of hermeneutics is endless."[6] Only an approximation to meaning is possible.

Although he believes that meaning is ultimately found in the author's intentions, convention also plays a significant role. While Schleiermacher emphasizes the reader's sympathetic understanding of the author, or what he calls "divination," interpretation involves more than understanding the author's consciousness. Language is a shared system, and as such limits the possibilities of meaning.[7] Understanding therefore involves two types of interpretation, which Schleiermacher calls the grammatical and the psychological or technical. Grammatical interpretation concerns the workings of the linguistic system (the conventional aspects of meaning); psychological interpretation attempts to grasp the author's individual use of language (the subjective aspects of meaning). Any utterance must be understood as the coalescence of these two aspects. While Schleiermacher aims to establish methods for interpretation, he also suggests (a claim that recurs in much hermeneutic discourse) that correct interpretation requires something like sensitivity or intuition, that is, something that is apparently beyond method.[8]

Schleiermacher did not put his lectures on hermeneutics into a completed form. His lectures were first published in 1838 from student notes, with his own handwritten lecture outlines remaining unpublished until the twentieth century. His ideas greatly influenced his students, including the future classicist August Boeckh, who extended Schleiermacher's ideas to philology and the study of human culture. A student of Boeckh's, the historian Johann Droysen, brought the methods of philological hermeneutics to the study of history. All of these theorists articulated the concept that came to be known as the hermeneutic circle, according to which the parts can be understood only in terms of the whole, and the whole only in terms of the parts. Wilhelm Dilthey, also a student of Boeckh's, was a transitional figure between Romantic linguistic hermeneutics and twentieth-century philosophical hermeneutics. His work marked the next important turning point in hermeneutics, in its move away from textual interpretation to an interest in the human (social) sciences, which, he argued, depended on interpretive knowledge. Hermeneutics now concerned itself with the interpretation of all phenomena, linguistic and otherwise, in what Dilthey referred to as "life-expressions."

If nineteenth-century hermeneutics was primarily methodological, twentieth-century hermeneutics moved away from epistemology to questions of ontology, most importantly in the work of Martin Heidegger. For Heidegger (who first studied theology), hermeneutics became centrally philosophical, concerned with the understanding of human existence, itself regarded as fundamentally interpretive. Heidegger emphasized the necessity of forestructure in interpretation, that is, a version of the view that understanding is governed by the hermeneutic circle. In *Truth and Method* Hans-Georg Gadamer (a student of Heidegger's) developed philosophical hermeneutics in the context of the human sciences and subsequently became the most influential figure in contemporary hermeneutic thought. "The understanding and the interpretation of texts," writes Gadamer, "obviously belongs to human experience of the world in general."[9] For Gadamer, interpretation is always a historical process and always linguistic. Meaning necessarily occurs in the present, as it is impossible to transcend one's historical horizon. Gadamer seeks to rehabilitate the notion of "prejudice," attacked in the Enlightenment (and in much nineteenth-century interpretive discourse as well). Prejudice or tradition, he contends, is what allows any understanding. Other contemporary thinkers in the hermeneutic tradition developed their own conceptions of hermeneutics, often in reaction to Gadamer's views. Emilio Betti, for instance, sought to rehabilitate an intentionalist and objectivist hermeneutics, while Jürgen Habermas introduced psychology and ideology critique into the debate. The lineage of these hermeneutic theorists, one a student of another, indicates the interconnections in the thought that has been regarded as making up the hermeneutic tradition. Hermeneutics sees itself in light of the tradition it both continues and transforms.

II

Extensive debates over the theory of interpretation were, of course, carried on in twentieth-century Anglo-American literary criticism among writers and schools of theory not directly tied to the hermeneutic tradition I've outlined above. Although that theory is not part of the hermeneutic tradition per se, it is equally involved in hermeneutic debate, and its main positions are sometimes very close to those we have already seen engaged inside the tradition. A brief summary of the positions on interpretation in these familiar debates in literary criticism will underscore the ways in which more recent criticism has carried on nineteenth-century controversies.

In the second half of the twentieth century, criticism largely abandoned the pursuit of authorial meaning. With the development of poststructuralist theories, the primary interests of criticism became the subjectivity of the interpreter and the indeterminacies of language. Jacques Derrida's argument that a text always "breaches, divides, expropriates the 'ideal' plenitude or self-presence of intention, of meaning, and, *a fortiori,* of all adequation between meaning and saying" profoundly influenced Anglo-American literary theory.[10] Meaning, without transcendental signifiers to ground it, is always sliding and undecidable. Earlier, the New Criticism, most influentially in the work of I. A. Richards and later Cleanth Brooks and W. K. Wimsatt, tried to shift critical focus from the historical/biographical emphases of the previously dominant literary history to the formal structures and language of the texts themselves. New Critics sought to dismiss the author, although they (for the most part) argued that meaning is objective and determinable. Wimsatt and Beardsley in their much-discussed essay "The Intentional Fallacy" (1946) famously asserted that authorial intention is neither "accessible or desirable."[11] In rejoinder, E. D. Hirsch claimed in *Validity in Interpretation* (1967) that if meaning is to be determinate, then it must be grounded in the author's intentions: "To banish the original author as the determiner of meaning was to reject the only compelling normative principle that could lend validity to an interpretation."[12] Semantic meaning alone, Hirsch argues, is not sufficient to determine meaning, since words can plainly mean many different things. Textual meaning is objective and unchanging, but can only be recognized as such in relation to the author's intentions.

Most late-twentieth-century criticism rejects Hirsch's contentions, and, further, explicitly defines itself as antihermeneutic. Jacques Derrida and Michel Foucault denounce the hermeneutic project, which they regard as intentionalist and founded upon the pursuit of the true and secret meaning of the text. Derrida has criticized even Gadamer's non-objectivist hermeneutics, arguing that it retains vestiges of metaphysical ideas such as intention and totality. But poststructuralist theory's desire to distinguish itself from hermeneutics cannot disguise that it is a clearly hermeneutic project. Although poststructuralism sees itself as disrupting prior views on meaning, the difference is only one of emphasis. Poststructuralist critics focus more emphatically on the features of language that complicate interpretation and believe those problems cause even greater difficulties for understanding than some earlier theorists thought, but poststructuralist ideas are central to earlier hermeneutic speculation as well.

Roland Barthes, Foucault, and Derrida contend that their theories of interpretation refuse the postulates of theological interpretation, which, they correctly insist, orthodox theories of hermeneutics have retained. Barthes in his essay "The Death of the Author" (1968) rejected the model of sacred hermeneutics that seeks original meaning, in favor of a structuralist account on which language rather than the author speaks: "We know now that a text is not a line of words releasing a single 'theological' meaning (the 'message' of the Author-God), but a multi-dimensional space in which a variety of writings, none of them original, blend and clash. The text is a tissue of quotations drawn from innumerable centres of culture."[13] If one renounces the theological scheme that grounds meaning in intention, Barthes argues, one refuses "to assign a 'secret,' an ultimate meaning, to the text (and to the world as text)" (147).

Foucault, likewise, regards traditional hermeneutics as still mired in a conception of interpretation that turns "through the whole apparatus of Revelation, to the Word of God, ever secret, ever beyond itself."[14] Derrida also charges that hermeneutics is moored in a "metaphysics of presence," resting on the belief that "the intelligible face of the sign remains turned toward the word and the face of God."[15] Hermeneutics, according to these theorists, depends on the promise of an absolute and determinate intentionalist meaning. While they are right to see the secular theory of interpretation as intimately related to the biblical hermeneutics from which it has developed, they are wrong to see their theories as radically disconnected from theological modes of exegesis, as this book will demonstrate.

Deconstruction, as well as other poststructuralist theory, has instead understood itself as continuing in the tradition of interpretation instituted by Friedrich Nietzsche. Nietzsche shows us that there is no "hidden secret" in a text, such as standard hermeneutics searches for. Derrida says of Nietzsche's thought that "the hermeneutic project which postulates a true sense of the text is disqualified under this regime."[16] Hermeneutics, conversely, remains "content with doubling the text" (*Grammatology,* 158). Nietzsche's insights result in a new conception of interpretation, which Derrida describes as "Nietzschean *affirmation*—the joyous affirmation of the freeplay of the world and without truth, without origin, offered to an active interpretation."[17]

There is no question that Nietzsche insists on the interpretive nature of existence. We must, he writes, give up the idea of "an eye turned in no particular direction, in which the active and interpreting forces, through which alone seeing becomes seeing *something,* are supposed to be lacking."[18] In a well-known statement of his perspectivist epistemology, he draws attention to the hermeneutic dimensions of human life: "How far the perspective character of existence extends or indeed whether existence has any other character than this; whether existence without interpretation, without 'sense,' does not become 'nonsense'; whether, on the other hand, all existence is not essentially actively engaged in *interpretation*—that cannot be decided even by the most industrious and most scrupulously conscientious analysis and self-examination of the intellect; for in the course of this analysis the human intellect cannot avoid seeing itself in its own perspectives, and *only* in these."[19] He contends that we cannot know mind-independent truths or transcend human perspectives to discover which interpretations correspond to the way things really are (if such exists).

Nietzsche's thoughts on interpretation, however, fit squarely into the nineteenth-century development of hermeneutics. Given that Nietzsche began his career as a philologist, it ought not to be surprising that he maintains that there is an "art of reading rightly, which is called philology."[20] Throughout his texts he comments on the necessity of standards in interpretation: "The restoration and keeping pure of texts, besides their explanation, carried on in common for hundreds of years, has finally enabled the right methods to be found; the whole of the Middle Ages was absolutely incapable of a strictly philological explanation, that is, of the simple desire to comprehend what an author says—it *was* an achievement, finding these methods, let it not be undervalued!" (*Human*, 270). Not only does he repeatedly denounce interpretations that he identifies as distorting a text, but like others in the Victorian tradition this book examines, he extends his comments on "bad" textual interpretation to the understanding of the world: "A great deal of understanding is required to apply to Nature the same method of strict interpretation as the philologists have now established for all books with the intention of clearly understanding what the text means, but not suspecting a *double* sense or even taking it for granted. Just, however, as with regard to books, the bad art of interpretation is by no means overcome . . . so it is also with regard to Nature" (*Human*, 8).

Revising the old notion of nature as a book of God, he conceives of the world as a text. Far from regarding interpretation as unconstrained, he condemns arbitrary readings: "He who has interpreted a passage in an author 'more profoundly' than was intended, has not interpreted the author but has obscured him. Our metaphysicians are in the same relation, or even in worse relation, to the text of Nature. For, to apply their profound interpretations, they often alter the text to suit their purpose—or, in other words, corrupt the text."[21] Nietzsche argues, in other words, that good interpretation involves diminishing the imposition of one's own interests on the text. The vocabulary and the ideas are familiar from nineteenth-century controversies in biblical exegesis. Even a text as late as *The Anti-Christ* stresses the necessity of interpretation that tries to get things right, both in the case of written documents and in the case of phenomena not conventionally considered textual: "What is here meant by philology is, in a very broad sense, the art of reading well—of reading facts without falsifying them by interpretation, without losing caution, patience, delicacy, in the desire to understand. Philology as *ephexis* in interpretation."[22]

Nietzsche stands as a central representative of the widespread nineteenth-century preoccupation with hermeneutics that this book examines.

III

Henry Sidgwick examined the pervasive turn to historical understanding in the late Victorian period, seen, for example, in the ways in which "evolution" took on a general explanatory power. "It is undeniable," he wrote, "that in every department of thought either the objects of our present thought or our thoughts about them, or both, are conceived by us as a present that had a past different from it."[23] Historicism posits that every phenomenon must be understood as a product of its own time; one must not apply present standards to the past. "Nothing man has projected from himself is really intelligible except at its own date, and from its proper point of view," said Pater, articulating the central premises of a historicist hermeneutics. "Every intellectual product must be judged from the point of view of the age and the people in which it was produced."[24]

If perspectivism and the cultural situatedness of understanding are accepted, however, then questions arise about how fixed meaning is possible. In Chapter 1, therefore, I examine the two general models of biblical exegesis dominant in Victorian exegesis, both of which acknowledged the cultural and historical determinants of interpretation in different ways. The first is Benjamin Jowett's model: a hermeneutics that sought to understand by attempting to transcend its own perspective and enter into that of the past in order to reconstruct the text's original meaning. The second is John Henry Newman's mode of exegesis, in which new meaning is found in the present and interpretation takes into account the history of the reception of a text. That the debates over scriptural hermeneutics were widespread is manifested by W. H. Mallock's parody of Victorian intellectual life, *The New Republic,* in which each of the characters offers his own view of historical interpretation. Mr. Jenkinson, reading from his manuscript on biblical interpretation, asserts that the books of Scripture must be "interpreted in their context": "To understand the meaning of any text, we must try to see what, from his position and education, the writer could have meant by it; not what this or that Father, living long afterwards, fancied that he meant."[25] Jenkinson (identified as Jowett by Mallock) pits his interpretive theory against one that resembles Newman's.

The Victorian interest in hermeneutics develops not solely from controversies over biblical exegesis but also from frequently related debates on language and classical philology. Classical studies in the Victorian period followed a path that parallels the debates in biblical interpretation in many ways. German scholarship entered into the study of classics at Cambridge early in the period when liberal Anglican scholars such as Julius Hare and Connop Thirlwall brought the methods of Schleiermacher and Barthold Georg Niebuhr to bear on the classics. As the period proceeded, criticism moved to reconsider the classics in the light of archeological discoveries and to situate the texts in their social, cultural, and historical contexts.[26] As in other areas of textual study, the belief that the present viewpoint is different from that of the past became dominant. Classicist Alexander Grant, although not imagining that this view of understanding caused problems for knowledge, follows Newman in believing that the present finds new meaning in a text: "Our age (whose gift it is to know the past) had to read Aristotle for itself anew. . . . We now look with different eyes upon antiquity. We bring to the remains of the ancient philosophers new ideas to guide us in our study."[27]

Philological inquiry was also essential to the development of hermeneutic thought in England. Interest in the workings and origins of language was widespread in the period, as the immense popularity of F. Max Mueller's lectures, and books such as Richard Chenevix Trench's *On the Study of Words* (1851) and John William Donaldson's *New Cratylus* (1839) indicate.[28] In the early Victorian period, defenders of transcendental conceptions of language opposed supporters of materialistic views: Was language natural and developed over time or of divine origin and revealed? William Whewell argued the latter in his *Indications of the Creator* (1845) in response to Robert Chambers's naturalization of language in *The Vestiges of the Natural History of Creation* (1844). As the naturalistic theories of language were accepted, historical philology, based on the idea that language develops over time, became dominant. The meaning of words, philology explained, is not fixed and immutable, but rather grows and changes in history.

Such a view obviously has consequences for the interpretation of texts from earlier periods, since words as used in the past might have different meanings in the present. But understanding the meanings and evolution of words was also regarded as a way of interpreting past societies and cultures. The work of the historian or the anthropologist, some suggested, was most successfully accomplished through the study of words. Trench, a theologian and professor of the "exegesis of the New Testament," wrote in his well-received study: "Language is the reflexion of the thoughts and beliefs of communities from their earliest days; by tracing its changes and its fortunes, by discovering the origin and history of words and their meanings, one can read those thoughts and beliefs with greater certainty and minuteness than had they been traced by the pen of the historian."[29]

Language, he and other students of philology maintained, allows us to understand the minds and the cultures of the past.[30] John Herschel also emphasized the hermeneutic dimensions of philological inquiry: "Words are to the anthropologist what rolled pebbles are to the Geologist— Battered relics of past ages often containing within them indelible records capable of intelligible interpretation."[31]

Max Mueller, the Oxford philologist—whose *Lectures on the Science of Language* at the Royal Institution in London in 1861 were attended by many literary figures, scientists, and other leading intellectuals of the day— took up questions of language's relation to reality. He insisted that there is no important connection between words and concepts, that—in other terms—the signifier is arbitrary. Nor did he believe that language merely names things that preexisted it: "There never was an independent array of determinate conceptions waiting to be matched with an independent array of articulate sounds."[32] Nor can words be conceived as merely a tool for expressing thought: "Language and thought," he argued, "are inseparable" (*Lectures*, 1:527). Mueller suggests, as Saussure would do later, that language does not transparently represent the world, but rather carves it up: "But you may say, cannot a concept exist without a word? Certainly no, though in order to meet every possible objection, we may say that no concept can exist without a sign, whether it be a word or anything else. And if it is asked, whether the concept exists first, and the sign comes afterwards, I should say No; the two are simultaneous; but in strict logic, the sign being the condition of the concept, may really be said to come first" (369). In this case, language can be understood as itself already a kind of interpretation.

Lewis Carroll's *Alice's Adventures in Wonderland* and *Through the Looking Glass* also consider questions about meaning and the relationship of signifier to signified. "Take care of the sense and the sounds will take care of themselves," the Duchess advises Alice.[33] But, of course, this is precisely the view that Mueller has dismissed and that Carroll here pushes to absurdity.[34] Carroll's play with language and logic is so sophisticated that current philosophers regard the books as touching on all the central topics in the philosophy of language, and Alice's famous exchange with Humpty Dumpty has resulted in a theory of meaning named for the latter:[35]

> "I don't know what you mean by 'glory,'" Alice said.
>
> Humpty Dumpty smiled contemptuously. "Of course you don't—till I tell you. I meant 'there's a nice knock-down argument for you!'"
>
> "But 'glory' doesn't mean a 'nice knock-down argument,'" Alice objected.

"When *I* use a word," Humpty Dumpty said, in rather a scornful tone, "it means just what I choose it to mean—neither more nor less."

"The question is," said Alice, "whether you *can* make words mean so many different things.

"The question is," said Humpty Dumpty, "which is to be master—that's all." [36]

The conversation is meant to be funny, but at the same time, Carroll underscores crucial issues in linguistic interpretation. If meaning were grounded solely in intention, as Humpty Dumpty wants to claim, then understanding would be impossible. Clearly, as Schleiermacher had contended, a shared system of language is also indispensable. At the same time, words can mean many things, even in a shared linguistic system, and that aspect of language does present problems for understanding. Further, if Humpty Dumpty's theory of meaning is accepted, then interpretation is a form of violence or appropriation, a will to power rather than understanding—as some poststructuralist theory believes interpretation to be.

The King of Hearts' mode of interpretation in the trial scene in *Alice* underscores that even when words are used in apparently conventional ways, meaning may not be evident. While Carroll, known for his parodies of current controversies (for instance, of the debates following the publication of *Essays and Reviews*) is probably to some extent satirizing legal practices, he also exhibits the ways in which general features of language cause problems for interpretation. The poem (the whole of which continues in the manner of these first stanzas) that the King uses as evidence against the Knave of Hearts, on trial for stealing tarts, is largely uninterpretable; that is, it is nonsense.

> They told me you had been to her,
> And mentioned me to him:
> She gave me a good character,
> But said I could not swim.
> He sent them word I had not gone
> (We know it to be true):
> If she could push the matter on,
> What would become of you?
> I gave her one, they gave him two,
> You gave us three or more;
> They all returned from him to you,
> Though they were mine before. (158)

It is impossible to interpret these lines with any specificity, since they lack all context and contain numerous indexicals without clear references. Alice shrewdly says of the poem, "I don't believe there's an atom of meaning in it" (159). The King, however, after pronouncing, "I seem to see some meaning in them after all" (159) proceeds to perform a complex interpretation of the verses. Moving line by line, he reads the poem in accord with the present context, assuming that it was written by the knave about the stealing of the tarts and that the pronouns with no antecedents refer to the persons involved in the crime. The "we" refers to the jury; the "she" in one case refers to the Queen and in another, where it does not describe her, is deemed a pun; the one, two, and three are tarts; and the cardboard Knave of course cannot swim. The King's theory obviously shapes the reading, and illustrates the necessity of context for interpretation. Jean-Jacques Lecercle believes that the King stands in for the literary critic, but Carroll would have been more familiar with theological interpretations that forced the words of the Bible into accord with preconceptions. It is hard to agree with Lecercle that the King's reading is the paradigm of all interpretation.[37] Carroll's satire makes clear that the reading is no more supported by the evidence than is the King's assertion that the absence of the Knave's signature on the verses he did not write proves his guilt. The reading, however, does underscore what one can do with language.

Carroll's play with meaning and interpretation indicates that as hermeneutics became of widespread interest to Victorian thinkers in many fields, they began to ask increasingly complicated questions about the act and the theory of interpretation: Is meaning determinate? Is it grounded in the author's intentions? Are these intentions available? Is meaning discovered or created? Does meaning emerge somewhere in between reader and text? Are preconceptions escapable? Will interpretations necessarily vary from interpreter to interpreter? Over time? What contextual information is necessary? Can principles that guide interpretation be established? Are there norms that transcend particular acts of interpretation? Can the conventions of language and semantic features provide determinacy? When should constraints on interpretation enter in? In what should these constraints consist? How does one adjudicate between interpretations? Is interpretation connected to authority? Is something like disinterest possible? What standards are to be used in assessing interpretations? Can subjective bias be eliminated in interpretation? Is the creativity of the interpreter of more interest than original meaning? The very multiplicity of questions and problems that the Victorians considered is the subject of this book.

For the Victorians, theories of interpretation are often connected, in one way or another, to ethical principles. Their efforts to articulate the interdependence of ethics and interpretation take several distinct forms. One view, the deontological, demands an ethical stance toward a speaker and respect for an author's intentions. A second variation, really a traditional form of moral intuitionism, is that ethics, as innate moral law, will provide the necessary constraints on interpretation; this view requires special virtues and skills in the interpreter. A third variation, consequentialism, is the belief that interpretations are to be constrained (or, on the contrary *not* constrained) according to their ethical effects on the world. This is not to argue that the ethical content of the work to be interpreted is the primary focus of attention—the sort of criticism that the Victorians have been so derided for—but rather that the means taken to limit permissible interpretations of a text always grow out of ethical considerations.

These questions as they emerge from the inquiries of various writers will be seen in more particular forms in the chapters that follow. Many Victorian authors beyond the principle ones examined here could equally well have been central to this study. It is common to see Pater in a line of thinkers that runs from Arnold through Wilde, with Pater transforming Arnold's objectivist premises to subjectivist ones, which are later fully realized by Wilde. But Pater's concern with interpretation is far more extensive and complex than that.[38] Nearly all of his writing is deeply concerned with hermeneutic questions. Matthew Arnold's work is likewise informed by hermeneutic problems. His writings on theology are briefly treated in the first chapter, but his literary criticism deserves thorough examination as well. (His notorious advocacy of disinterest in interpretation is a view that has been the object of much recent attention.)[39] Influenced no doubt both by Carlyle and by some of the same German writers that Carlyle had drawn upon, Arnold refers to "the interpreting power" of the poet.[40] "Poetry," he writes, "is the interpretress of the natural world, and she is the interpretress of the moral world" (3:30). On this formulation, poetry trumps the old theory of the two books of God, Scripture and Nature, requiring different interpretive enterprises, each in its own sphere (with the hope that they would not conflict). Arnold makes poetry the queen interpreter and so avoids problems of reconciliation.

Arnold's thought on hermeneutics is also of interest because although he sets out criteria for interpretation and advocates "objectivity," it turns out that it is not method alone that results in a good reading. Interpretation, he believes, also requires special perspicuity. As so often in hermeneutic speculation, a quality like tact comes into the picture. Schleiermacher, as we've seen, makes a similar move, and Jowett also contends that "interpretation is the province of the few; it requires a finer perception of language, and a higher degree of cultivation than is attained by the majority of mankind."[41] Is it method that provides standards for interpretation, these critics asked, or is it something like "tact," a special, perhaps intuitive quality in the interpreter, that affords correct meaning?

John Ruskin's work is also concerned with hermeneutic questions, as several studies focusing on his use of typology have shown.[42] Ruskin transfers the modes of interpretation that he has learned from biblical exegesis to secular literature and particularly to art.[43] In *Sesames and Lilies,* he offers detailed advice on the process of textual interpretation. To correctly understand the texts of others, he writes, one must

> have a true desire to be taught by them, and to enter into their thoughts. To enter into theirs, observe; not to find your own expressed by them. . . .
>
> Be sure you go to the author to get at *his* meaning, not to find yours. Judge it afterward, if you think yourself qualified to do so, but ascertain it first. And be sure also, if the author is worth anything, that you will not get at his meaning all at once—nay, that at his whole meaning you will not for a long time arrive in any wise. . . .
>
> The metal you are in search of being the author's mind or meaning, his words are as the rock which you have to crush and smelt in order to get at it. And your pickaxes are your own care, wit, and learning; your smelting furnace your own thoughtful soul. . . . And therefore, first of all, I tell you, earnestly and authoritatively (I *know* I am right in this), you must get into the habit of looking intensely at words.[44]

Ruskin's theory of interpretation is resolutely intentionalist, and, like many later Victorian critics, he warns against the error of imposing oneself on the text (a view that Wilde's Gilbert will reverse). His comments are especially interesting in the emphasis he puts on close reading, a process that he goes on to model in his interpretation of Milton's "Lycidas" (a reading that clearly manifests its origins in biblical hermeneutics).

Robert Browning's poetry is equally concerned with interpretive issues. Critics have demonstrated the ways in which the Higher Criticism deeply influenced the content and the methods of his work.[45] His poetry, of course, insists on the limitations of individual perspective, and *The Ring and the Book* is essentially a poem about interpretation and the difficulties of arriving at a correct account of events when we are limited to individual and subjective points of view. The list of Victorian literary authors who take up hermeneutics could in fact be long extended. George Meredith deliberates on the workings of figurative language and the problem of interpreting others throughout *The Egoist*. Dickens and Thackeray often satirically transfer the language of scriptural exegesis to secular matters in their novels. Hardy also insists on the interpretive nature of human experience: "In making even horizontal and clear inspections we colour and mould according to the wants within us whatever our eyes bring within."[46] The new genre of the detective novel, largely developed in the Victorian period, has been understood as a form that permits readers to perform successful acts of interpretation. Wilkie Collins' *Moonstone* certainly draws attention to hermeneutic questions from its onset. From the first narrator's declaration of having been misinterpreted; through Franklin's disquisition on "objective" vs. "subjective interpretation";[47] through the many references to the problems of interpreting the stained gown, documents, the behavior of others, and finally even oneself, the novel underscores the act of interpretation.

It was not just among literary figures that interpretation became pervasive. In opposition to the positivistic treatments of history that came to dominate institutional historiography in the last decades of the period, historians such as J. A. Froude—who wrote that "it is not questioned that if we *could* arrive at a full daguerreotyped objective account of things, such an account would be of profit to us. But judging from universal experience no such account is possible"—emphasized the hermeneutic dimensions of the writing of history.[48] To characterize the totality of Victorian historiography as imitating the objective methods of empiricist science and naïvely believing in language's ability to represent what really happened in the past is to ignore those writers, Carlyle among them, who recognized the interpretive nature of the enterprise.

The new field of psychology also depended on interpretive models, alongside the more quantitative methods used in laboratory studies. James Sully, one of the founders of the first philosophy and psychology journal (at that point, the two fields were not yet clearly demarcated), *Mind*, sought to demonstrate in *Illusions: A Psychological Study* that in perception and in all other forms of human cognition, "illusions of interpretation" are rife.[49] "Every interpretation of another's look or word," he says, sounding much like George Eliot, is likely to involve "hasty projection of our own feelings, thoughts, etc., into other minds" (223), and, when reading, "we usually approach an author with a predisposition to read our own habits of thought and sentiment into his words" (223). Despite his often pessimistic account of people's capacity for correct interpretation Sully is confident that the problems will be minimized as intuitive insight evolves. The "sciences" of physiognomy and phrenology have also been understood as hermeneutic, in their assumption that the "signs" of the body could be "read" to reveal character and psychological attributes. Even medical diagnosis in the nineteenth century has been understood as semiotic in nature, the interpretation of symptoms to identify diseases that could not be directly seen.

Victorian anthropology also used hermeneutic methods from its inception.[50] We need not ignore the worst of the Victorian anthropologists' views to notice that they were aware of the interpretive nature of their project and the difficulties of correctly knowing others. E. B. Tylor accuses Herbert Spencer of misinterpretation in his *Principles of Sociology:* "It may here be remarked that the besetting sin of us all who study primitive ideas is to treat the savage mind according to the needs of our argument." Spencer is "prone to a tightness of interpretation," Taylor charges, "in dealing with the phrases by which rude races convey their thoughts" and notes that this "may give wrong notions of what actually passes in their minds."[51] Spencer, however, in the same text on sociology had acknowledged: "In dealing with other beings and interpreting their actions, we must represent their thoughts and feelings in terms of our own. The difficulty is that in so representing them we can never be more than partially right, and are frequently very wrong."[52] And, as we will see, it was not just the human sciences that relied increasingly on the notion of interpretation in the Victorian period, but also the natural sciences.

After such a roll call, it should be clear that while the twentieth century has been called the century of interpretation, the name might apply as well to the nineteenth. The recent concern with interpretation is much influenced by Victorian Britain. The belief that there was a "hermeneutic turn" in the twentieth century is a myth. Instead a clear continuity can be established between the nineteenth- and the twentieth-century preoccupations with interpretation. Early in the twentieth century Heidegger placed hermeneutics at the center of philosophy. Sociology also conceived of itself as a hermeneutic discipline early in the century, with Max Weber defining it as "a science concerning itself with the interpretive understanding of social action" and dependent on empathy and the understanding of subjective perspectives.[53] By mid-century, interpretation was understood to be crucial in almost every field. Hermeneutics became the focus of Continental philosophy, Peter Winch reasserted the hermeneutic nature of the social sciences, and Clifford Geertz characterized anthropology as an interpretive enterprise. By the final decades of the century, the concept of interpretation had become ubiquitous, in literary studies, in the social sciences, even in the natural sciences, against whose methods hermeneutics originally defined its own. But the groundwork for all of this conceptual activity was laid in the nineteenth century.

This book may therefore make recent interpretive discourse more aware of its history. As I have already been showing, the debates are not new. Late twentieth-century and early twenty-first century theory continues a nineteenth-century project; it borrows much from the Victorians and from the concerns of theological hermeneutics. But while I want to emphasize continuities, I want to insist on differences as well. To take one example, Victorians did not inevitably see indeterminate models of interpretation as aligned with freedom from authority. On the contrary, many believed that aiming at some form of objectivity of meaning was a safeguard against the abuse of authority. To take another, many Victorians, although well aware of the difficulties of attaining certain knowledge, nevertheless upheld that as an ideal. As Robert Browning wrote:

> Knowledge means
> Ever-renewed assurance by defeat
> That victory is somehow still to reach.
> (22–24) [54]

To the extent that we might locate a prominent disposition, many of the Victorians examined in this book can be characterized as acknowledging the epistemic problems, yet persisting in believing correct interpretation to be possible. The close look at Victorian hermeneutics that follows should both help us gain new perspectives on issues central to current theory and give us a better understanding of the origins of our concerns about meaning.

CHAPTER ONE

Victorian Scriptural Hermeneutics

History, Intention, and Evolution

> First, it may be laid down that Scripture has one meaning—the meaning which it had to the mind of the prophet or evangelist who first uttered or wrote, to the hearers who first received it.
> —Benjamin Jowett, "On the Interpretation of Scripture"

> In a higher world it is otherwise, but here below to live is to change, and to be perfect is to have changed often.
> —John Henry Newman, *Essay on the Development of Doctrine*

Critics no longer insist upon "a dogmatic faith in the plenary verbal inspiration of every one of Shakespeare's clowns," quipped Pater in an essay on the history plays, satirizing the practices of literary critics, but showing at the same time that he recognized the close ties between literary interpretation and theological exegesis in his day.[1] Victorian speculation on literary interpretation is deeply indebted to nineteenth-century controversies over scriptural hermeneutics, and, indeed, current literary theory is unthinkable without nineteenth-century debates over biblical interpretation.

This chapter examines the rethinking of the Bible as historical narrative in the Victorian period and traces the significance of this enterprise for the project of literary interpretation. Victorian controversies over scriptural hermeneutics reveal that biblical exegetes were deeply concerned with the interpretive issues that preoccupy literary theorists today.

I focus most closely on Benjamin Jowett and John Henry Newman, who represent two poles in the controversy over the locus of textual meaning. As I will argue, the interpretive methods that they advocated also became key to late-twentieth-century literary debate, with Newman's views largely winning out in their transfer to literary theory in our time. Tracing Victorian exegetical debate makes distinct the trajectory of hermeneutics in the nineteenth century from theology outwards into secular interpretation; by the century's end, literary criticism had become the ascendant practice.

I

Nineteenth-century disputes over the Bible's meaning and status shook Victorian society in ways that we find hard to imagine today.[2] Confronted with serious challenges—new scientific findings that contradicted literal readings of Genesis (it had, of course, been apparent before the Victorian period that accepting the biblical account of creation as historical fact presented problems), the introduction of the historical-critical methods of the German Higher Critics in England (in controversial and highly public texts such as Bishop John Colenso's study of the composite nature of the Pentateuch [1862]), and Darwin's *Origin of Species* (1859), among others—theology responded with new exegetical principles that acknowledged the growing evidence of the Bible's historicity. Figural approaches such as typology with its synchronic tendencies became less influential, as the claim that Scripture was a unified work designed and supervised by God became less credible.[3] Exegetes adopted interpretive schemes that could somehow account for the evident lack of knowledge of scientific laws demonstrated in the stories or the obvious contradictions between narratives. Hence, theories involving the ideas of accommodation and of development became prominent, as did rationalist, naturalist, and mythical approaches to Scripture (although many theologians continued to uphold orthodox interpretive doctrines such as the inerrancy of Scripture and plenary inspiration).[4] One crucial consequence of this hermeneutic innovation was the dissolution of the boundaries that traditionally separated the Bible from other literature. Methods of analysis developed in disciplines such as classics and philology entered into theological exegesis, and, conversely, approaches developed for interpreting Scripture would eventually be extended to literary hermeneutics.

As exegetes contended with challenges to received views, questions of interpretive authority became increasingly significant. The Church of England, for example, held doctrines that were plainly contradicted by recent scientific findings. The liberals advocated an approach that essentially removed the Bible from ecclesiastical control. Like Spinoza before them, they contended that Scripture could be understood from Scripture itself; it did not require the supplement of church doctrine. The interpreter must be left alone with the text itself. The Conservative church, on the other hand, endeavored to maintain church doctrine and account for the seeming discrepancies between the findings of science and a fully inspired and infallible Bible. Proponents asserted that a special hermeneutics is required for Scripture alone, a move that would be imitated by some later literary critics.

While the traditionalists attempted to hold on to orthodox interpretations of the Bible, the liberals, many of whom were familiar with the German Higher Criticism, advanced new approaches.[5] A number of the Broad Church Anglicans were German scholars, and through them (along with writings by Coleridge and Carlyle), German biblical hermeneutics made its way into English thought.[6] The contributors to *Essays and Reviews,* for instance, are known to have read Niebuhr, Strauss, Schleiermacher, and Kant, among others.[7] The liberals rejected the tenet that Scripture is fully inspired, either the directly dictated word of God or the inspired writing of men chosen by God to deliver his message. They also abandoned the orthodox belief that the Bible is wholly infallible, and denied the status of the narratives as reliable historical report. In the wake of these disputes, questions about biblical meaning became more pressing: Where does meaning reside? Is it fixed in the past in the intentions of the original writer? In God's intentions? In the church's authoritative reading? Does it alter over time? How are interpretations to be justified?

Recognition of the historicity of Scripture resulted in two broad trends in hermeneutic methodology. The first, influenced by German Romantic hermeneutics, concluded that the biblical narratives must be understood in the context of the time when they were written. Since Scripture is a record of the consciousness of that time, one must seek to put oneself in the place of the original writer. Biblical meaning is fixed in the past and is reconstructed through historical and philological criticism. A second method of reconciling the text with history held instead that, although there is (in practice) some ultimately fixed thing behind Scripture (that is, God's message), the text, in order to present that message, must constantly transform, become something new. Meaning can only be unfolded historically.

II

The very controversial *Essays and Reviews* (the collection of writings by Anglican liberals that became a best seller and evoked four hundred books, pamphlets, and articles in the five years following its publication in 1860) caused an uproar in Britain, although the historical criticism it offered was by that time common in Continental theology. British theology, however, like Casaubon's research on mythology in *Middlemarch,* tended to proceed in ignorance of developments beyond England. The essayists all accepted that the Bible was a historical document (although there are marked differences in their stances and approaches). As Frederick Temple writes: "It is a history; even the doctrinal parts of it are cast in a historical form, and are best studied by considering them as records of the time at which they were written."[8] Benjamin Jowett in his essay "On the Interpretation of Scripture" does not so much offer a specific praxis for scriptural interpretation.[9] He is instead concerned with the problem of historical understanding itself. Unlike some of the other essayists, his aim is not to demonstrate the results of the application of the historical-critical methods of interpretation to the Bible but rather to develop an intentionalist account of meaning. He writes of "the interpreter, whose business it is to place himself as nearly as possible in the position of the sacred writer," echoing Schleiermacher's views (all of whose published works Jowett owned).[10] Only by reconstructing the historical context of a text can one come to understand the intentions of the writer, Jowett asserts, and only when one has successfully reproduced the individual consciousness from which an utterance originates can one truly be said to have understood the meaning of a text. "The true use of interpretation," he writes, "is to get rid of interpretation, and leave us alone in the company of the author" (508).

While insisting on the autonomous role of the interpreter, Jowett nevertheless believes that there is one correct reading of the text. This meaning, however, is to be discovered individually, "gathered without reference to the adaptations of the Fathers and Divines; and without regard to *a priori* notions about its nature and origins" (519). Jowett aims to liberate readers from ecclesiastical authority. Placing the texts in their historical contexts, he maintains, is a means of ridding them of all the false meaning that has accumulated over the centuries. (In this way, Jowett's theory of interpretation is the exact opposite of Gadamer's, who, in attempting to reverse the Enlightenment's rejection of prejudice, argues that a text's interpretive history in large part constitutes its meaning.) In arguing that ecclesiastical interpretations should be disregarded, Jowett historicizes church doctrine and even calls for a history of theological interpretation to be written— because such a study would reveal that church dogma reflects the biases of its own historical period. He suggests that "it becomes almost a political question how far we can venture to disturb" the false readings of the church (505). (Matthew Arnold was later to protest that the essayists "turn religion into mere politics.")[11] Ecclesiastical readings, Jowett insists, often represent only the interpreter's erroneous projections: "They throw an intensity of light upon the page of Scripture. . . . But it is not the light of interpretation. . . . it is the element in which their own mind moves which overflows on the meaning of the text. The words of Scripture suggest to them their own thoughts and feeling" (504). By the end of the century, Oscar Wilde would argue that projection is not an error to be avoided, but an inevitable truth of all interpretations. For Jowett, however, such projection is to be countered by the attempt to determine the writer's intentions, particularly through close attention to the use of language at the time the text was written.

Jowett hardly believes exegesis is easy or that we will ever fully grasp the meaning of the text. His intentionalism is not naïve; he takes into account that the writer may not have been fully aware of his meaning: "All that the Prophet meant may not have been consciously present to his mind" (506). Nevertheless, he firmly resists interpretive methods that allow for changes in meaning over time. "The book itself remains as at the first unchanged amid the ever changing interpretations of it" (481). Accommodation, the theory that God delivered his message in terms that an ancient consciousness could understand and so must be translated into new terms for the present, is, he contends, a tool that allows the church to justify whatever beliefs it puts forward. He also argues against imposing figural and typological interpretive schemes on the biblical texts for similar reasons: "That is one of those mischievous notions which enables us, under the disguise of reverence, to make Scripture mean what we please" (507).

Presentism (as we would now call it) is to be avoided, though Jowett acknowledges that it is hard to resist: "The present is nearer to us than the past, the circumstances which surround us pre-occupy our thoughts; it is only by an effort that we reproduce the ideas, or events, or persons of another age" (520). Nevertheless, he criticizes those who "read and explain the thoughts of former times by the conventional modes of their own" (483). In opposition to Newman, he disapproves of interpreting the Bible in the light of doctrines and traditions to follow, asserting that "Scripture has become confused, by the help of tradition, in the course of ages, under a load of commentators" (481). Bringing presuppositions to the text means that we distort it in order to find what we wish to find. He cautions that much "interpretation" is in fact overinterpretation: "The minuteness of the study in our own day has also a tendency to introduce into the text associations which are not really found there" (512). Unlike Wilde later, Jowett insists that interpretation is not creative: "The office of the interpreter is not to add another, but to recover the original one" (480). Readings that do not attempt to determine the "original meaning" of the text do not qualify as "interpretations"; he instead calls those readings "applications" and warns against the "confusion of the two" (520). Applications are extensions of meaning, connections of the text to other ideas or to life. Such applications can be valuable; but they are not to be mistaken for the text's meaning.

This insistence on meaning's grounding in intention does not show that Jowett is conservative, a common charge in contemporary discourse against those who support a notion of fixed meaning. Rather, he understands his hermeneutic theory as a defense against the text's political use. If one does not ground Scripture's meaning in intention and historical context, where Jowett believes it is legitimately found, biblical interpretation can only become an interested activity, as demonstrated by "unfair appropriation" and obvious "party efforts to wrest its meaning to different sides" (484). Jowett's position works against the tendency to ascribe fixed ideological stances to particular interpretive methodologies. His aim in grounding meaning in authorial intention is not to control the proliferation of signification, but is instead to overturn the church's authoritative control of meaning.

Schleiermacher had proposed universal principles of linguistic interpretation, and Jowett similarly seeks to establish that the Bible does not require a special hermeneutic:

> *Interpret the Scripture like any other book.* . . . The first step is to know the meaning, and this can only be done in the same careful and impartial way that we ascertain the meaning of Sophocles or Plato. . . . No other science of Hermeneutics is possible but an inductive one, that is to say, one based on the language and thoughts and narrations of the sacred writers. And it would be well to carry the theory of interpretation no further than in the case of other works. Excessive system tends to create an impression that the meaning of Scripture is out of our reach, or is to be attained in some other way than by the exercise of manly sense and industry. Who would write a bulky treatise about the method to be pursued in interpreting Plato or Sophocles? Let us not set out on our journey so heavily equipped that there is little chance of our arriving at the end of it. The method creates itself as we go, beginning only with a few reflections directed against plain errors. (504)

Jowett's stance is largely antisystematic, because he believes that the adoption of a system prevents one from seeing what it cannot encompass. Once we recognize that understanding involves the historical reconstruction of an author's subjective intentions, we can proceed without recourse to many specific hermeneutic rules. The interpreter must only, he says, "confine himself to the plain meaning of words and the study of their context" (483). His allusion to "manly" common sense marks interpretive ability as a masculine skill, a point left undeveloped, but one that only underscores that the turn to intentionalism affords no escape from politics. Jowett's remarks on complex methodologies for secular texts are amusing in the light of events to follow, but they underscore that secular interpretation was only beginning to come into its own. And it is in part as a result of claims such as his ("*Interpret the Scripture like any other book*") that literary hermeneutics became the more pervasive practice.

Despite—or more correctly *because of*—Jowett's assertion that there is one correct interpretation of the text, his essay came under attack in the furor that followed upon the appearance of *Essays and Reviews*. His method was said to encourage subjectivism, by insisting on the primacy of individual interpretation and refusing the validity of the church's authorized interpretations. Jowett defended his hermeneutic by affirming a connection between interpretation and morality, arguing that a correct grasp of meaning is confirmed in a person's conduct. Similarly, Frederick Temple answered the accusations against his method by insisting that "conscience is the supreme interpreter" (*Essays*, 162). The strategy of averting charges of subjectivism by appealing to the ethical sense of the interpreter appears frequently in Victorian writing on exegesis. The Scottish clergyman John Tulloch (echoing Kant) argued that freedom of interpretation does not lead to relativism because "the highest freedom is always bound fast in moral law."[12] Whereas for Spinoza reason had been the guarantor of correct meaning, these writers give a central position to morality as a guide to and a brake on interpretation.

III

The competing position in the debate over meaning—that meaning changes over time—had been introduced in a well-developed account sixteen years before the publication of *Essays and Reviews*, in John Henry Newman's *Essay on the Development of Christian Doctrine* (1844, revised 1878). Newman set his theory of interpretation against growing challenges to ecclesiastical control, in a bid to win back the church's absolute authority in exegetical questions. An ardent defender of church dogma, Newman was in every way opposed to what he regarded as the subjectivism of the Broad Church movement. His method of interpretation is based on development: revelation unfolds progressively in time. The traditional version of progressive revelation, used to explain contradictions between the Old and the New Testaments, is that the views represented in the biblical texts change between the two testaments. Newman adds that the human capacity to interpret the revelation contained in the Bible changes, so the same text's "meaning" is necessarily different for a nineteenth-century reader than it would have been for a third-century reader. We can grasp biblical meaning only from certain viewpoints at any particular historical moment.[13] Interpretations inevitably vary both diachronically and from person to person. Variety in interpretation does not necessarily entail error, but instead shows that no interpretation can be entirely adequate to an utterance or idea. Newman hangs on to the belief that determinate meaning exists (in God's intentions), but, for all practical purposes, the text is indeterminate, given that we will never be able to fully grasp that meaning. Hence sanctioned interpretations will alter radically over time. Although he seeks to establish the authority of Catholic doctrine in all matters, Newman's method results in a tension between relativism—both in textual interpretation and in an epistemology that is essentially interpretive and grounded in individual subjectivity—and the "dogmatic principle" he supports.[14]

Newman's career can be seen as a series of hermeneutic debates, the outcomes of which had very real consequences for his life and self-conception. Valentine Cunningham astutely notes that "none of Newman's writings fail to be obsessively preoccupied with the nature of textuality, of words, or reading and writing, of meaning, words about words, i.e. problems of interpretation."[15] Newman's dispute with Charles Kingsley over the interpretation of one of his own texts is at once an almost comical instance and an indication of how seriously Newman took interpretation, when we see how a seemingly inconsequential disagreement came to have far-ranging consequences. From this hermeneutic debate Newman's *Apologia Pro Vita Sua* grew.

The disagreement began, notoriously, with an offhand comment by Kingsley in an unsigned review of Froude's *History of England:* "Truth for its own sake has never been a virtue of the Roman clergy. Father Newman informs us that it need not, and on the whole ought not to be."[16] Kingsley refers to Newman's comments on equivocation found, among other places, in his "Sermon on Wisdom and Innocence." The review precipitated a lengthy series of letters and pamphlets, all concerned with valid interpretation. Newman's taxonomy of the various ways that words can be used to deceive or mislead demonstrates his acute interest in the workings of language. Here he explains how lying is to be distinguished from equivocation: "Another mode of verbal misleading is equivocation or a play upon words; and it is defended on the theory that to lie is to use words in a sense which they will not bear. But an equivocator uses them in a received sense, though there is another received sense, and therefore, according to this definition, he does not lie."[17] Newman's restriction of lying to the use of "words in a sense which they will not bear" is an odd definition of lying, more typically understood to be the statement of something known to be untrue by the speaker. But he cuts meaning from intention in this definition. He suggests that if a speaker is fully aware that his words can be understood in a sense that is not true and, further, intends that they should be understood in this way, but there is also a sense in which the words count as truthful, then the speaker has not lied. In the *Essay on Development,* Newman makes a similarly odd distinction, claiming that verbal evasion or misleading should not be called equivocation: "Supposing a person were to ask me whether a friend, who has told me the fact in confidence, had written a certain book, and I were to answer, 'Well if he did, he certainly would tell *me,*' and the inquirer went away satisfied that he did *not* write it—I do not see that I have done anything to incur the reproach of the English word 'equivocation.'"[18] The fine and questionable discriminations he makes between lying, evasion, and equivocation may seem to corroborate Kingsley's views, but they also show that Newman is well aware of the subtleties and the elasticity of linguistic interpretation.

The ensuing debate, in fact, shows that both clergymen know that the question—to borrow Stanley Cavell's famous phrase—"Must we mean what we say?" is always at issue. In response to Newman's rejoinder, Kingsley wrote: "I am most happy to hear from you that I mistook (as I understand from your letter) your meaning" (*Apologia,* 360). Newman demanded that an apology be made. Kingsley complied, sending Newman a copy of the retraction that was to appear in *Macmillan's Magazine* along with a letter, which stated that "the tone of your letters (even more than their language) makes me feel, to my very deep pleasure, that my opinion of the meaning of your words was a mistaken one" (*Apologia,* 365). Kingsley's reply to Newman carries ironic undertones, emphasizing that understanding a statement involves more than grammatical and lexicographical knowledge. In formulations that bring Humpty Dumpty's theory of meaning to mind, Kingsley manages to suggest that Newman makes words mean whatever he wants them to mean.

Newman (not surprisingly) was unsatisfied with the apology. His response again points to how easily intention (though here it is likely that Newman also means something other than what he seems to say when he ascribes "intention" to Kingsley) can be divorced from linguistic meaning: "Its main fault is, that, quite contrary to your intention, it will be understood by the general reader to intimate, that I have been confronted with definite extracts from my works, and have laid before you my own interpretations of them" (*Apologia,* 266). Since Kingsley had never used specific passages from Newman's work to support his claims, Newman protests against what he takes to be the likely sense in which Kingsley's words would be taken. He wants to discredit the impression that Kingsley's interpretation of his words is "the fair and natural and primary sense of them" (concepts that do *not* play a role in Newman's scriptural interpretation) and that, therefore, Kingsley had cleared Newman only because he found that Newman "did not mean what" he "really in effect said" (*Apologia,* 370).

Simultaneously ascribing and undercutting meaning, the two clergymen conduct their debate on intention with a sophistication that can only be accounted for by their familiarity with biblical interpretation. Newman's response, despite his defense of equivocation, implies both that a good interpretation needs solid grounding in the text and that it is a simple matter to make words seem to mean what they were never intended to mean. He includes a two-column gloss of what he takes to be the likely understanding of Kingsley's claims:

Mr. Kingsley's Letter	*Unjust, but too probable,* *popular rendering of it*
. . .	. . .
2. Dr. Newman has, by letter, expressed in the strongest terms his denial of the meaning which I have put upon his words.	2. I have set before Dr. Newman, as he challenged me to do, extracts from his writings, and he has affixed to them what he conceives to be their legitimate sense, to the denial of that in which I understand them.
3. No man knows the use of words better than Dr. Newman; no man, therefore, has a better right to define what he does or does not, mean by them.	3. He has done this with the skill of a great master of verbal fence, who knows as well as any man living, how to insinuate a doctrine without admitting himself to it. (*Apologia,* 367)

Whether Newman's readings are in fact the "popular" interpretations of Kingsley's words is questionable, but by showing that language can be used to do much more than make literal assertions, Newman also works to make his own enterprise of proving that Kingsley misinterpreted the real meaning of his words more problematic. Hence Kingsley could ask: "*What proof have I, then, that by 'mean it? I never said it!' Dr. Newman does not signify,* I did not say it, but I did mean it?" (*Apologia,* 383). After a series of pamphlets on the conflict, culminating in Kingsley's "What, Then, Does Dr. Newman Mean?" Newman resolved to vindicate himself by presenting an interpretation of his entire life in his *Apologia Pro Vita Sua.* As Newman explains it there, this battle over meaning, which often seems most profitably compared to Lewis Carroll's verbal play in the *Alice* books, is in fact a battle over Newman's very self: "He asks what I *mean;* not about my words, not about my arguments; not about my actions, as his ultimate point, but about that living intelligence, by which I write, and argue, and act" (*Apologia,* 390).[19]

Central to the *Apologia* is Newman's representation of an earlier hermeneutic conflict over the interpretation of the Thirty-nine Articles. In that particular case, an interpretation led Newman to part permanently from family and friends to become a Roman Catholic priest. Newman's Tract Ninety interpretation of the Thirty-nine Articles sought to show that they were not unquestionably Protestant in nature; the Articles did not oppose all of Catholic dogma, only later corruptions, and could reasonably be interpreted according to Catholic belief. Attempting to reconcile Catholicism with Anglicanism and halt the Church of England's increasing Protestantism, he was eager to take on the challenge of proving that the Articles were not against Rome, remarking that when it came to posing his interpretation against a Protestant one, "'Two can play at that'" (*Apologia,* 171). In retrospect, he claimed that his intention had been to show only what the words might be *made* to mean, not what they *did* mean (a hermeneutic exercise relevant to his debate with Kingsley): "As regards the 39 Articles, my method of inquiry was to leap in *media res.* —I wished to institute an inquiry how far, in critical fairness, the text *could* be opened; I was aiming far more at ascertaining what a man who subscribed it might hold than what he must" (*Apologia,* 73). Interpretation, on such an account, is easily disconnected from conviction: "I have no need or intention at this day to maintain every particular interpretation which I suggested in the course of my Tract, nor indeed had I then" (*Apologia,* 79). He was pleased to find that "there was no doubt at all of the elasticity of the Articles" (*Apologia,* 72). Newman again reveals a fascination with language and meaning, reporting that "even my own Bishop has said that my mode of interpreting the Articles makes them mean *anything* or *nothing*" (*Apologia,* 199).

Even while Newman implies that he was to some extent engaged merely in interpretive play, his conviction in some of the principles underlying his interpretation of the Articles assured serious consequences. He reports in his autobiography that the Tract caused a huge public controversy at Oxford and throughout the country: twenty-five hundred copies were sold in two weeks. Asked to suppress his interpretation, Newman refused and became convinced that he was forced to choose between Catholicism and Anglicanism.

IV

At about this time, Newman wrote the following in a letter to a friend: "If you knew all, or were here, you would see that I have asserted a great principle, and I ought to suffer for it:—that the articles are to be interpreted, not according to the meaning of the writers, but (as far as the wording will admit) according to the sense of the Catholic Church" (*Apologia*, 199). The interpretive principle he offers in the passage might be understood in this way: any statement can be interpreted in multiple ways, meaning cannot be fixed and is easily severed from intention, and it is this feature of language that allows the church to claim authoritative control over meaning. That, at least, is the suspicious reading. To put it in less skeptical terms, and ones that are consonant with some recent theories of interpretation, Newman rejects the idea that the meaning of the text is to be found in the intentions of the original writer, arguing instead that the text should be understood in the context of an interpretive community and in the light of tradition. If on the one hand, Newman may seem to construct interpretive principles in accordance with the results he wants to achieve, thus supporting assertions that the paradigm of ecclesiastical hermeneutics is the imposition of a desired meaning on a text, on the other hand, in his appeal to Catholic doctrine, Newman introduces a principle that he consistently upholds in his theory of textual interpretation: that interpretations are inevitably made in the light of previous interpretations, that tradition plays a central role in all understanding.

In *An Essay on the Development of Christian Doctrine*, Newman provides his most detailed account of his scriptural hermeneutics. As noted, his theory aims to justify historical shifts in the understanding of Scripture. The Catholic Church had supplemented Scripture with many other doctrines, and it was Newman's aim to demonstrate that those teachings were not corruptions but instead valid interpretations of what was already there, necessary and anticipated developments of the text. Hence, he needed to show that because our understanding is historically conditioned, ideas are understood differently at different times. Unlike Schleiermacher and Jowett, then, Newman rejects the idea that an interpreter should attempt to overcome historical differences in understanding, instead asserting that a text must necessarily be understood from the perspective of one's own historical moment. In his dissent from Schleiermacher's view, Newman anticipates Gadamer, who contends that we are always bound by our historical horizons.[20]

Yet certainly not all interpretations are correct for Newman. Believing the principle of private judgment to be false and dangerous, he supports the infallible judgment of the Catholic Church and condemns those who believe "that Scripture is a sufficient guide in matters of faith to the private Christian, who may put on it whatever sense he thinks the true sense."[21] Correct interpretations are those legitimated by the Catholic Church. Newman sets himself the difficult tasks in the *Essay on Development* of supporting the validity of radical changes in the interpretation of the Bible over history, of accounting for additions to Catholic teaching, and of excluding other—often more commonsensical—interpretations of Scripture, and all this while continuing to preserve the notion of a fixed (if unattainable) meaning.

Consequently, his theory must explain why Scripture is capable of sustaining such diverse interpretations. His claim in the *Essay on Development* is that the Bible "is written on the principle of development" (93). "From the nature of the human mind time is necessary for the full comprehension and perfection of great ideas" (67). Scriptural exegesis is compared to legal interpretation, where reinterpretation for the present historical moment is required; the Bible is like a text "such as legislators propound, and scribes and lawgivers comment on. . . . a legislature in germ afterwards to be developed" (95). Revisions in understanding are unavoidable, given the inadequacies of human language and what might be regarded as the literary features of the text, that is "the structure and style of Scripture, a structure so unsystematic and various and a style so figurative and indirect that no one would presume at first sight to say what is in it and what is not" (98). What may look like new meanings are merely apprehensions of other aspects of the total meaning, and this process of supplementary understanding will continue indefinitely, since humans are incapable of apprehending the totality. Correct interpretations have grasped a part of the meaning, whereas the complete meaning "is commensurate with the sum total of its possible aspects, however they may vary in the separate consciousness of individuals" (71). To explain this notion, Newman uses the analogy of a physical object: ideas "admit of being walked round, and surveyed on opposite sides, and in different perspectives, and in contrary lights" (71). (Wilde will use this same image when explaining the workings of the dialogue form.) A text, then, can take on what appear to be radically different meanings, all of which may be valid interpretations.

For Newman, in opposition to Jowett, the aims of the earthly writers of Scripture are not significant in determining whether an interpretation is correct. "We make it no objection," says Newman, "that the sacred writer did not contemplate" an interpretation" (122). Newman does not entirely cut meaning from the concept of intention, however, maintaining that the historically changing church-sanctioned interpretations of Scripture *are* intentional meanings, though they were not necessarily a part of the human author's intentions: "These natural and true developments . . . were, of course, contemplated and taken into account by its Author, who in designing the work, designed its legitimate results" (101). Just as God was soon to be taken to be the operative agency behind evolution, here he is the designer of the shifting meaning of the Bible through history.

Correct understanding rests upon what Newman calls "antecedent probabilities," extratextual beliefs that guide the interpretive process and anticipate interpretations. In this, he is quite opposed to the liberal belief that interpretation should be presuppositionless. Since not all interpretations are correct, adjudication is required to establish which are in fact true developments of the original text. Recognizing the disadvantages of proclaiming the church as the final judge without offering any hermeneutic principles, Newman suggests rough tests of an interpretation's validity. Often these work metaphorically, as in his commonly used organic analogy: "The earlier prophecies are pregnant texts out of which the succeeding announcements grow; they are types. It is not that first one truth is told, then another; but the whole truth or large portions of it are told at once, yet only in their rudiments, or in miniature" (93). Most of the *Essay on Development* is a practical illustration of how each of these tests can be applied to historical developments. True developments are "mathematical," "physical," "material," "logical," "political," "historical," "ethical," and "metaphysical," but, as the mere naming of these tests makes apparent, they are inadequate for the task Newman wishes them to do. He claims, for example, that a true development must maintain the original idea of the text: "This process will not be a development, unless the assemblage of aspects which constitute its ultimate shape really belongs to the idea from which they start" (73). Yet this is a rather vacuous rule, given that he does not offer a method for determining the original idea.

Newman ultimately falls back on the need for authority, laying out the consequences of doing without it: "If things are left to themselves, every individual will have his own view of them, and take his own course; that two or three will agree today to part company tomorrow; that Scripture will be read in contrary ways . . . that philosophy, taste, prejudice, passion, party, caprice will find no common measure, unless there be some supreme power to control the mind and to compel agreement" (112). He worries, as will some twentieth-century literary critics, that without some standard of authoritative interpretation, readings will proliferate endlessly, making agreement impossible. It is difficult to overlook his use of the words "control" and "compel" as the means of obtaining consensus, but despite the appearance of simply deciding the issue by fiat, Newman's argument is consistent with his views on the role of tradition in understanding.

As I've said, Newman believes tradition legitimately informs interpretation: "Texts have their illuminating power, from the atmosphere of habit, opinion, usage, tradition, through which we see them."[22] He sees tradition (precedence, conventions, beliefs held in common, cultural determinants) as forming a communal basis that is a necessary condition for understanding. This claim supports his contention that the doctrines of the Catholic Church should be read back into the Bible, although they do not appear to be there under any literal construal. We properly understand a text in the context of previous interpretations of it: "We elucidate the text by the comment, though, or rather because, the comment is fuller and more explicit than the text" (*Essay on Development*, 121). Understanding is the product of communities of interpreters; it is "carried on through and by means of communities of men and their leaders and guides" (74).[23]

Sanctioned interpretations change over time for a number of reasons. Social and cultural differences make new understandings necessary: "Principles require a very various application according as persons and circumstances vary, and must be thrown into new shapes according to the form of the society which they are to influence" (88). Interpretations also vary from person to person. Interpreters are situated, "exposed to the prejudices of birth, education, place, personal attachment, engagements, and party" (101). Life experiences unavoidably impact the way a person interprets a text. By stressing the inevitability of differences in perspective among interpreters, Newman renounces for all practical purposes the possibility of determining one correct meaning of a text.

Newman's theory of language underlies his account of interpretation and understanding. Newman believes that because ideas and thoughts are pre-linguistic, words are not equal to the task of expressing them. An idea has "to wrap itself in clothing" in order to be communicated (*Essay on Development,* 102). Words can adequately describe the objects of sense experience, and in these cases, references are shareable. In the case of concepts, however, words can only weakly suggest meaning. Human conceptual resources are far more powerful than linguistic resources. "Moral Truth," for example, "cannot be adequately explained and defended in words at all. Its views and human language are incommensurable. For, after all, what *is* language but an artificial system adapted for particular purposes, which have been determined by our wants."[24] Language is just a tool, useful in some situations, but, for Newman, it is not instrumental in the construction of reality.[25]

The distinction he makes between "real" and "notional" propositions in *The Grammar of Assent* is central to Newman's theory of language. Real propositions are those that refer to concrete particulars or individuals, while notional propositions are particulars "diluted and starved into abstract notions."[26] Notionals have no real existence; we experience individual things, not universals. Full meaning involves real propositions: "All that fullness of meaning which I have described as accruing to language from experience, now that experience is absent, necessarily becomes to the multitude of men nothing but a heap of notions, little more intelligible than the beauties of a prospect to the short-sighted, or the music of a great master to a listener that has no ear" (28). Yet it is only when language is used in notional propositions that meaning can be fully transmitted, only when it has been virtually emptied out. The more words "approach to being mental abstractions, and the less they have to do with the concrete reality" then "the more closely they are made to express exact, intelligible, comprehensible, communicable notions" (172).

Full meaning, then, is possible with the symbols used in algebra, signs which "have no colour, no motion, no heat, no qualities which address themselves to the ear or to the palate" (173), says Newman, who plainly adores words, despite the "imperfections of human language" (89). Logic and mathematics rely on notional language, and there symbols and numbers can convey clear, shareable notions; in "arithmetic 1 is 1, and just 1, and never anything but 1; it never is 2, it has no tendency to change its meaning" (173). Words, however, accrue layers of connotations through tradition and individual experience. If we want easily communicable notions, we must starve "each term down till it has become the ghost of itself . . . so that it may stand for just one unreal aspect of the concrete thing to which it properly belongs, for a relation, a generalization, or other abstraction, for a notion neatly turned out of the laboratory of the mind, and sufficiently tame and subdued, because existing only in a definition" (174). Linguistic communication on Newman's formulation

involves paring meaning down to the lowest common denominator, sub-
jugating and restraining it.

Newman's beliefs about notional and real propositions have clear consequences for his theory of interpretation. "The notion and the reality
assented-to," he says, "are represented by one and the same proposition,
but serve as distinct interpretations of it" (82). This entails that no two
interpretations will be perfectly alike, for we can apprehend a text only by
understanding its words in a real rather than a notional sense. Since the
writer also uses language in its real sense, no interpretation can be a perfect doubling of the author's meaning.[27] Newman's views on language
open the way to subjectivist accounts of meaning such as the one that
Wilde will later present, grounding interpretation in an individual
reader's response. Newman believes that the deficiencies of language
cause serious problems for shared understanding. Understanding
"depends on personal experience and the experience of one man is not
that of another. Real assent, then, as the experience which it presupposes,
is proper to the individual, and, as such, thwarts rather than promotes the
intercourse of man with man" (60).

That the deeply religious Newman is in fact deeply skeptical was a commonplace among his contemporaries, and his skepticism is obvious in his
doubts about shared meaning. By way of contrast, consider what Pater,
who is often pegged as radically relativist and skeptical about interpretation, says about universals:

> Abstract or common notions come to the individual mind through lan-
> guage, through common or general names, Animal, Justice, Equality, into
> which one's individual experience, little by little, drop by drop, conveys
> their full meaning or content; and, by the instrumentality of such terms
> and notions, thus locating the particular in the general, mediating between
> general and particular, between our individual experience and the com-
> mon experience of our kind, we come to understand each other, and to
> assist each other's thoughts, as in a common mental atmosphere.[28]

For Pater, abstractions become robust through individual experience,
enabling us to organize particulars into conceptual schemes that allow
shared understanding. For Newman, the particularities of experience
and the inadequacies of language keep us apart.

Much of Newman's thought verges on the skeptical, subjectivist accounts
of understanding seen in some recent interpretive theory. The principles
he uses to justify the development of biblical meaning are those that underlie theories of indeterminacy in current discourse: that words have multiple

significations, that meaning is always cut from intention, that each interpreter brings her own perspective to bear on a text, and that it is, above all, always understood from within history. His theory stands as another Victorian example that indeterminacy need not be aligned with any particular politics; indeed, in Newman's case, the assertion of the inevitability of shifting meaning becomes a way of maintaining the church's control of the text. Newman's ultimate aim is to demonstrate that, despite the personal and perspectival nature of any experience, certain knowledge is attainable. But he does this by insisting on historical contingency.

V

Development became a central term for Victorian exegesis after Newman's *Essay* appeared.[29] Late in the period, it increasingly became a synonym for evolution, as the clergy sought to harmonize theology and science. In "The Critic as Artist," Wilde's dialogue on interpretation, he writes: "The nineteenth century is a turning point in history, simply on account of the work of two men, Darwin and Renan, the one the critic of the Book of Nature, the other the critic of the books of God. Not to recognize this is to miss the meaning of one of the most important eras in the progress of the world."[30] The two forms of interpretation that Wilde identifies as transforming his age—new biblical criticism and new biological theory—were brought together in an evolutionary model of exegesis in the last decades of the period.

Much has been written about the attempts to reconcile evolution with Christian theology following the publication of Darwin's *Origin of Species*.[31] Less attention has been paid to the way in which in the last half of the nineteenth century Darwin's theory (or versions of it) itself entered and transformed religious hermeneutics, marking it with recognizably evolutionary metaphors. Following the publication of Darwin's work, a new response to the apparent historicity of Scripture became prominent: a theory of interpretation, based on evolutionary analogies, which argued that the meaning of Scripture alters over time. The emergence of a theory that combines an evolutionary model of history with textual exegesis is a significant development in the history of hermeneutics. This model of textual interpretation, arising primarily as a means of defending the Bible against science and history by incorporating the very explanatory models that seem to threaten it, was secularized and radicalized by the century's end and became the basis for some dominant interpretive trends in literary studies in the twentieth century.

Forerunners of evolutionary theories are seen in British theology earlier in the century. An important example is found in Thomas Arnold's elaboration of a traditional accommodation theory of interpretation, used as a means of defending Scripture against error in his essay "On the Right Interpretation and Understanding of the Scriptures" (1829). Arnold develops a historical scheme of interpretation to explain the discrepancies and contradictions that were becoming apparent in the Bible, as well as to account for incidents that were morally objectionable to a modern consciousness. He uses the established concept of accommodation, relativizing biblical meaning insofar as the particular formulations of God's revelation that we have access to are not aimed at the nineteenth-century level of understanding: "The revelations of God to man were gradual, and adapted to his state at the several periods when they were successively made."[32] The truths of Scripture are timeless, but their particular formulations are not. Hence, a process of translation through historical study is required to make the universal truths contained in the Bible relevant for the present. Although this theory is keenly aware of historical change, it does not yet posit an evolving text.

As we have seen, Newman's *Essay,* appearing sixteen years before the *Origin,* but almost contemporaneously with Robert Chambers' *Vestiges of the Natural History of Creation* (1844), can also be taken as an important predecessor of the models of biblical exegesis that appear after Darwin. In Newman, we see a crucial, early anticipation of the evolutionary ideas that would transform biological science a few years later. F. D. Maurice, in fact, links the *Essay* to evolution in 1846, claiming that in it Newman regards Scripture as "a living [system]—such a one as the author of the *Vestiges of Creation* recognizes the system of nature to be—a system of generative powers, vital energies; in unceasing movement . . . gradually evolving itself in the course of these workings."[33] Newman's theory of development relies on hermeneutic principles that will be central to the new evolutionary exegetical theories. In the years of controversy following the publication of Darwin's work, however, (and Darwin's theory was rather quickly assimilated by many in the established church), the language of the biblical hermeneut will alter strikingly.

A number of methods were adopted to reconcile Scripture and evolution, most prominently various schemes of a teleological evolution directed by God; evolution, as one theologian put it, is "merely one way of describing what we can observe of God's continuous action upon the physical world."[34] But even if a theory of providential evolution is accepted, the problem of the discrepancies between the Genesis account of creation and Darwin's account remains. The same kinds of defenses that appeared before Darwin's work was published, and that have been so comprehensively examined in Charles Gillispie's *Genesis and Geology,* remained available. These included appeals to the historical limitations of the original writers, elaborate figurative readings of Genesis that proved it in agreement with scientific findings, or symbolic and poetic readings that relegated the Bible to a sphere different from the scientific. But new evolutionary modes of interpretation, which brought the methods of scientific study into biblical exegesis, become pervasive in the last decades of the century.

What is remarkable in the post-Darwinian theories is their very explicit borrowing of evolutionary language and scientific modes of explanation. A. F. Kirkpatrick, a late-Victorian theologian, writes that we have come to realize that "God's revelation of himself is a more gradual process than we had supposed it to be. . . . There is an analogy between the process of revelation and the process of creation as we now understand it "[35] These theories of interpretation generally rely on a version of the concept of progressive revelation, a theory initially used to explain contradictions in the Old Testament and to account for those parts of it that were considered objectionable. As W. Robertson Smith explains that theory: "There is a method in Revelation as much in Nature, and the first law of that method, which no careful student of Scripture can fail to grasp, is that God's Revelation of himself is unfolded gradually."[36] Revelation, by analogy to the physical world, is progressively developed, and Scripture itself operates according to "method" and "law." The view is extended in the new theories to the idea that present-day readers will necessarily understand the Bible differently than those in other times. Development is seen not only across the testaments; instead, revelation continues to progress in the changing understandings of it in each age. One might argue that the old idea of progressive revelation has merely been dressed up in the new language of evolution and presented in au courant metaphors. But the use of evolutionary language is more than decorative. The widespread adoption of evolutionary models in all areas of thought in the late nineteenth century signals new ways of understanding the world. In hermeneutics, the incorporation of evolutionary theory requires the revision of widely established interpretive aims.

In theological writing of the late century, the use of evolutionary language became increasingly detailed. One theologian, discussing the Bible and revelation, writes: "When truth passes from one phase of development into another higher up on the scale, it often happens that features are preserved that have no vital connection with the organs of the later type, and which, as evolution proceeds, declare more and more plainly their useless and obstructive nature."[37] Here a particular interpretation is assimilated to a stage in the development of species.

Doctrines, as well, evolve according to the same mechanisms by which species evolve. The church "has been in religion the natural ground for that struggle of existence between ideas, that struggle between the past and the present and that struggle between authority and the individual, in which alone a survival of the fittest becomes possible, and order and continuity are united with progress, advance, and development."[38] Church doctrines, like species, continue to exist if adaptations make them fit: "History tests doctrines by their power of survival. A doctrine is evolved in the heat of a great controversy. Has it anything more in it than the adaptation which it exhibits to a passing phase of thought?"[39]

Frederic W. Farrar, in the single *History of Interpretation* written in the period, calls on evolutionary language in similar ways. Farrar's history, originally delivered as the prestigious Bampton Lecture in 1885, is particularly significant because it explicitly takes up meta-theoretical questions about interpretation.[40] In both his commentary on the history of scriptural hermeneutics and in his account of correct method, he is importantly influenced by evolutionary thought. His survey of biblical interpretation itself relies on a teleological development that places nineteenth-century hermeneutics above its predecessors. He repeatedly compares the history of scriptural interpretation to that of scientific understanding: "It is as impossible to interpret the Bible now by the methods of Aquiba or Hilary as it is to interpret Nature by the methods of Pythagoras. The History of Exegesis leads us to the complete transformation of a method."[41] Farrar is not interested in justifying any particular interpretation, but rather is concerned to argue for a new interpretive methodology: "Revision of the principles and methods of exegesis is rendered absolutely necessary by the ever-widening knowledge of modern days" (xviii). For Farrar, the Bible is "an ever-advancing revelation" and "the gradual development of the canon of interpretation is just what we should have expected from the gradually developed conditions under which revelation is presented to us" (9).

Scientific method is used on a number of levels to support his case: "Exegesis has often darkened the true meaning of Scripture," he claims, "not evolved or elucidated it. This is no mere assertion. If we test its truth by the Darwinian principle of 'the survival of the fittest,' we shall see that, as a matter of fact, the vast mass of what has passed for Scriptural interpretation is no longer deemed tenable, and has now been condemned and rejected by the wider knowledge and deeper insight of mankind" (9). This fascinating passage appeals to a scientific theory as the adjudicator of conflicts over scriptural meaning. Note also how for Farrar "evolve" becomes simply a synonym for "elucidate."

The evolutionary theories provided new principles of textual meaning and at the same time offered new ways out of some of the exegetical problems that had arisen as a consequence of scientific and historical findings. Various attempts to bring the Bible into accord with present knowledge had, many admitted, resulted in contorted schemes of interpretation. "Is it consistent with sanity, not to say accuracy of interpretation," asks one theologian, "to make the word 'waters' stand for great and small primitive nebulae?"[42] Such interpretations enraged Nietzsche, who wrote of exegetes: "Again and again they say, 'I am right, for it is written,' and the interpretation that follows is of such impudent arbitrariness that a philologist is stopped in his tracks, torn between anger and laughter. . . . How the Bible is pricked and pulled and *the art of reading badly* formally inculcated."[43] Feuerbach likewise condemned the "arbitrary exegesis" of biblical hermeneuts, describing interpretations that rested on the view that the Bible is infallible as a "disingenuous, sophistical, tortuous mode of thought, which is occupied with groundless distinctions and subterfuges, with ignominious tricks and invasions."[44] He turned a scathing irony on the convenience of ever shifting meaning. But if changes in interpretation become not evidence of arbitrariness or even error, but rather the sole form of understanding possible, as observation of the natural world reveals, then biblical meaning must inevitably alter over time.

Developmental theories made the texts increasingly more elastic. The late-century theologian Robert Jamieson asserts in his commentaries that "Moses, writing under the influence of Divine inspiration seems to have been led . . . to employ language which contains a latent, expansive meaning, the full import of which time only can evolve, and which, if rightly interpreted, would be capable of adjustment with all the research and discussion which the progress of scientific light might shed."[45] Here we are on familiar ground; "interpretations," as George Eliot says, "are illimitable."[46]

Exegetes who employed these new methods were well aware of their radical nature, and one finds them carefully defending themselves against various charges. James Bannerham, for example, attempting to reestablish a special hermeneutic sphere for the Bible, writes that "it may be a true canon of criticism in regard to any human book, that one sense and no more than one, is to be sought for in any ordinary writing and *that,* the sense that was in the mind of the author when he wrote. But such a canon is inapplicable to Scripture."[47] Elsewhere, Robertson Smith worries that "some will say" that his methods are "giving an unbounded play to unrestrained subjectivity."[48] Indeed, this was said. One theologian who denies "the evolutionary reading of biblical history" complains that the new interpretation places meaning not in the text or in the author's intentions, but in the reader's mind: "We make our own thought the measure of all things, then the Bible is not what the writers made it, but we think it to be. . . . What I think, not what the Bible says, is true." His rapidly accelerating argument soon arrives at the hyperbolic conclusion that such a method "leads to the annihilation of all objective realities."[49]

It is not surprising that the shift in interpretive thought provoked the same objections and battles over meaning that we observe in current debate on literary interpretation. Milton S. Terry, a theologian influenced by German Romantic hermeneutics, wrote in his overview of biblical hermeneutics: "Twisting words out of their naturally established usage and foisting onto them the ideas of a later age is a process essentially at war with all safe and sound methods of interpretation."[50] The dissenters were right that exegetes had to significantly revise what had until that point been commonly accepted interpretive ideals in the history of hermeneutics. Evolutionary theories require a substantial shift in methodology: the goal is no longer, for all practical purposes, ascertaining the one correct meaning. Instead it is to understand the text at a particular moment in history. The new developmental theories more fully dismissed the notion of a text's stable meaning and the belief that it is located in the consciousness of the intending mind than did Newman's theory of development. They revealed meaning to be historically shifting.

VI

What is of the greatest significance for literary theory is the way in which these evolutionary theories of exegesis were secularized and entered into the emergent discipline of literary criticism, which in the last decades of the nineteenth century was transformed into the institution of literary studies as we now recognize it.

The emergence of modern literary criticism owes much to Matthew Arnold's transformation of the Bible into a literary text.[51] Arnold adopts the evolutionary view of meaning in his treatment of the Bible in *St. Paul and Protestantism* (1870). "We entirely agree with Dr. Newman and with the great Anglican divines that the whole Bible is written on the principle of development" (*CPW* 6:92), Arnold says (although he protests that Newman's absolutist tendencies are in tension with his theory of development). Reading St. Paul figuratively rather than literally, he asserts that his interpretation is not to be taken as the final, correct reading, but instead as itself a "development," a current interpretation of meaning:

> We by no means put forth our version of St. Paul's line of thought as true, in the same fashion as Puritanism puts forth its *Scriptural Protestantism or gospel* as true. Their truth the Puritans exhibit as a kind of cast-iron product, rigid, definite, and complete, which they have got once and for all, and which can no longer have anything added to it or anything drawn from it. But of our rendering of St. Paul's thought we conceive rather as of a product of nature, which has grown to be what it is and which will grow more; which will not stand just as we now exhibit it, but which will gain some aspects which we now fail to show, and will drop some which we now give to it; which will be developed, in short, further, just in like manner as it has reached its present stage by development . . . Thus we present our conceptions neither as something quite new nor as something quite true. (*CPW* 6:111–12)

With unmistakably biological language—interpretation continues to evolve just as species evolve—Arnold implies that interpretations are provisional and historically situated.[52] Even more strikingly, he begins to dislodge the idea of the truth of an interpretation.

Like the liberal theologians, Arnold contended that Scripture should be approached like any text. In *Literature and Dogma* (1873), he protests that "it is as if a hand had been put out of the sky presenting us with the Bible, and the rules of criticism which apply to other books did not apply to the Bible" (*CPW* 6:249). He rejects rationalist methods, however, arguing that the Bible should be interpreted like a literary text (not a historical document), since it is, in essence, poetry that has been mistakenly understood as science: "The Bible-language is not scientific, but the language of common speech or of poetry and eloquence, approximative language thrown out at certain great objects of consciousness which it does not pretend to define fully" (*CPW* 6:244). Representative of the extension of hermeneutic thought in the nineteenth century, Arnold regarded poetry itself as interpretation: "More and more mankind will discover that we have to turn to poetry to interpret life for us" (*CPW* 9:16). Poetry "interprets by expressing, with magical felicity, the physiognomy and movement of the outward world, and it interprets by expressing, with inspired conviction, the ideas and laws of the inward world of man's moral and spiritual nature" (*CPW* 3:33).

While apparently seconding Schleiermacher's call for a general hermeneutic in arguing for the breakdown of special forms of interpretation applicable only to Scripture, Arnold in fact opens the way to a special literary hermeneutics. Shifting the interpretation of the Bible away from theologians, who are "catching at the letter of the Scriptures, and mistaking this play with words for serious argument" (*CPW* 6:263), he emphasizes the poetic nature of the text and argues that its interpretation should be turned over to trained literary critics:

> It is as if some simple and saving doctrines, essential for men to know, were enshrined in Shakespeare's *Hamlet* or in Newton's *Principia* (though the gospels are really a far more complex and difficult object of criticism than either); and a host of second-rate critics, and official critics, and what is called "the popular mind" as well, threw themselves upon *Hamlet* and the *Principia,* with the notion that they could and should extract from these documents, and impose on us for our belief, not only the saving doctrines enshrined there, but also the right literary and scientific criticism of the entire documents. A pretty mess they would make of it! and just this sort of mess is our so-called orthodox theology. (*CPW* 6:277)

Having rejected theological exegesis, he proceeds to set out the requirements for proficient criticism: "This literary criticism *is* extremely difficult," he writes. "It calls into play the highest requisites for the study of letters; great and wide knowledge of the manner in which men have thought, of their way of using words and what they mean by them, delicacy of perception and quick tact, and besides all these, a favourable moment and the 'Zeit-Geist.' And yet everyone among us criticises the Bible, and thinks it is the essence of the Bible that it can be thus criticised with success!" (*CPW* 6:276). The tools and qualities of the specialist in literature must be applied to theological works. Literary studies take ascendancy over theology.[53]

Arnold's appropriation of Scriptural exegesis for the literary interpreter is representative of the trajectory of interpretation in the Victorian age. He transfers the authoritative reading of the Bible out of the hands of theologians and into the hands of skilled critics: "Now, we all know what the literary criticism of the mass of mankind is. To be worth anything, literary and scientific criticism require, both of them, the finest heads and the most sure tact" (*CPW* 6:276–77). Thus he forecasts the emergence of a new professional literary critic and the reinstitutionalization of interpretation in the study of literature in the universities. By the century's end, as my second intertext shows, literary interpretation had come into its own.

It was not until Pater and Wilde, however, both of whom were well aware of the controversies over biblical exegesis and deeply influenced by

Darwinian and evolutionary theory, that Victorian literary critics began to propose theories of interpretation that *entirely* do away with the quest for authorial intention and the attempt to discover the correct meaning of the text.[54] In these theories, any vestigial notion of objective meaning is dismissed, and the focus turns from the author's to the interpreter's subjectivity. Wilde is widely regarded as being influenced by Darwin in his social theory, but his literary criticism is not only a revision of Arnold and Pater, as the usual narrative goes, but also a reaction to evolutionary thought. Wilde, as chapter 4 shows in detail, presents through his character Gilbert in "The Critic as Artist" an anti-intentionalist theory that celebrates the proliferation of interpretations. Art works "by their imaginative beauty make all interpretations true, and no interpretation final."[55]

Darwinian theory, then, as it transformed scriptural hermeneutics, also had a profound effect on literary interpretation in the late-Victorian era. But related theories of interpretation became ever more prominent in the twentieth century, not only in the rejection of intentionalist criticism, but more strikingly in reception theories and in Gadamer's *Truth and Method,* which asserts that a text's meaning is a product of its history. Gadamer believes that interpretations are inevitably changing because always conditioned by what he terms *tradition*—conventions, beliefs we hold in common, cultural and historical determinants. Or consider Hans Robert Jauss's reception theory, in which he argues that a literary work contains an ever-unfolding potentiality of meaning, which is actualized in various interpretations at various historical moments.

Even Derrida's hermeneutics (as I've said, Derrida would reject the designation "hermeneutics" for his theory) might be seen as emerging from the Victorian move away from intention and fixed meaning in post-Darwinian biblical exegesis. Derrida explicitly severs his view from theological hermeneutics. He regards his thought as instead indebted to a Nietzschean view that breaks from the theological tradition, which, Derrida argues, rests on the belief in a transcendental meaning, a semiotic that he describes in this way: "a sign signifying a signifier itself signifying an eternal verity, eternally thought and spoken in the proximity of a present logos."[56] And yet, the theologians themselves effectively dissolved the view Derrida counters here.

Contemporary literary criticism has not sufficiently recognized its connections to nineteenth-century scriptural exegesis. Greater knowledge of our origins would illuminate theoretical discussions and perhaps help us reconsider some current views. Let me return to Wilde once more. Near the end of Wilde's "Portrait of Mr. W. H.," a story about literary interpretation, it appears that one of the main characters has killed himself because of his failure to "convert" others to his theory on Shakespeare's sonnets. Wilde's narrator exclaims: "To die for one's theological opinions is the worst use a man can make of his life; but to die for a literary theory! It seemed impossible."[57] While on the one hand, this might be read as a parody of the new professional literary critic, it also shows that Wilde, like Pater, was quite aware of the close links in his own day between the new field of literary interpretation and biblical exegesis. Wilde foresaw that in a secular age literary criticism would increasingly become a sphere where questions of belief and morality would be broached.

❧

Victorian Legal Interpretation

> Would you some day inform them that in a legal document words have to be interpreted in a legal sense: and not by private feelings of whatever kind they may be. . . . They do not understand that legal documents are things that have to be carefully, rightfully, interpreted.
>
> —Oscar Wilde

Charles Dickens's *Bleak House,* as critics have often noted, is concerned with the problems of interpretation in many ways, with Chancery's interminable delay in the interpretation of one particular legal document standing at the center of the novel's world. Given the political, social, and individual consequences of legal judgment, it makes sense that *Bleak House* (and the Victorian novel is in general obsessed with the law) marks legal hermeneutics as the central site of interpretive anxiety. Moreover, the novel suggests that legal interpretation would be less confused—less foggy—if interpreters held the right morals. As Ada Clare says: "It seems very strange, as there must be right somewhere, that an honest judge in real earnest has not been able to find out through all these years where it is."[1] In contrast to *Bleak House*'s disquiet, an interesting confidence about the ease of legal interpretation is expressed at the start of most nineteenth-century treatises on jurisprudence. Authors devote many pages to problems of right interpretation of the law only after asserting that, in most cases, interpretation is not required. The plain or literal sense of the words alone will do. Once the difficulties have been admitted, however, Victorian legal theorists also often move to grounding right interpretation in ethics.

The history of Victorian hermeneutics is incomplete without a discussion of hermeneutics in law, which, like scriptural interpretation, has a tradition that precedes the Romantic hermeneutics I've discussed. Jurisprudence was one of the traditional areas of hermeneutic inquiry prior to the extension of interpretive theory to a universal hermeneutics, and Victorian jurisprudence often looked back to specialized methods and vocabularies developed during the Enlightenment for the interpretation of the law. As in exegesis of the Bible, a lot is at stake in the interpretation of the law. A consideration of the arguments that marked legal hermeneutics shows how the hermeneutic problems that were later to become crucial to literary interpretation were first treated in highly nuanced ways in what is a more immediately practical context.

In 1871, Parliament passed the Interpretation Act, according to which particular words in laws were to be interpreted in fixed ways. The Act stipulated that there were to be no exceptions, unless explicit directions were given in the original text that the words were to be interpreted in other ways. The wording of the Act is uninteresting, appearing to do no more than define terms in roughly the same way a dictionary does. Yet its passing points to the recognition of pervasive problems in ascertaining the meaning of documents. It attempted to provide a law of interpretation, a rule for interpreters to follow that would render meaning determinate. That Parliament felt that there was a need to put such a key to interpretation into law makes manifest that, despite the underplaying of the difficulties, legal hermeneutics like biblical hermeneutics was riven by the obstacles in the way of establishing an authoritative account of meaning.

Legal and biblical hermeneutics were brought together in James Fitzjames Stephen's defense of Rowland Williams, in the aftermath of the publication of *Essays and Reviews*. Scriptural interpretation was both the occasion for the trial and the key to Stephen's defense of the theologian.[2] The prosecutors charged that Williams's essay demonstrated that he did not subscribe to the Thirty-Nine Articles, as required for clergy in the Church of England, and they sought to excommunicate him. Stephen's defense was built on "the liberty of interpretation."[3] He argued that Williams's views were not in conflict with the Articles as he interpreted them, and maintained that interpretive questions were "designedly and intentionally left open by the Articles" (66). Like Newman before him, Stephen aimed to show that the words of the Articles can mean many different things. The ordination vows, he contended, do not bear on questions of interpretation. They say nothing about meaning, and a clergyman is free to interpret them as he sees fit. Stephen uses the indeterminacy of language not, as Newman does, to support the authority of the Church on questions of meaning, but rather to resist it.

Stephen's command of the language of biblical interpretation is apparent, as he discusses with ease key topics in exegesis. As Matthew Arnold was to do more influentially several years later, Stephen asserts that the Bible should be understood as a literary not a historical text. Different sorts of narratives, he contends, require different modes of understanding. As it makes no sense to say, "I believe in a poem" (54), so it makes no sense to approach the Bible on those terms of understanding. Stephen does not, however, seek to sever meaning from authorial intention: "I do not say that any one is at liberty to understand the Bible in a sense which the authors do not intend. I say he is at liberty to form his own opinion as to what the sense was they did intend" (56). So unlike many of the Higher Critics, his method of interpretation does not require reading the text against the intentions of the original writers (for whom perhaps the account was understood to be literal). Rather, Stephen believes that the writers intended much of the Bible to be understood as poetry and legend.

The defense, however, rested not only on questions of the interpretation of theological documents but also on those of legal interpretation, and, more importantly, on the distinction between the two. The case poses particular problems, Stephens contends, because passages from the Bible are used as evidence in the trial. As he points out to the judge, this practice raises questions of authority, and in a civil court, the judge, not the Church, is the arbiter: "The whole authority of the Bible in this court is derived from the law; and therefore you must decide what authority the law gives to the Bible before you can quote the Bible itself as authority" (15). Secular authority trumps ecclesiastical authority. The judge, an expert in legal interpretation, must in this context "adjudicate and put a judicial construction on Bible passages" (12). Drawing on the familiar terminology of Victorian jurisprudence, Stephen asks that the judge consider the "plain sense" of the Articles. He wants to show that the commonsensical interpretive principles used in the law can and should be used to interpret the Bible. In other words, the Church cannot uphold special and authoritative interpretations that are not supported by ordinary methods of understanding. The prosecutor, however, objects that legal and theological interpretations are fundamentally different. Appealing to ethics as the grounds of interpretation, the prosecutor argues that in the case of the Articles "the obligation is a moral one and [Stephen] tries to convert it into a legal one; therefore I say he cannot complain that the defendant contends for the strictest legal construction of the words in question" (45). A key principle of the legal positivism that dominated Victorian law was the separation of legality and morality, and the prosecutor may here be insisting on that separation while exempting theological interpretation from legal treatment on the grounds that, as many had argued before, the Bible requires special methods of interpretation (the opposite of what Jowett argued in *Essays and Reviews*). But he is also implying that "moral obligation" constrains interpretation—in other words, that it here limits interpretation to the ways in which the Church would interpret the Articles. In any case, the decision was against Williams (though he was later reinstated), and Stephen's attempt to subordinate theological to legal interpretation was at least temporarily frustrated. His defense, layering legal hermeneutics on biblical hermeneutics, shows scriptural hermeneutics on its descent, its privileged position and special modes of hermeneutics under siege.

Outside of theology, the most extended examination of hermeneutics written in the English language in the nineteenth century treated legal interpretation. Francis Lieber's 1839 *Legal and Political Hermeneutics; or, Principles of Interpretation and Construction in Law and Politics,* though not strictly a "Victorian" text (it was written and published in the United States) deserves mention because of its extensive treatment of intentionalist hermeneutics.[4] Lieber, who studied with Schleiermacher, Wilhelm von Humboldt, and F. A. Wolf in Jena before becoming a United States citizen (and was the first to introduce the word hermeneutics into Anglo-American legal discourse), aimed to apply the insights of Romantic hermeneutics to legal interpretation. His book, however, as might be expected given the premises of Romantic hermeneutics, also concerns the general difficulties of linguistic interpretation, and therefore underscores the ways in which Victorian jurisprudence maintained some innocence about problems central to its practice.

Like Carlyle, Lieber regards words as the most important signs. Given that there is "no direct communion between the Minds of Men; Signs are Necessary."[5] Communication through signs, however, means that understanding is always in question, since (and here he anticipates Newman) "no absolute language, by which is meant that mode of expression, which absolutely says all and every thing to be said, and absolutely excludes everything else, is possible, except in one branch of human knowledge, namely mathematics" (39). For this reason, "interpretation of some sort or other is always requisite, whenever human language is used" (39). Meaning is grounded in intention, and there is one "true" meaning to an utterance, which it is the interpreter's task to reconstruct. But intention alone is not enough to guarantee meaning; convention also plays a role.

If people did not use language "according to rules generally adopted," Lieber says, "there would be no such thing as understanding one another among men" (22–23). Nevertheless, intention trumps the conventions of language, and the "true sense" of an utterance is "the meaning which the person or persons, who made use of the words, intended to convey, whether he used them correctly, skillfully, logically or not" (23).

Having straightaway established authorial intention as the locus of meaning, Lieber turns to examine at length the difficulties of discovering that intention. He critiques the idea of "literal" meaning, a common conception in Enlightenment and Victorian jurisprudence, showing that he understands language to work in ways that might be regarded as literary: "Literal meaning ought to mean, of course, that which takes the words in their literal sense, which is hardly ever possible, since all human language is made up of tropes, allusions, images," and so on (66). He charges that claims of literal meaning have often been misused: "Enormous crimes, and egregious follies have been committed under the pretended sanction of literal interpretation, using interpretation as a means to promote certain objects" (68). Although Lieber's aim is to provide "Principles of Sound Interpretation," he does not offer much in the way of methodology, beyond the attempt to ascertain the author's intentions.

Primarily, Lieber presents a remarkably detailed and nuanced taxonomy of various forms of misinterpretation. He warns against biased modes of interpretation, those that make texts conform to what the interpreter wants to find in the text: "Be it repeated, our object is not to bend, twist, or shape the text, until at last we may succeed in forcing it into the mould of preconceived ideas" (89). He identifies a series of hermeneutic errors, giving them designations such as "sinister interpretation" (32); "extravagant interpretation"—"that mode of interpreting, which substitutes such meaning as is evidently beyond the true meaning" (71); and "limited interpretation," in which the interpreter has already concluded something about the text, such as "that the scriptures were written by inspired men" (71), and so interprets it in accordance with those presumptions. His main target is (as Jowett's will be) interpretive preconception, a category of error that he refers to as "predestined" interpretation (recalling the theological roots of hermeneutics). Predestined interpretation occurs when the interpreter, perhaps unconsciously, "makes the text subservient to his preconceived views, or some object he desires to arrive at" (72). A "peculiar form" of this mode is "artful interpretation"; "that, which, by cunning and art, attempts to show that the text means something, which was not according to the interpreter's own knowledge the meaning of the author or utterer" (72). Lieber acknowledges the tendency of interpretation to move toward projection, but he

argues that if interpreters become aware of this propensity, they can miti-
gate against it. Lieber tries to reign in interpretation with a consistent
appeal to intention, and in so doing reveals the problems that always
attend intentionalist accounts of meaning. The cumulative effect of his
careful examination is, overall, an underscoring of the difficulties of
establishing meaning.

One of Lieber's most striking claims is that interpretation and liberty
go hand in hand. "The freer a country the more necessary becomes interpretation," he argues (53). For Lieber, one of "the main ingredients of
civil liberty" is "the supremacy of the law," which protects people against
caprice, violence, and the abuse of power. Law, in his traditionally liberal
view, is not the authority that seeks to control and limit interpretation,
but instead that which guarantees freedom. His argument is not that
interpretation should be unconstrained in a free society. Rather, the laws
that guarantee freedom must be administered fairly, and this involves
careful and accurate interpretation: "It is necessary to remember well,
that in general, nothing is so favorable to that great essential of all civil
liberty—the protection of individual rights, as close interpretation and
construction. Most laws lose in their protective power . . . according as
they are loosely interpreted" (136). Lieber, like Jowett, suggests that linking indeterminacy with freedom from authority, and determinacy with
the misuse of authority, is not inevitable. Strict interpretation of law is a
protection against arbitrary treatment by those in power: "The laws of the
European continent were, for a long time, loosely interpreted," says
Lieber, "whenever there was a question of right between the individual
and the one who possessed the power" (137). Thus "the same law was differently interpreted on different occasions" (137). In other words, Lieber
believes that if one does not place authority in an intentional text, it is
turned over to whoever is presently in power. Grounding interpretation
in intention is for Lieber both a political and an ethical move. As disputes
over meaning in the law make apparent, debates over interpretation are
always concerned not only with epistemology—questions of what we can
know—but also with ethical questions about the ends and purposes of
interpretation.

Lieber's investigation of legal hermeneutics is more complicated and
more candid in its acknowledgment of the difficulties involved in establishing meaning (even if his reliance on intention may now seem too
easy) than are many treatments of interpretation in the lengthy Victorian
overviews of jurisprudence. However, the same issues arise at least implicitly in the texts and Victorian legal theorists plainly do recognize that
interpretation is more uncertain than they make it out to be in their

ordered presentation of the issues. Discussions of interpretation in Victorian legal writing indirectly (unintentionally?) yet sharply emphasize the problems surrounding an intentionalist account of meaning, and in some ways are more illuminating than Lieber's speculations precisely because of their failure to fully acknowledge the dilemmas.

When Carlyle in 1843 insisted that human laws are not laws unless they match divine laws, he looked back to the eighteenth-century model of natural law promoted by Blackstone.[6] The dominant legal theory in Victorian England was instead the legal positivism that grew from Bentham's work on jurisprudence and was more fully articulated and disseminated by fellow Utilitarian John Austin in his book *The Province of Jurisprudence Examined* (1832). In brief, legal positivism does not see law as attempting to correspond to legality as it really exists in the world. There is no ideal law "out there" that we try to match. Humans create law rather than discover it, and the authority of the law comes only from the authority of the lawmaker. In a theory of natural law, however, the law attempts to get at an objective legality, and it can fail to do that. For Austin and other positivists, law is simply "the command of the sovereign."[7]

Whether the law is moral is an entirely different question, and positive law insists on the separation of *is* from *ought*. One obeys the law not because it is right, but simply because it is the law. Although cutting legality from morality may seem to turn law entirely into a matter of power, Bentham and Austin, liberal Utilitarians, regard this separation as a route to social reform and a protection against the abuse of power. By insisting on a distinction between law as it exists and law as it ought to be, they make room for criticism of existing laws. Laws are not absolute decrees; they are made by humans in power. It follows that the law must be strictly interpreted; it cannot be made to conform to what the judge thinks it ought to be. Bentham (like Lieber) contended that if one does not take the words (and the intention) of the original lawmaker as the limit to meaning, the judge can attempt, in H. L. A. Hart's words, "in the misleading guise of finding what the law behind the positive law really is, to invest his own personal, moral, or political views with a spurious objectivity as already law" (*Essays*, 157). This concern with legal authority and arbitrary interpretation mirrors ecclesiastical conflicts over exegesis, in which censurers charged that the Church twisted the words of the Bible to force them into conformation with its current doctrines. Victorian theorists, as we've seen, often connected indeterminacy with a misuse of power.

If law is understood as a command, then the law's meaning must be sought in the intentions of the commander. Classical positivist discussions of interpretation presume that meaning is always intentional. As Austin

writes in his *Lectures on Jurisprudence:* "The discovery of the intention with
which the statute was made, is the object of genuine interpretation."[8]
Austin, however, still holds the pre-Romantic view, on which interpretation is not usually in question, since one typically understands the lawmaker's intention without problem: "Generally, the interpreter assumes it
tacitly, and without hesitation or inquiry" (1024). Only occasionally is the
meaning "indeterminate and dubious" (1024), and then rules for determining intention are required. Austin makes a division between literal
(or grammatical) and logical meaning, terminology used also in
Enlightenment discussions of legal hermeneutics and still widely adopted
throughout the nineteenth century. Literal meaning is "the meaning
which custom has annexed to [words]. It is the meaning attached to them
commonly by all or most persons who use habitually the given language"
(1024). Thus literal meaning (what others call "plain meaning") is conventional meaning (a concept that Lieber, with his deeper consideration
of interpretive difficulties, has rejected on the grounds that language is
often figurative and vague). In interpreting law, Austin looks first to conventional meaning; not, however, because he assumes that meaning is
located in the text. He is not a formalist. He seeks authorial intention and
believes that the literal meaning is the best indication of intent, although
he does acknowledges that it does not always reveal intention: "The intention, however, of the legislature, as shewn by that literal meaning, may differ from the intention of the legislature, as shewn by other *indicia;* and
the presumption in favour of the intention which that literal meaning
suggests, may be fainter than the evidence for the intention which other
indicia point at" (1024). In these cases, logical interpretation is required,
which involves extending interpretation beyond conventional meaning,
in order to ascertain "the actual intentions of the lawgiver" in other ways.

   The problems with this account of the discovery of intention are obvious. How does one know when "literal" interpretation will do the job and
when, on the contrary, "logical" interpretation is required? And what
extensions of meaning (in the aim of finding intention) are legitimate? In
On the Interpretation of Statutes (1879), Sir Peter Benson Maxwell begins by
declaring that "when the language is free from ambiguity, the task of interpretation can, indeed, hardly be said to arise. It is not allowable to interpret . . . what has no need of interpretation."[9] Yet he almost immediately
admits that this rule of construction is not very useful, because "language
is rarely so free from ambiguity as to be incapable of being used in more
than one sense" (17). Over four hundred pages of principles to aid in the
ascertainment of meaning follow. Maxwell, like other Victorian theorists
of interpretation, shifts the ground from the epistemological to the ethi-

cal, without any signaling of having done so. One is justified, he argues, in departing from the "primary and literal meaning of the words," if *not* doing so would result in an "unjust" or "mischievous" enactment. Similarly one can reject any construction that would lead to such an outcome, in favor of another reading that would result in a "wholesome" one (179). "It is obvious," says Maxwell, "that the latter must be adopted as that which the Legislature intended" (179). The attribution of intention (ostensibly the locus of objective meaning), then, is based on the subjective; intention depends on what one adjudges the moral construction of a statute.

Some late Victorian works on legal interpretation confront its problems more fully, though the premise that meaning is found in intention remains constant. By 1896, Sir Frederick Pollack acknowledges that interpretation is always at issue and defends this as a vital aspect of the law: "The need of interpretation is not in itself any reproach to the law. Rather law without interpretation is but a skeleton without life, and interpretation makes it a living body."[10] Sheldon Amos, professor of jurisprudence at University College in London, discusses in detail the difficulties of ascertaining intention in his *Science of Law* (1875). Examining the "Nature and Grounds of Interpretation," he asserts that only "in the rare and almost impossible case of a legislator condescending to step down into the judgment-seat, and, as occasion required, to interpret his own laws, can the integrity of the meaning really intended by the legislator in the use of the words he employed be infallibly preserved."[11] (Notice the use of the theological term infallible, a word frequently used in Victorian discussion of legal hermeneutics.) Amos seems initially not to question that the lawmaker would fully know his intentions. He goes on to concede, however, that the pursuit of intention "presuppose[s] that (at least) the legislator is a man of a single mind, and really had a distinct and single meaning" (60), and acknowledges that there may not be a consistent intention in a law. Still, he believes that interpretation should begin with the supposition that intention will reveal itself in the language of the law. When problems arise, one turns to "extensive" interpretation: "It is only when the words are ambiguous, and the meaning therefore uncertain, or when it is held desirable, for some reason or other, to put the undoubted meaning upon the word, that other clues to the probable policy of the legislator can be made available" (67). This formulation—"when it is held desirable, for some reason or another"—opens out the discovery of intention in ways that seem impossible to systematize.

John Salmond's discussion of interpretation in *Jurisprudence* similarly moves from the contention that interpretation seeks "the true intention of the legislature" to an opening out of the concept of intention.[12] In wording that echoes *Alice in Wonderland,* Salmond initially asserts that judges must "take it absolutely for granted that the legislature has said what it meant, and meant what it has said" (182).(As Alice learns, those two statements are not the same.) But it soon becomes clear that Salmond also recognizes that intention is often very difficult to determine and that words do not always clearly reveal it. Language, he says, may be ambiguous or may have no meaning at all. The writer may not have had a clear intention, may have been confused, or may not have considered all cases. Salmond more fully separates intention from language than Austin does, and in terms that once again invoke scriptural hermeneutics: "The essence of the law lies in its spirit, not in its letter, for the letter is significant only as being the external manifestation of the intention that underlies it" (182). There are many cases in which an interpreter must go beyond the grammatical sense to seek intention, for instance, when "the text leads to a result so unreasonable that it is self-evident that the legislature could not have meant what it has said" (184). Salmond acknowledges that there is a fine line between creating meaning through interpretation and gaining the lawmaker's intention: "Undue laxity, on the one hand, sacrifices the certainty and uniformity of the law to the arbitrary discretion of the judges who administer it; while undue strictness, on the other hand, sacrifices the true intent of the legislature and the rational development of the law to the tyranny of words" (183). Intention gets slippery here, and Salmond offers an increasingly complex analysis of it, introducing finely nuanced categories such as "latent intention," "real intention," and "conscious intention." The section moves fascinatingly from a presumption that systematic rules and methods govern the process of discovering intention toward what appears to be an elaborate justification of why one might not take what the text seems to say as revealing its intention. His presentation is orderly, scholarly, and confident in the techniques it offers, but the implications are apparent. The difficulties in determining original intent that are manifested in these accounts opened the way for the argument of twentieth-century legal realism that the interpreter creates the text.

Victorian commentators became more conscious not only of the problems involved in discovering intention but also of the ways in which historical distance exacerbates those problems, particularly in the case of the law, where the judge seeks not only to interpret the law, but to apply it in the present. Amos, for instance, notes that over time language has taken on supplementary meanings, or has lost meanings it once had, and these linguistic changes "render it doubtful which of the meanings the legislator intended at the time of composing the law" (61). This leaves the judge with two options. Either he can "institute a historical and philo-logical inquiry" in order to "revert to the true meaning of the terms intended" or "he may be directed to consider the probable modification in his expressions which the legislator would have made had he been liv-ing at the present day, and had he shared in all the social conditions by which the judge himself is surrounded" (61). Amos outlines two now familiar modes of interpretation: the interpreter can try to get back to original intention in the past, or he can extend "intention," making the text relevant to the present moment.

In jurisprudence, the notion that law must be reinterpreted in and for the present is inevitable given that the interpreter seeks not only to understand the words but also to put the law into practice in the present. Hence the same problems of application that arose in biblical exegesis as interpreters sought to make Scripture relevant to contemporary society arose in legal interpretation. Not only is the judge faced with the diffi-culty of knowing what the lawmaker in the past thought, but the judge must also apply a law that was not framed for current society. One cannot simply try to understand what the intentions of the lawmakers were, in any strict sense, but must instead translate their terms for application in situations they could not have foreseen. A sixteenth-century legislator could not, to take one example important to the Victorians, have had any intentions about trains, since trains were yet to be invented. Thus there are many things about which the lawmaker could have had no intentions whatsoever. Yet if one restricts the meaning of the law to what appear to be the *strict* intentions of the lawmaker as revealed by the plain meaning of the words, then one may not in fact be acting on the genuine inten-tions of the lawmaker, because one does not take the purposes of the law into consideration. In that case, the law must be understood in new ways, and, as Amos suggests, the judge must attempt to discern what the law-maker would have thought about things he could not have known about. The historical account of intention takes on a broad definition, and has more to do with a notion of general purpose than with the conscious con-tents of the mind of the lawmaker.

Interpretation of the law, then, makes unavoidable the recognition of the historical situatedness of understanding. Precedent can be seen as a form of development, in which the history of a law's interpretation becomes a part of its meaning. In this view, meaning is located in legisla-tive history, as in the church, meaning is found in doctrinal history. In fact, arguments analogous to Jowett's (or to Spinoza's before him) have been advanced in jurisprudence; such arguments attack the adherence to precedent on the grounds that the text of the law should be stripped of the judicial accretions that have grown up over the years and assert that interpreters need only the original text.

Victorian legal interpretation parallels Victorian theological interpretation in its movement between a notion of original meaning found in intention in the past and a conception of historically changing meaning found always in the present. (Compare Jowett versus Newman.) Pollack, like Newman, constructs a theory in which history and change are understood as a part of original intention: "It may with equal verbal correctness be affirmed in one sense, and denied in another, that interpretation (whether performed by judges or by text writers) makes new law. . . . On principle, however, it seems that the result of authentic interpretation, whether it is to be treated as always having been law or not, is an integral part of the law from the moment it is fixed" (240–41). It is not possible, however, to argue (as one could about the "author" of the Bible) that the human lawmaker could have known and intended the changes in understanding, and if both historical change and original meaning in the past are collapsed under intention, an expanded conception of intention emerges.

This division between historically situated and original meaning continues to be played out in contemporary debates on legal hermeneutics.[13] Gadamer speaks of "The Exemplary Significance of Legal Hermeneutics," and regards the judge's need to understand the law as it applies to the present as a model for all interpretation.[14] Interpretation for Gadamer always means mediation in light of the present. The legal scholar Emilio Betti, on the other hand, contends that the tasks of the judge and the legal historian are different. While the former applies the law, the latter determines the objective meaning of the law as it is found in the intentions of the lawmaker in the past, and the historian's task is what interpretation consists in. Variations on the historical and the original modes of understanding drive all of the Victorian theories examined in this book; these are the two poles between which theories of interpretation shuttle. Carlyle, as the next chapter will show, brings these two modes together in a hermeneutic that treats the world as a manuscript.

CHAPTER TWO

𝒵

Carlyle

Between Biblical Exegesis and Romantic Hermeneutics

History is a real Prophetic Manuscript, and can be fully interpreted by no man.

—Thomas Carlyle

For indeed it is well said, "in every object there is inexhaustible meaning; the eye sees in it what the eye brings means of seeing."

—Thomas Carlyle

In a review article of 1891 Wilhelm Dilthey describes Carlyle as "the greatest English writer of our century."[1] It is not surprising that Dilthey, the transitional figure between nineteenth-century Romantic hermeneutics and twentieth-century philosophical hermeneutics, greatly admired Carlyle, since he would have found in Carlyle's work a preoccupation with the same hermeneutical issues that absorbed him. Carlyle's connections to German idealism and romanticism have been clear since his time, but the affinities of his thought with the Romantic hermeneutics which developed in the context of transcendental philosophy have not been sufficiently recognized.[2]

Carlyle is not only deeply influenced by the Romantic hermeneutic tradition, but his own major work is centrally about hermeneutics. Chaotic and often contradictory in his writing, his strong connection to nineteenth-century hermeneutics—indeed, his claim to be one of the shapers of that tradition—has not been readily seen. His thought lacks the conceptual rigor of Romantic and scriptural hermeneutics with their attempts to provide systematic accounts of interpretative procedures. But taken together, his works still offer a complex inquiry into the role of interpretation, and the variety of genres in which he writes allows him to put his hermeneutic principles into practice in ways not possible in a purely theoretical context.

While it is more or less a truism that Carlyle joins German philosophy with Calvinism, there has been little detailed examination of the role of the latter in his work and still less attention to the relationship between the two.[3] Carlyle derives from his German sources an epistemology that regards all human experience as interpretive and appends to that a hermeneutic that is largely Calvinist. As we will see, for Carlyle, ethics and practice ultimately provide the grounds for both creating and adjudicating between interpretations.

Carlyle's thought is valuable for current thought in that his writing makes visible the transition from religious to secular hermeneutics. Observing that shift as it occurs, we see the ways in which secular hermeneutics, even when it sees itself as radically new, remains deeply immersed in the presumptions and methods of sacred interpretation. Further, while recent criticism has shown that it is easy to read him as anticipating poststructuralism, Carlyle, while fully acknowledging the role of human construction in knowledge, remains a realist in his assumptions about truth and meaning.

I

Whether Carlyle was directly familiar with the hermeneutic theory that began to proliferate in Germany around the turn of the century is uncertain. We know that he was acquainted with some of the works of the central figures of Romantic hermeneutics. He mentions Schleiermacher's *Speeches on Religion* and much admires Friedrich Schlegel, sometimes quoting him, sometimes paraphrasing his ideas without acknowledgment. Comments in letters indicate that Carlyle was also acquainted with the work of the historian Leopold von Ranke, and it was against Rankean objectivism that historical hermeneutics defined itself. Precise influences are unnecessary, however, for Carlyle knew and was fascinated by the concepts and works from which Romantic hermeneutics developed.

Carlyle's deep attraction to the transcendental philosophy of Kant and Fichte, his admiration for the Romantics Schlegel and Novalis, and his high regard for Goethe and Schiller, are well known. He is, however, above all affected by the roles that the concepts of understanding and interpretation play in that thought. By far the most crucial and enduring idea Carlyle develops as a result of his German readings is his fundamentally hermeneutic view of human experience.

The idealist split between appearance and reality is central to Carlyle's worldview. From Kant, he derives the belief that time and space are not absolutes: "Time and Space themselves are not external but internal entities: they have no outward existence, there is no Time and Space *out* of the mind."[4] They are, nevertheless, inescapable categories of human thought. Primarily through radicalizations of Kant's philosophy, Carlyle adopts a modified version of the distinction between the noumenal and phenomenal. He is impressed by the idea that the mind plays a powerful synthesizing role in our perceptions of appearance, and from this he develops the notion that interpretation is essential to all human experience.

It is widely accepted that Carlyle does not really comprehend the technicalities of the German philosophy he presents to the Victorian public. But what matters here is not Carlyle's failure to understand but the way he consistently brings to the philosophy an interpretive emphasis modeled on textual exegesis. In Carlyle's hands, transcendental idealism takes a decidedly textual turn: "The Revelation of the Infinite in the Finite; a majestic Poem (tragic, comic, or epic), couldst thou but read it and recite it!"[5] He takes interpretation, in fact, to be the focus of transcendental philosophy, attributing to Kant the belief that "the ultimate aim of all Philosophy must be to interpret appearances,—from the given symbol to ascertain the thing" (26:79). Needless to say, this interpretive twist is his own.

This is not to suggest that Carlyle wholly projects a concern with interpretation onto Kantian philosophy. The emphasis on the conditions of human understanding in German idealism is crucial to the development of Romantic hermeneutics. He would have found in Goethe, Schelling, and Novalis the idea of appearance as symbol that in some way reveals the Infinite. But Carlyle's own views are thrown into relief by his glossing over the important differences between idealist philosophers. What lies behind appearance for Carlyle is not the noumenal world, absolute ego, ideal activity, or mind. Nor, in Carlyle's view, can the finite influence the infinite; the symbol, cannot, as it can for Novalis, transform the non-ego that it represents. Although Carlyle in part takes his notion of the symbol from the German writers he admires, his use of it is profoundly shaped by Christian tradition. For Carlyle, the relationship between the world of appearance and the absolute is analogous to that between text and meaning. A symbol points to stable and absolute divine meaning, the intention of God, to be interpreted on the model of textual exegesis. Carlyle consistently recasts the transcendental philosophy he encounters to bring it into accord with the model of scriptural exegesis.[6]

He also accepts the idea, widespread in post-Kantian German idealist thought, that the infinite is in part discernible in the finite and unites this with the belief, found in Christian theories of accommodation and in various forms in the early Schlegel, Schiller, and Schleiermacher (all of whom were also Protestants), in the impossibility of ever doing more than endlessly approximating to the infinite: "It is true all goes by approximation in this world" (10:11). This epistemology translates for Carlyle into a two-leveled obligation to interpret the infinite by giving it form in the finite world and then in turn to interpret the forms of the finite world to understand the divine. Because human understanding is historically conditioned, attempts at articulating divine meaning will necessarily take on different forms in different historical periods. This does not, however, amount for Carlyle to an interpretive relativism that releases understanding from the constraints of an originating intention. Meaning is grounded in divine intention, but its entirety is always beyond our grasp. Here, Carlyle is in agreement with Schleiermacher, who brings transcendental tenets to his hermeneutic, writing "interpretation gives finite form to infinite intuition."[7]

What did Carlyle discover in German transcendental thought that he did not find in Christian idealism? Notoriously, at the time of his German studies, Carlyle was in the throes of religious skepticism. He claimed that his encounter with Goethe enabled him to revive his dwindling faith. Goethe's more generalized form of idealism, that is, allowed Carlyle to free himself from specifically Christian doctrines while he still maintained what amounted to the same general understanding of reality.

Carlyle came away from his German reading convinced that the Infinite takes many forms in our world and that each of these forms is a product of its historical context. This conviction allowed him to reassert his spiritual belief while relegating Christianity to a position of just one among many historical embodiments of the divine—although a particularly successful one. In this, Carlyle rejected Calvin's conviction that God is revealed only through Scripture. If the absolute is everywhere manifest in the finite, then the task of interpretation extends beyond the Bible to all experience. Carlyle grafts on to the ideas he finds in German idealism the Christian notion of the world as a text, and the synthesis makes unending interpretation in pursuit of meaning a necessity. Having established this more encompassing conception of the divine text, however, Carlyle returns to his Presbyterian roots.

One finds everywhere in Calvin's *Institutes* ideas that are central to Carlyle's thought, particularly in Calvin's extensive theory of biblical exegesis.[8] Carlyle's family was deeply committed to the Burgher sect, a strongly Calvinist evangelical community, which put great emphasis on the importance of the word of God in Scripture, and in particular on the question of how one was to understand that word.[9] The meetings regularly attended by the Carlyle family were devoted to expounding biblical texts. Exegesis played a large role in Carlyle's early life.

Many of Calvin's principles for the interpretation of Scripture underlie Carlyle's account of how one ought to go about interpreting the world. Calvin's fundamental rules are that we must attempt to determine the intentions of the author; that there is one correct meaning of the text, but that a complete reproduction of that meaning is beyond human capacities; that we should investigate the historical, geographical, and linguistic contexts in which a text was composed; and that despite these more technical aspects of interpretation, the grasping of the meaning of a text is in the last analysis an intuitive act.

The limited capacity of humans to know the divine is an insistent note in Calvin's thought. The meaning of Scripture always exceeds human conceptual representation. God's intentions may appear "hidden and fugitive" from our point of view.[10] Any interpretation of the Bible, then, will be partial and approximate. Calvin believes, however, that "we must nevertheless endeavor, as much as in us lies, to approach it more and more by continual advances."[11] Carlyle will echo this in his assertion that we must continue "working more and more on Reality, and evolving more and more wisely *its* inexhaustible meanings" (28:53).

Despite the obstacles in the way of full understanding, Calvin is insistent that there is a "true meaning of Scripture." We must not, he cautions, "twist Scripture without restraint, thus making anything we please out of anything" (*Institutes*, II.viii.8). The text provides severe constraints on meaning, even though our inability to achieve complete understanding results in diverse interpretations: "Scripture they say is fertile and thus bears multiple meanings. I acknowledge that Scripture is the most rich and inexhaustible fount of all wisdom; but I deny that its fertility consists in the various meanings which anyone may fasten to it at his pleasure."[12] The telos remains divine intention, the goal to see "the Lawgiver's pure and authentic meaning faithfully rendered" (*Institutes,* II.viii.8).

Carlyle's indebtedness to Calvin's hermeneutic is most pronounced in his adoption of one of Calvin's fundamental principles: accommodation, the belief that God must always adjust the expression of his meaning to the finite limits of human understanding, a view that is crucial to Victorian scriptural hermeneutics as well. God, says Calvin, presented his meaning in ways attuned to the consciousness of the time: "He accommodated diverse forms to different ages, as he knew would be expedient for each" (*Institutes,*

II.ii.13). Calvin believes that the Bible records the word of God, as given to the inspired writers, but the texts were written by individual men in particular historical circumstances, in a style and in language distinctive to each.

Language, Calvin argues, is inadequate to a full grasp of God's intentions. The symbols of the Bible always fall short of the meaning they represent, yet it is only through the vehicle of the word that God can be known.[13] One can never dispense with this deficient medium and have direct access to God. Similarly, Carlyle is critical of language's inadequacies, complaining of the "fundamental infirmity, vitiating insufficiency, in all *words*."[14] Nevertheless, at least in his early writing, language is the most significant symbol system we have, and essentially conditions all other thinking of which we are capable.

The highest use of language, Carlyle maintains, that which most clearly allows us some comprehension of the divine, is that used by the hero.[15] In that view, Carlyle reproduces the strongly elitist component of Calvin's hermeneutic. Calvin believed that he was especially chosen by God to expound the Scripture, just as the original writers had been elected by God to present his message. "Only those to whom it is given," says Calvin "can comprehend the mysteries of God" (*Institutes,* I.vii.5). Carlyle, likewise, believes that only certain heroic figures have the ability to read the text of the world adequately: "Facts are engraved hierograms for which the fewest have the key" (1:161). "Heroes" are superior interpreters of the text of appearance, both in that they are better able than others to read the infinite in the symbols of appearance and in that their lives are the highest symbols. Thus Carlyle was to write eight volumes on Frederick the Great and proclaim him "the supreme ultimate interpreter" (2:72).

II

Like the German Romantic hermeneuts, Carlyle extends the sphere of hermeneutics from the interpretation of texts within a particular discipline to an attempt to grasp the conditions for all understanding. In extending hermeneutics beyond the interpretation of texts per se to the understanding of all experience, Carlyle might be seen as anticipating philosophical hermeneutics. For the Romantic hermeneut the interpretive endeavor remained primarily a linguistic one. Carlyle anticipates Dilthey's expansion of hermeneutics to the understanding of all meaningful human action in his concern with the interpretation of human events, institutions, and practices.[16] Yet he can also be seen as reversing this movement by reinstating biblical hermeneutics with a vengeance.

The world becomes one large text on which to practice Calvin's hermeneutics. "Life in itself [is] a Bible" (27:100), the world is "universal divine Scripture" (28:176) "whose Author is God" (26:444).

For Carlyle, interpretation is not one method of knowing among others. It is the fundamental mode of all human knowledge. He sees the whole world as purposeful, immanent with meaning, and so approaches it as if it were made to be interpreted. His model for understanding the world is that of an obscure text that will always remain partly opaque. Carlyle alters Calvinist exegesis, however, not only by extending the sphere of revelation beyond Scripture but also by adopting the distinctively Romantic view of the productive imagination. While Calvin wants to guard against human creativity leading away from the divine will, Carlyle insists that it is only through human creativity and action that God's intentions can be revealed. The text, therefore, takes on a dual aspect in Carlyle's view. For while we interpret the text to realize divine intention, the text is always also one that we write in our attempt to "body forth" the divine in material form. Thus he blurs the boundaries between reading, writing, and translation, interpretation and creation, speaking of the "Bible of World-History that all men, in all times with or without clear consciousness have been unwearied to read, what we may call *read;* and again to write, or rather be *written!* What is all History, and all Poesy, but a deciphering somewhat thereof, out of that mystic heaven-written Sanscrit; and rendering it into the speech of men?" (28:251). Here, as so often, Carlyle has it both ways. Interpretation is both devising and discovery, invention and revelation. This seeming contradiction is essential to Carlyle's view. While he does not want to allow for complete freedom in interpretation, he wants individual agency to matter.

The image of the world as a text of God is, of course, an old Christian (though not Calvinist) concept, but filtered through the ideas that Carlyle adopts from German idealism, it takes on a new character.[17] In Carlyle's view, the idea is more than a metaphor:

> Singular what difficulty I have in getting my poor message delivered to the world in this epoch: things I imperatively need still to say.
>
> 1. That all history is a Bible—a thing stated in words by me more than once, and adopted in a sentimental way; but nobody can I bring fairly into it, nobody persuade to take it up practically as a *fact*.[18]

Carlyle puts his emphasis not, as most previous thinkers had, on understanding nature as a book of God. Instead he emphasizes the interpretation of history and those things produced by human thought and actions: language, artworks, symbol systems, beliefs, cultural practices and institutions.

He further transforms the idea by insisting that the temporal nature of human existence makes the text dynamic. There is no stable correspondence between the signs of the world-text and the divine intention they represent. While the meaning they point to remains fixed and unchanging, the signs (the signs themselves are interpretations for Carlyle) of the text will inevitably change.[19] Attempts at articulating divine meaning will take different forms in different historical periods, because forms are not like the eternal reality they give a glimpse of, but mere signs in the shifting world of temporality and history, symbols through which the eternal is given sensible existence.[20] All symbols "exist for a time only" (1:55), wear out, become outmoded, and no longer succeed in revealing divine meaning. Transferring the concept of accommodation to the understanding of all human experience allows Carlyle to pay close attention to diachrony while continuing to assert that there is a fixed intention behind events.

Carlyle ends, then, by locating meaning somewhere between authorial intention and the interpreter's understanding. His theory of interpretation is at once intentionalist and relativistic, grounded simultaneously in intuitionism and in aesthetic subjectivism. Yet Carlyle insists that there is a transcendent ground beyond history that guarantees determinate meaning. Accounts of the meaning change, but not the meaning itself. Nor are all interpretations equally correct or incorrect. Some adequately (though temporarily and incompletely) reveal divine intention, while others are no more than false symbols of the world of appearance.

III

Underlying Carlyle's theory of interpretation is a clearly articulated perspectivist epistemology. He believes that absolute truth is always beyond human cognitive capacities and he condemns wholly logical or rationalist approaches to knowledge. Although this attitude is derived in part from his Calvinist antirationalism, with its emphasis on suprarational ways of knowing, he gives the view a philosophical basis that carries it into the sphere of hermeneutics: purely objective knowledge is an impossibility because there is no God's-eye view available to humans. In a notebook entry, Carlyle comments on the limits of our knowledge: "For the present, I will confess it, I scarce see how we can reason with *absolute* certainty on the nature of fate or *any*thing; for it seems to me we only see our own perceptions and their relations; that is to say, our soul sees only its own partial *reflex* and manner of existing and conceiving"(*Notebooks,* 97). He stresses the relativity of human perspective in ways that will be echoed later in the century in scientific theory. Our knowledge is inevitably conditioned by our epistemic faculties: "Nine tenths of our reasonings are *artificial* processes, depending not on the real nature of things but on our peculiar mode of viewing things, and thereby varying with all the variations both in the kind and in extent of our perceptions" (*Notebooks,* 4). Carlyle goes so far as to claim that all truths to which we have direct access, all truths of appearance, are contingent truths: "If it be, as Kant maintains, that the logical mechanism of the mind is arbitrary, so to speak, and might have been made different, it will follow, that all inductive conclusions, all conclusions of the Understanding, have only a relative truth, are true only for *us,* and *if* some other thing be true" (27:27).

Not only are we restricted to ways of understanding determined by our constitution, but our individual viewpoints also condition our perceptions of the world. In quintessentially Carlylean terminology, he expounds on the limitations of subjective vision: "Each individual takes up the Phenomenon according to his own point of vision, to the structure of his optic organs;—gives, consciously some poor crotchety picture of several things; unconsciously some picture of himself at least. And the Phenomenon, for its part, subsists there, all the while, unaltered; waiting to be pictured as often as you like, its entire meaning not to be compressed into any picture drawn by man" (29:2). Carlyle's skepticism, however, always implies the reality of the inaccessible truth, and always assumes its value; he takes human limits as an obstacle on the way to that truth. Despite the unavailability of purely objective knowledge, there are standards for adjudication between interpretations. For Carlyle, these take, in various ways, an ethical form.

One of Carlyle's most striking claims, which operates both in his views on the interpretation of existence and in his more specific hermeneutic practices, is that knowledge is inextricably tied to morality. Interpretive constraints enter through the ethical attitude of the interpreter. Carlyle insists that one can best understand something not by adopting an unbiased, objective viewpoint (in his view, an impossibility, in any case), but rather through sympathy and love. Moral sentiments give one the needed perspective for a more correct understanding.

In Carlyle's early thought, he regards literary works as the highest mode of interpretation of the divine: "Literary Men are the appointed interpreters of this Divine Idea; a perpetual priesthood, we might say, standing forth, generation after generation, as the dispensers and living types of God's everlasting wisdom, to show it in their writings and actions

in such particular form as their own particular times require it. (26:58).
His model for the interpretation of these interpretations is a coaxing of
the meaning from the depths of the text. He writes, for example, of
Goethe's *Helena:*

> In truth, the outward meaning seems unsatisfactory enough, were it not
> that ever and anon we are reminded of a cunning, manifold meaning
> which lies hidden under it; and incited by capricious beckonings to evolve
> this, more and more completely, from its quaint concealment. (26:148)

We seek the meaning behind what is given, a meaning that is "altogether
provoking and impenetrable" to "hasty readers" (28:148), and one that,
as in the case of the Bible, which becomes Carlyle's model for all great literary texts, is "manifold."

In his essays on literature Carlyle provides specific practical rules for
interpreting texts.[21] Among these are the principles that interpretation
requires strenuous effort from the reader and that a text must be read
"unhurriedly," that is "close read": "In fact, *Faust* is to be read not once
but many times, if we would understand it: every line, every word has its
purport; and only in such minute inspection will the essential significance of the poem display itself" (26:153). Carlyle also deems that a
select group will be superior interpreters and he appeals to readers of
particular proficiencies, "the sympathising reader" (1:61), the reader
with "metaphysical acumen" (1:9). While this focus on the talented no
doubt reflects the elitism of Carlyle's Calvinism, the idea that some are
innately superior interpreters is, as we have seen, pervasive in nineteenth-
century hermeneutics. Arnold's interpretive "tact" is another version of
the view that correct interpretation depends upon a particular sensibility
and an intelligence that cannot be determined by any prescribed
method.

Carlyle's principal rule involves the psychologizing mode of Romantic
hermeneutics that requires a sympathetic projection into the author's
perspective: "Herein lies the highest merit of a piece, and the proper art
of reading it. We have not *read* an author till we have seen his object,
whatever it may be, as *he* saw it" (26:150). Given his commitment to the
idea that great literary works are ultimately revelations of divine intention, Carlyle's interpretive method might be expected to seek to bypass
human intention altogether (as does Newman's). But his emphasis falls
on reconstructing the intention of the human artist as the means of
grasping divine intention: "While looking on the *Transfiguration,* while
studying the *Iliad,* we ever strive to figure to ourselves what spirit dwelt in

Raphael; what a head was that of Homer. . . . We partially and for the time being become the very Painter and the very Singer" (28:45–46). Just as in Calvin's view, God's will can be understood only in the concrete form of the biblical narratives, so for Carlyle the divine intention embodied in a literary work can be approached only through understanding the writer's vision from within.[22]

But like all nineteenth-century theorists of interpretation, Carlyle knows that we can never exactly replicate the author's meaning: "No perfect clearness may be attained, but only various approximations to it; hints and half-glances of meaning" (26:152).[23] An accomplished reader can succeed in partially recreating the meaning, by discovering the "centre" of an author's thought and replicating the perspective that gives the work cohesion: "The further we advance into it, we see confusion more and more unfold itself into order, till at last, viewed from its proper centre, his intellectual universe, no longer a distorted incoherent series of air-landscapes, coalesces into compact expansion" (26:13–14). We attempt to enter into the author's viewpoint, "see the world with his eyes, feel as he felt, and judge as he judged" (27:50). Carlyle here comes very close to Schleiermacher's belief that correct interpretation requires a sympathetic entering into a speaker's perspective.

Carlyle's theory of biographical interpretation is also informed by this sympathetic method of understanding. He believes that all lives are texts to undergo exegesis, although the hero, as the most accurate interpreter, himself most deserves interpretation. He begins his biography of Goethe by asking: "How shall we interpret, how shall we even see him?" (26:199). His answer is that we begin to see him or any subject of biography, by, in a sense, becoming him. The biographer's aim is "to see into [his subject], understand his goings-forth, decipher the whole heart of his mystery: nay, not only to see into him, but even to see out of him, to view the world altogether as he views it" (28:44).

One must, it seems to follow, lose some of one's own sense of self in order to enter into the viewpoint of another. But, remarkably, Carlyle carries this idea beyond psychological empathy with other people, extending the view to all acts of knowing. There is, he claims, a moral dimension to all understanding: "And how much of *morality* is in the kind of insight we get of anything; 'the eye seeing in all things what it brought with it the faculty of seeing'! To the mean eye all things are trivial, as certainly as to the jaundiced eye they are yellow" (5:94). Understanding for Carlyle depends on entering into an ethical relationship with the thing one attempts to know. It can never proceed on the model of an impartial knowing; the knower must be *affected* by the person or thing he attempts to understand. "Sympathy," he writes "is the first essential toward insight" and "a loving Heart is the beginning of all Knowledge" (28:57).

These claims might be taken to mean that an interpreter's ego-centered perspective is inevitably distorting and that the attempt to "see" from another's point of view is a first step toward a more objective perspective. Since each subjective perspective colors and distorts what is interpreted, and the values with which we approach something affect our understanding of it, Carlyle might be expected to advocate sympathy as a means of ridding oneself of one's subjective perspective, as a partial escape from unmitigated egocentricism. Certainly, Teufelsdroeckh's injunctions to self-annihilation would be consistent with this model.

In fact, however, Carlyle is saying something quite different. Rather than advocate sympathy as a step toward objectivity and disinterested impartiality, he asserts that sympathy and love—interestedness and partiality—are essential conditions of all knowledge, even of ordinary empirical knowledge: "He could not have discerned the object at all, or seen the vital type of it, unless he had, what we may call, *sympathized* with it" (5:93). Affect is not simply added to what is essentially a cognitive act. It is instead the basis for any successful act of understanding. One does not gain knowledge by ridding oneself of emotions; rather emotions are the preconditions of knowledge.

Here Carlyle shows himself to be opposed to standard canons of rational inquiry. Rather than recommend escape from the distortion of a subjective point of view to an objective perspective, he asserts, in effect, that an interested and partial approach is essential to knowledge. For sympathy requires seeing from a particular viewpoint and love necessarily implies a tendency to find interest and value. Understanding demands *partiality*, and morality and knowledge are inextricably connected: "A thoroughly immoral *man* could not know anything at all! To know a thing, what we can call knowing, a man must first *love* the thing, sympathize with it: that is, be *virtuously* related to it" (5:107).

IV

Sartor Resartus brings together many of the facets of Carlyle's hermeneutic thought, putting into practice ideas on interpretation that he had previously presented only in abstract form. It is Carlyle's attempt to produce what he terms a phantasmagory, and he underscored the hermeneutic obstacles the form presents: "The difficulties of interpretation are exceedingly enhanced by one circumstance . . . namely, that this is no

Allegory; which, as in the *Pilgrim's Progress*, you have only once for all to find the key of, and so go on unlocking" (27:449). *Sartor* is a text that models and requires multiple orders of interpretation—readers trying to interpret Carlyle's book, the Editor trying to interpret Teufelsdroeckh, Teufelsdroeckh trying to interpret history and appearance.

From the start, interpretation is the Editor's task, and Teufelsdroeckh is his major "text." In turn, Teufelsdroeckh is the expounder of Carlyle's own view that life is an ongoing hermeneutic endeavor, the world a symbol that is to be interpreted to reveal the divine meaning that lies behind it: "We speak of the Volume of Nature: and truly a Volume it is,—whose Author and Writer is God. To read it! Dost thou, does man, so much as well know the Alphabet thereof? With its Words, Sentences, and grand descriptive Systems, and Thousands of Years, we shall not try thee. It is a Volume written in celestial hieroglyphs, in the true Sacred-writing; of which even Prophets are happy that they can read here a line and there a line" (1:204–5). Extravagantly, even ironically, Carlyle makes concrete his notion that divine meaning is revealed in a form appropriate for human understanding by making Teufelsdroeckh's topic "clothes." Clothes are essentially interpretations that do not fully reproduce intention since they are a translation from the mode of the absolute and eternal to that of the temporal and finite.

In keeping with the hermeneutic preoccupation with meaning-making, Carlyle might be said to make *Sartor* a book about its own creation. The material for Teufelsdroeckh's autobiography turns out, famously, to be six bags "in the inside of which sealed Bags lie miscellaneous masses of Sheets, and oftener Shreds and Snips" (11:61). The organization by zodiac signs is unintelligible, and although the Editor makes the claim that the clothes philosophy will be incomprehensible without some knowledge of Teufelsdroeckh and his history, the biography is just as difficult to interpret as the text on clothes. The clothes narrative itself shifts, without signal, in the course of any given paragraph from a literal account of the history of clothes in society to a metaphorical presentation of the symbolic manifestation of the divine.

While it would be easy, given our current emphasis on undecidability, to see *Sartor* as a text whose main point is the instability of interpretation, Carlyle's object is almost the reverse. That is, he wants his readers to recognize that firmly entrenched ideas, customs, social practices are modifiable and that *better* interpretations are possible. His emphasis is on the difficulty of seeing in new ways, and he tries to dramatize how interpretations take hold and become very difficult to shake off. Things we accept as necessary, "the whole fabric of Government, Legislation, Property,

Police, and Civilised society" (1:48) turn out to be only clothes, symbols we have created. As for many recent theorists, part of Carlyle's purpose in insisting on the interpretive nature of experience is related to his desire to alter contemporary social institutions and overcome ossified beliefs. In this sense, it is not unreasonable to see Carlyle's hermeneutic as a kind of pre-Habermasian ideology critique.

A number of recent commentators have argued that *Sartor* is a proto-postmodern text, a text that reveals the indeterminability of all signs.[24] But in *Sartor* Carlyle attempts to show that despite the difficulties of interpretation, objective meaning does exist and can in part be grasped. That is, the religious model I discussed earlier lingers crucially in Carlyle's hermeneutic theory. Interpretations are inexhaustible for Carlyle not because of the iterability of the sign or because meaning always surpasses intention, but because divine intention always surpasses human conceptual representation. While he does set up a persistent tension between the historically changing and a stable absolute, Carlyle never lets go of his faith in a fixed locus of meaning behind the world of appearance. His work fits into the nineteenth-century hermeneutic tradition precisely because he believes that there is such a thing as correct interpretation and that finding it, though ultimately impossible, is the goal of interpretation.

He is, then, a long way from a Derridean view. The attempt to replicate the original meaning or intention remains the aim of interpretation for Carlyle, an aim that deconstruction dismisses, so that despite his emphasis on textuality, Carlyle's position is precisely the view that Derrida interrogates. It is with the notion of the text as a book of God that Derrida begins *Of Grammatology* and it is from this notion of the signified as eternal truth that he derives his views on the concepts of presence, the absolute logos, and the transcendental signifier. Hermeneutics for Derrida, as we have seen, relies on the theological and metaphysical notion that a text is unified and informed by a univocal, unchanging intention. These charges apply to Carlyle's views on text and interpretation.

Sartor's concluding shift away from its account of Teufelsdroeckh's philosophy and its depiction of his vanishing into the sphere of social reform and politics have often puzzled critics. But for Carlyle this move to ethical action is the necessary consequence of any glimpse into divine meaning, and it would be more puzzling if he did not represent this, his central conclusion, at the end of his text on interpretation. Carlyle's insistence on a reality that interpretation attempts to approximate leads him toward social reform just as contemporary assertion of the constructed nature of "reality" is designed to move toward change. Action becomes the most trustworthy form of interpretation for Carlyle, as the passage he is so fond of quoting from Goethe indicates: "In action alone can we have certainty" (28:26). Throughout the text Carlyle stresses the interplay between interpretation and practice. The final aim of interpretation is ethical action; we interpret in order to act, we interpret by acting.

There is, then, a second way in which ethics is fundamental to Carlyle's account of interpretation. Despite his insistence on the multiplicity of adequate but partial possible interpretations, Carlyle maintains a means of adjudicating between readings through his emphasis on the ethical. It is not only that a certain ethical stance is required in an interpreter. For Carlyle, morality provides a ground from which to assess all interpretations. The standard for a good interpretation of the divine is that which results in the most ethical action.

Of course, this begs the question of how we know what it is to be moral. How do we learn which sentiments are morally required? If an ethical attitude is fundamental to correct interpretation, we are still left with the tremendous problem of how to derive ethical judgments. Yet Carlyle provides an answer even to this seeming gap in his theory, and one that continues to rely on the interpretive paradigm.

In his *Reminiscences* Carlyle tells of meeting Dr. Chalmers, an important Calvinist minister, in the early 1820s. Carlyle explains that Chalmers discussed "some scheme he had for proving Christianity by its visible fitness for human nature." Chalmers is reported as saying "'All written in us already . . . in *sympathetic ink*. Bible awakens it; and you can read.'" Carlyle describes his reaction as lukewarm; he listens "not with any real conviction."[25] Yet, although he may have rejected the idea that the Christian Bible is the route to truth, the notion of an inner text appears in Carlyle's writings from beginning to end. In one of his final works, for instance, Carlyle writes of the divine message: "Men at one time read it in their Bible. . . . And if no man could now see it by any Bible, there is written in the heart of every man an authentic copy of it direct from Heaven itself: there, if he may have learnt to decipher Heaven's writing . . . every born man may still find some copy of it" (30:67). Carlyle's controlling idea of experience as text to be read pertains not only to external appearances but also to this interior text, which amounts to something like innate ideas or intuition.

Carlyle is, of course, a moral realist. He also believes that we have some intuitive access to the moral law: "Without some ulterior sanction, common to all minds; without some belief in the necessary, eternal, or which is the same, in the supermundane, divine nature of Virtue, existing in each individual, what could the moral judgment of a thousand or a thousand-thousand individuals avail us?" (26:464). One might wonder, in fact, whether Carlyle's concept of understanding depends so heavily on the notion of intuition, an immediate apprehension of truth, that it moves out of the sphere of hermeneutics. After all, Carlyle sometimes suggests that correct interpretation is entirely superrational, an act of knowing without logical proof: "To *know;* to get into the truth of anything, is ever a mystic act—of which the best Logics can but babble on the surface" (5:57). Moreover, that sympathy and love are moral attitudes is seemingly an unquestioned ethical judgment. In its appeal to a universalist ethic of reciprocity, his account ultimately seems to be founded on an innate faculty for gaining moral truth.

Although at times it sounds as though he thinks we can gain direct insight into truth, even intuition and innate ideas turn out to require interpretation. He rarely refers to intuitive knowledge without also bringing in his exegetical paradigm. He explains the idealist focus on intuition, for example, in the context of hermeneutics: "Their Primitive Truth, however, they seek not historically and by experiment, in the universal persuasions of men, but by intuition, . . . they find these things written as the beginning of all Philosophy, in obscured but ineffaceable characters, within our innermost being" (26:81).

In his belief that intuitive knowledge is itself like a text, Carlyle accepts that intuitions do not constitute immediate or complete understanding of the "Divine." Even these are interpretations in forms commensurate with human understanding. As Teufelsdroeckh says "All forms whereby Spirit manifests itself to Sense, whether outwardly or in the imagination, are Clothes" (1:215).

In the end, then, Carlyle might be seen as abandoning his interpretive principles by falling back on ethics as the ground for assessing interpretations, but even here he remains within the hermeneutic circle. It is only through human intentional activity that divine intention is revealed. Hence human actions and lives must be interpreted as a text of divine origins. But it is only if we have an ability to read divine meaning that we can act ethically. (Again, Carlyle appears to adapt an idea from Christian theology, that of application, whereby one shows that one has correctly understood Scripture by acting it.) Right interpretation results in ethical action, but, in a self-referential movement, it is only through the interpretation of action that we can recognize the divine. This circular reasoning is a basic structure of Carlyle's thought, and should be seen as a version of the hermeneutic circle. The parts can be understood only in terms of the whole, the whole only in terms of the parts. Action reveals to us the ethical as we see it in practice, and yet vague intuitions of it serve as our original impetus to action.

V

Carlyle's dominant concern with ethics further complicates his hermeneutic position, in particular as he engages with questions of history.[26] As we've seen, Carlyle shares with the Romantic hermeneuts the view that correct interpretation of a literary work requires the reader's projection into the consciousness of the author. In tension with his views on empathetic reconstruction, however, Carlyle suggests in discussing literary works from earlier periods that the historical gap cannot be bridged. The forms of ancient myths and epics, for example, can no longer speak to us: "We believe it to have been believed, by the Singer or his Hearers; into whose case we now laboriously struggle to transport ourselves; and so, with stinted enough result, catch some Reflex of the Reality, which for them was wholly real and visible face to face" (28:50). Time obstructs our ability to reconstruct the author's "centre," and Carlyle is generally more skeptical than Schleiermacher or Jowett about our capacity to disengage ourselves from our own historical circumstances. Older texts, again on the model of biblical accommodation, must be translated for the present, as they embody the spirit of their time: "Each age, by the law of its nature, is different from every other age, and demands a different representation of the Divine Idea, the essence of which is the same in all; so that the literary man of one century is only by mediation and reinterpretation applicable to the wants of another" (26:59). Despite his extensive remarks on empathetic interpretation, then, Carlyle is principally interested in a text's ethical effect in his own time, and this orientation toward the present is strongly felt in his histories. His historical hermeneutics is strikingly presentist, denying the notion that one can know the past on its own terms.[27] Historical knowledge is instead always conditioned by present circumstances and needs.

If in Carlyle's early thought the works of a great writer are "truer than reality itself, since the essence of unmixed reality is bodied forth in them under more expressive symbols" (6:51), he later reverses that view, having found "that History, after all, is the true Poetry; that Reality, if rightly interpreted, is grander than Fiction; nay that even in the right interpretation of Reality and History does genuine Poetry consist" (4:17). Carlyle comes to regard accounts of real events as fundamentally different from imagined narratives: "Let any one bethink him how impressive the smallest historical *fact* may become, as contrasted with the grandest *fictitious event;* what an incalculable force lies for us in this consideration: The Thing which I here hold imaged in my mind did actually occur" (28:54). This strict demarcation between fact and fiction is both interesting and bewildering, given the idealism that undergirds Carlyle's sense of the no more than provisional reality of the historical world. If everything in the human world is symbolic, why, one wonders, aren't the imaginative incidents of a literary text as revealing of the divine as historical occurrences. Why are events and people as "signs" more in touch with the divine reality than products of the imagination expressed in words as sign? Is not a literary work itself a historical fact? Carlyle never adequately explains this; but "facts," things that really happened and really existed (as those terms are understood in the phenomenological world) take on profound value in his later writing. We might speculate that Carlyle comes to regard fiction as being further removed from divine intention, because it involves an additional level of symbol on top of the order of the material signs he regards as divine text (although he is the first to recognize that our access to history is textual). Or it may be that his intense sense of the symbolic and illusory nature of experience led him to deeply crave the concrete and the embodied. His ontological distinctions remain unclear, but whatever the explanation, the "Past" becomes the most significant of texts.

As I've tried to show, Carlyle brings together two domains, biblical exegesis and Romantic philosophy, in his hermeneutic. His writing on history extends this hermeneutic into a historical method:

> Let us search more and more into the Past; let all men explore it, as the true fountain of knowledge. . . . For though the whole meaning lies far beyond our ken; yet in that complex Manuscript, covered over with formless-inextricably-entangled unknown characters,—nay, which is a *Palimpsest*, and had once prophetic writing, still dimly legible there,—some letters, some words, may be deciphered; . . . well understanding, in the mean while, that it is only a little portion we have deciphered; that much still remains to be interpreted; that History is a real Prophetic Manuscript, and can be fully interpreted by no man. (27:89–90)

The idea that history is textual later became widespread, but its origins in religious hermeneutics have nearly been effaced. In Carlyle, we witness the transition to a more encompassing notion of textuality in history: "Great Men are the inspired (speaking and acting) Texts of that divine BOOK OF REVELATIONS, whereof a Chapter is completed from epoch to epoch, and by some named HISTORY; to which inspired Texts your numerous talented men, and your innumerable untalented men, are the better or worse exegetic Commentaries" (1:142). The "textuality" metaphor (though more than a metaphor according to Carlyle) manifests its roots in biblical exegesis. Carlyle's language remains explicitly theological, consonant with his belief in the actuality of history as Bible.

Just as some theologians argue about readings of Scripture, Carlyle believes that interpretations of the text of history must change as historical conditions alter: "Here also I will observe, that the *manner* in which men read this same Bible is, like all else, proportionate to their stage of culture, to the circumstances of their environment" (28:252). But the meaning of history changes also because the "text" itself is not yet completed; history is not at an end, and the full meaning is only in the whole. Thus the historicity of understanding is doubly emphasized, for the "text" not only takes on different meanings at different times, but it also continues to be written in time.

In crucial ways, then, Carlyle's theory of historical interpretation is directly imported from theology, being an extension of an accommodation theory from scriptural exegesis to human history. Although the biblical model does provide a broad framework for his general thought, his thought also bears comparison with that of the historians who applied interpretive theory to history and in so doing inaugurated the hermeneutic tradition in nineteenth-century historiography. Like them, Carlyle defines his historiography against the conception of objectivity that was to become the ideal methodology of historical positivism later in the century. Scholars have commented on the paucity of the theory of history in the first part of the nineteenth century, pointing to Wilhelm von Humboldt, Johann Droysen, and Leopold von Ranke as notable exceptions. Carlyle's historical texts, however, always preoccupied with problems of knowledge, also participated in that developing tradition.[28] Dilthey, a historian as well as theorist of hermeneutics, was one of the few to note that Carlyle's views resemble Humboldt's, particularly the Humboldt of "On the Task of the Historian" (1821).[29] In addition, Carlyle's theories resemble some of Droysen's in the *Historik* (1857). (Both historians are now considered central figures in the hermeneutic tradition and both, like Carlyle, were influenced by German idealism and romanticism). Again, this is not a matter of direct influence (Droysen's methodological work was not published until 1857), but of writers, who, working in comparable intellectual milieus, were drawn to interpretation as a central explanatory concept.

Carlyle's writings on history already manifest awareness of much that we regard as contemporary: the textuality of historical knowledge, the effects of representation, and the impossibility of giving a complete account of the past: "Nay, even with regard to those occurrences which do stand recorded, which at their origin have seemed worthy of record, and the summary of which we now call History, is not our understanding of them altogether incomplete; is it even possible to represent them as they were?" (27:87). In his texts, he poses theoretical and methodological questions that have become common in historiography.[30] Carlyle never claims objectivity for his histories and cannot be charged with the obfuscation or the naïveté about representation that Roland Barthes discerns in nineteenth-century historiography.[31] Nor does Carlyle take the writing of history to be a disinterested activity. For Carlyle, the historian's account is always partial, in both senses of the word. It is shaped by a particular consciousness with a particular aim in telling the story, and it is incomplete.[32]

In fact, his self-reflexivity about his project so emphasizes the problems involved in historical knowledge that they appear to be nearly insurmountable. To begin with, there are many gaps in our knowledge of history: "Of the *thing* now gone silent, named Past, which was once Present, and loud enough, how much do we know? Our 'Letter of Instructions' comes to us in the saddest state; falsified, blotted out, torn, lost and but a shred of it in existence; this too so difficult to read or spell" (28:168). Since we have access to history only through things that exist in the present, such as relics and documents (either contemporary accounts of historical events or later reconstructions), we cannot hope to have any real access to the past or a complete understanding of history.

History is told in narrative, Carlyle reminds his readers, and involves particular conventions of representation. One of these is that the historian must summarize experience: "History contracts itself into readable extent" (28:173). Another is that the writer must ignore some things and focus on others to create a coherent account. Ultimately narrative is inadequate to experience: "An Historian must write (so to speak) in *lines;* but every event is a *superficies;* nay if we search out its *causes,* a *solid;* hence a primary and almost incurable defect in the art of narrative; which only the very best can so much approximately remedy" (*Notebooks,* 124). The linearity of writing cannot encompass the reality of events because "narrative is, by its nature, of only one dimension; only travels forward towards one, or towards successive points" (27:89). Carlyle's histories both insist on their status as presentations of the real and call into question the representational capacities of realist narrative.

And yet his historical writing is pervaded by an intense sense of the reality of the past—and its reality is what makes it so pressing for the present. He is awestruck by the idea that the past, which once existed, is now gone: "The Past is a dim indubitable fact" (10:38); "no less obscure than undeniable" (10:52); "a *fact,* no dream" (10:62); "its characters *were,* and *are not.*" History's value lies in its being "fact," and yet he forces on readers the obscurity of the facts. So Carlyle is a skeptic, certain of the past's reality, but also certain that we do not know it as it was. On the one hand, the past is ontologically independent of the present; on the other hand, our *knowledge* of it is not: we can only know it in and for the present. These two conceptions structure Carlyle's historical writing, perhaps partially accounting for the sense of excess, the plethora of detail, as he tries to reproduce the past as thickly as possible, to bring it alive, if only to declare it irrecoverable.[33]

Not only is narrative an inadequate representational medium, but every eyewitness account of a historical event is limited and perspectival: "The old story of Sir Walter Raleigh's looking from his prison-window, on some street tumult, which afterwards three witnesses reported in three different ways, himself differing from them all, is still a true lesson for us. Consider how it is that historical documents and records originate; even honest records, where the reports were unbiased by personal regard" (27:87). For humans, there is no gaining the supra-historical position that is needed for full knowledge. We perceive events only from limited points of view (hence Carlyle's frequent use of visual metaphors), but it is only in that whole, available only to omniscience, that the complete meaning resides. In history, as in textual interpretation, we can achieve "at best a poor approximation" (27:89).

The problems of historical knowledge are further compounded for Carlyle, because he does not believe that we can successfully reproduce even the admittedly limited point of view of an actor or author in the past. The notion that each age has its own unique consciousness was pervasive in the nineteenth century. But this idea does not lead Carlyle to Pater's historicism, that is, the injunction to judge "from the point of view of the age."[34] Instead, as Carlyle remarked about myth and epic, the "spirit of the age" acts as an obstruction to knowledge: "Nothing harder than to form a true judgment of foreign minds and forms of character, especially if they are separated from us by a diversity of language, institution, date, and place" (*Notebooks,* 92). Rather than appeal to universal qualities shared by humans at all times (an idea he sometimes has recourse to), he instead insists on the differences: "Neither will it adequately avail us to assert that the general inward condition of Life is the same in all ages. . . . The inward condition of Life, it may rather be affirmed, the conscious or half-conscious aim of mankind, so far as men are not mere digesting machines, is the same in no two ages; neither are the more important outward variations easy to fix on, or always well capable of representation" (27:86). Carlyle's presentism, then, is in large part a matter of necessity. Given that we can see only from particular view-points, our accounts will inevitably reflect the present. But at the same time, he does not believe that presentist historiography is a compromise; rather, he believes that the object of history is its relevance and application to the present. Thus Carlyle examines Jocelin of Brakelond's manuscript "in hope of perhaps illustrating our own poor Century thereby" (10:39). For Carlyle, the ethical aims of historical interpretation are inseparable from a focus on the present.

While Carlyle's emphasis on the way history obstructs knowledge might seem to link his hermeneutic theory to poststructuralist historiography, it is important to keep in mind that his primary affinities are with nineteenth-century hermeneutics.[35] While that tradition has widely influenced poststructuralist views, it is distinct from them in essential ways. For Romantic historical hermeneutics presumes that history is underwritten by some set of transcendental values. Or, as Carlyle has it, although the historian must supply an imaginative glue that imbues the fragments with meaning, a determinate meaning exists. Since the whole is not available, coherence must be created by intuition and shaping. Here Carlyle again articulates a version of the hermeneutic circle. He writes that the "Artist in History" is distinguishable from the "Artisan in History," because an artist can "inform and ennoble the humblest department with an Idea of the Whole, and habitually know that only in the Whole is the Partial to be truly discerned" (27:90).

Carlyle sees the historian's project as twofold: "Stern Accuracy in inquiring, bold Imagination in expounding and filling-up; these are the two pinions on which History soars" (28:259–60). Successful interpretation calls for "the strictest regard to chronology, geography . . . , documentary evidence, and what else true historical research would yield" (28:330), but Carlyle's greater emphasis falls on the intuitive conjecture that draws the pieces together. Hence in his histories he deprecates Dryasdust, the empiricist historian who meticulously ferrets out facts but cannot draw them into coherence. Wilhelm van Humboldt, for whom history also depends on ideas that "lie beyond the finite realm," similarly emphasizes the importance of imagination for the historian.[36] "If," he says, "the historian in his depiction is able to attain to the truth of what has taken place only by supplementing and connecting what was incomplete and fragmented in his direct observation, he can do so, like the poet, only through the imagination" (Humboldt 106). The view that imagination is central to interpretation was to be extended beyond historiography and even into the natural sciences in the Victorian period.

Carlyle's views on history, as I've suggested, also have much in common with those of the idealist historian Droysen, a follower of Humboldt's and a friend of Schleiermacher's, who transferred the latter's views on textual interpretation to the study of history. Droysen, like Carlyle, is deeply concerned with the ontological status of the past. History, he asserts, is available only "as faded traces," only as it manifests itself in the present: "The data for historical investigations are not past things, for these have disappeared, but things which are still present here and now, whether recollections of what was done, or remnants of things that have existed and of events that have occurred."[37] Droysen likewise maintains that only divinity could know history in full. Again like Carlyle, he conceives of historiography in opposition to Ranke's objectivity. For Droysen, Ranke's method attends to unimportant details (Dryasdust's heaps of rubbish), while ignoring large questions, particularly ethical ones.

The apparent similarity between Carlyle's views and those of some post-structural theorists of historiography is in effect simply a condition of his participation in a tradition of nineteenth-century historical hermeneutics. Carlyle willingly acknowledges that what he produces is a kind of rhetoric, partial, shaped, and intended to persuade. He concedes that historical accounts find different meanings in the events they relate because of the interpretive presuppositions they depend on. The point, then, is not to attempt to be objective or to deduce meaning empirically, but instead to approach history with the "right" preconceptions. For Carlyle, these are ethical ones.[38] He believes, however, that the aim of interpretation—admitting perspective, the effects of systems of representation, of social construction, and of historical conditioning—is truth. So although he accepts that history is ideological (or, ethical, in his terms), and shaped by the historian, he also denounces what he takes to be false history. If one adopts the wrong presuppositions, Carlyle asserts, the past "cannot even be *not* seen; it is misseen" (10:239). Voltaire's accounts, for example, are to be condemned because he looks "through a pair of mere anti-catholic spectacles" (26:414).

Carlyle's perspectivism will only seem odd in conjunction with his views on truth and the absolute because in postmodern thought perspectivist accounts are typically thought to undercut traditional notions of truth and univocal meaning. Hermeneutic skepticism, however, is not only compatible with, but is in effect a condition of, any search for truth. Carlyle's thought is instructive in this respect because it belongs to the central philosophical tradition that unites a belief in the real with a skepticism about our ability to know it. If, after all, there is no reality to be gotten at, then the skeptical problem dissolves. In this regard, his perspectivism is concerned with what we can know, not what there is; its interest is epistemology, not ontology.

What needs emphasizing is that Carlyle proposes both a deep and skeptical reflexivity about our access to meaning and truth *and* a goal of objective meaning and universal truth. Carlyle's dogmatism is obvious. Nevertheless, he insists on historical critique, on the interrogation of the socially-accepted. He urges us to see the effects of systems of representation, to realize that all knowledge is situated, that interests and biases are always at work. Yet Carlyle continues to believe that there is an objective and determinate meaning behind the shifting interpretations of the world as text.

In Carlyle, the movement of hermeneutics from theology to the secular sphere is apparent. In laying bare this transition, Carlyle's work allows us to see some of the origins of current ideas on textuality and the ways in which those ideas have retained vestiges of the theological conceptions from which they developed. At the same time, in carrying interpretation beyond the confines of theology and written texts to a universal hermeneutics, Carlyle opened the way for the philosophical hermeneutics that would follow. Finally, Carlyle's transplantation of ethics as the limiting feature of interpretation from biblical to general hermeneutics underscores the ways in which interpretation is linked to moral questions and suggests that all theories of interpretation may implicitly appeal to some sort of ethical principle. As hermeneutics was further secularized, writers such as Eliot and Wilde rejected the idea that certain meaning is guaranteed in any manner, but they preserved the belief that moral considerations ground interpretation.

❧

Victorian Science and Hermeneutics

The Interpretation of Nature

The facts of the external world are marks, in which man discovers a meaning and so reads them. Man is the Interpreter of Nature, and Science is the right Interpretation.

—William Whewell

Carlyle, as we have seen, regarded all human knowledge as symbolic "interpretation" of the absolute. Notwithstanding his early training in the sciences and onetime aspiration to pursue a scientific career, he did not believe that science yielded absolute truths. Science should recognize that it provides knowledge only of phenomena, or, as Carlyle understands that idea, that it is interpretation. "Science," he writes, "has done much for us; but it is a poor science that would hide from us the great deep sacred infinitude of Nescience, whither we can never penetrate, on which all science swims as a mere superficial film."[1] Such a view might seem to call scientific knowledge into question, but in regarding science as provisional "interpretation," Carlyle anticipates, albeit in his sometimes blurry way, views that would become significant in scientific thought later in the period.[2]

Victorian philosophy of science encompasses a complex and diverse field of issues; in this section, I want to begin to suggest, in broad strokes, the way in which the discourse of interpretation became critical to significant strains of Victorian theory of science. In doing so, I will not attend in detail to some important distinctions between various theories and methodologies, ranging from realist through instrumentalist and pragmatist views. Nor will I look in depth at the different ways in which the concept of "interpretation" is understood in Victorian scientific literature. This intertext, in other words, does not seek to offer a thorough exploration of the subject, but only to show that even in areas that would seem to be far from hermeneutics, there was a hermeneutic tradition of some significance. Contrary to what we might expect, some prominent Victorian theorists of science came to understand science as interpretive in nature, and in ways that reproduce the debates and the range of views that we have already seen in discussions of textual hermeneutics.

Lorraine Daston and Peter Galison have shown that in the late nineteenth century a moralized form of objectivity became the ideal in scientific image making (in particular, in a turn to mechanical objectivity in atlas images). This new form of objectivity sought to neutralize the effects of the human observer by means of an "ethic" of self-restraint. It centrally involved what the authors refer to as "a ban on interpretation."[3] Scientists attempted to efface themselves, to render the facts simply and mechanically. While Daston and Galison are certainly correct that worries over the "dread subjectivity of interpretation" (117) arose in the period, their account should not be taken as a complete description of Victorian philosophy of science.[4] Interpretation was neither dreaded nor banned in significant strands of Victorian *theory* of science. Rather, among some of the most influential philosophers of science of the period, interpretation and subjectivity were recognized as the conditions of any understanding.

Daston and Galison's account, which focuses primarily on working anatomists, to some extent underscores the distinction between methodological principles involved in scientific practice and philosophical assumptions grounding the theory of science. Even scientists who accepted on the theoretical level that science involved interpretation, that it was fundamentally subjective and provisional, also insisted on the importance of strict measurements, careful observations, exacting experiments, and accurate images. Many were committed to restraint and deference to the data, as George Levine has shown.[5] In this we can see another common Victorian attitude: the recognition of the subjective nature of interpretation, combined with a resolve to nevertheless get it right. For most, notions such as the theory ladenness of observation and the inevitability of human interpretation did not result in serious doubts about the reliability of science as an account of the way the world is.

It may seem odd to claim that the preoccupation with interpretation carried over even to theorists in what is often regarded as a stronghold of empirical method (sometimes caricatured as monolithically, naively empiricist). Histories of hermeneutics normally treat hermeneutics as a special theory and method of knowledge in the human sciences opposed to the methods established for the natural sciences. When at the end of the nineteenth century Dilthey designated hermeneutics as the mode of understanding for the social sciences and the humanities, he explicitly defined the methodologies of the human sciences (*Geisteswissenschaften*) in contrast with those of the natural sciences. According to the standard model against which Dilthey posed his method, the knowledge produced by the empirical methods of the physical sciences is privileged; it is objective and conclusively verifiable, not situated and historical, and thus it is the only certain knowledge. It is often assumed that theorists did not begin to argue that hermeneutic methods were also central to the natural sciences until the second half of the twentieth century, when philosophers of science such as Michael Polanyi and Thomas Kuhn established the importance of preunderstanding for science, arguing that facts are not independent of scientific theories.[6] According to their accounts, there are no important methodological distinctions between the physical sciences and the humanities or social sciences. The latter need no longer try to emulate an inaccurate ideal of the objective methods of the natural sciences; rather, the methods of the natural sciences are also hermeneutic.

Interpretive views, however, were already present in Victorian scientific thought. There was, of course, a tradition that appealed to Baconian induction and absolute objectivity.[7] (This is itself a position analogous to the interpretive view that one must approach a text without preconception in order to discover its objective meaning, as Jowett recognized when he appealed to scientific method as support for his hermeneutic: "In natural science it is felt to be useless to build on assumptions.")[8] But the dominance of the empirical ideal does not adequately account for the full range of thought about science at the time. What I am particularly interested in establishing here is not so much that nineteenth-century science can be seen to anticipate the view that science is hermeneutic in nature in the senses that recent philosophy of science has understood that claim, but rather that some Victorian theorists of science understood their project as essentially interpretative and involving sign systems in ways that often closely replicate nineteenth-century debates over textual interpretation.

There was great interest in the philosophy of science during the period, and well-known scientists and philosophers wrote about methodological questions. Many theorists believed that there are constraints on human knowledge, either because it is limited to sense experience or because it is shaped by the faculties and categories of the human mind.

They maintained the inescapability of subjectivity, that the knower affected the known, and that we have no direct access to a mind-independent reality. As the minor philosopher Henry Jones put it: "This self of ours intrudes everywhere. It is only by resolutely shutting our eyes, that we can forget the part it plays even in the outer world of science. So active is it in the constitution of things, so dependent is their nature on the nature of our knowing faculties, that scientific men themselves admit that their surest results are only hypothetical."[9] The belief that there is an unbridgeable gulf between the world as known by human consciousness and the unknown reality that lies beyond it was sometimes expressed in the idea that science involves "interpretation." As Donald R. Benson and Jonathan Smith have shown, Victorian theorists of science came to regard the work of science as involving creative imagination and comparable to poetic creation.[10] Writers such as Karl Pearson, George Henry Lewes, and Hermann von Helmholtz argued in various ways that although we think we perceive things, we in fact apprehend only symbols or signs, from which we must discover meaning.[11]

The critiques that saw science as interpretation were based both on realist and idealist presumptions, and a number of theorists attempted to fuse both. For the scientific realists, correct representation of the natural world was the goal, but they were rarely naïve realists. They did not hold simple correspondence views of the mind unproblematically mirroring reality. Rather they offered revisionary accounts of how realism worked. They accepted that our forms of representing reality are always provisional, that science does not get certainty with its stories, and that we are limited by the power of our representational systems. The understanding of empiricist method by both realists and idealists was often more complex than it has sometimes been taken to be. They denied the myth of the naïve scientist who goes out with no commitments, gathers experience, and generalizes it. These theorists recognized that science had to dismiss the notion of the perfect passive recorder of facts. They believed instead that scientific inquiry involved creativity, accepted that hypotheses preceded (rather than grew from) observation, and often regarded data as context-dependent.

The idea that science involves interpretation is not a single view. Several general Victorian positions depend on the conception of science as interpretation, and these run the gamut from realist to antirealist, empiricist to rationalist views. The most benign form of the idea that science is interpretive (and one that would not count as a hermeneutic view of science in contemporary debate) arose in reaction to the radical empiricism of Locke, whereby only a passive recording of raw sense experience counts as knowledge. Theorists argued that scientific work is instead active, that it goes beyond experience by interpreting the given and theorizing about the existence and characteristics of unobservables. According to this realist view, the work of science depends on sense experience, but the empirical data must be "interpreted," which involves going beyond what is observable.

A stronger form of the idea that science is interpretive is seen in various positions that maintained that even the observables are not merely given, as they depend upon our shared conceptual scheme or our sensory apparatus. What seems to be given to us in sense experience is itself already theory laden; hence both the data and the scientific theories formulated about the data are interpretations. Finally, this position is further radicalized to become the view that we cannot know the world independently of our individual subjective thinking. Science varies over individuals and depends on personal characteristics. Variations on all these positions are found in the Victorian writings on the philosophy of science that the remainder of this intertext examines.

As early as the 1840s, hermeneutics made its appearance by way of the remarkable philosopher of science William Whewell.[12] As Robert E. Butts says, "Whewell thought the goal of science was to interpret nature, not to catalogue or describe it."[13] Trying to mediate between Lockean empiricism and Kantianism, Whewell sought to show that interpretive conceptions are crucial to the process of scientific discovery. Whewell was a realist about scientific knowledge, that is, he regarded it as providing a description that "conforms to the true order of nature."[14] But he also believed that conceptions are furnished by the mind, and argued that knowledge depends on a "fundamental antithesis" between mind and things (subject and object): "In all human KNOWLEDGE both Thoughts and Things are concerned. In every part of my knowledge there must be some *thing* about which I know, and an internal act of *me* who knows" (*PI*, 1:17). There is always a dialectical relationship between sensation and idea.

Resisting the empiricist model on which there is no room for thought to play a role and experience comes to us unmediated, Whewell maintains that "a certain activity of the mind is involved, not only in seeing objects erroneously, but in seeing them at all" (*PI*, 2:29). All perception is theory laden; it is always the result of a particular conceptual scheme: "Even in the case in which our perceptions appear to be most direct, and least to involve any interpretations of our own,—in the simple process of seeing,—who does not know how much we, by an act of the mind, add to that which our senses receive?" (*PI*, 1:42). There is no neutral observation, no data independent from interpretation. The mind is both creative and passive, according to Whewell, and he introduces Wordsworth's famous lines about what we "half create" and "half perceive" to illustrate his view.

Whewell likens science to the interpretation of a manuscript: "It has been well said that true knowledge is the interpretation of nature; and therefore it requires both the interpreting mind, and nature for its subject; both the document and the ingenuity to read it aright."[15] Whewell might be taken to be merely picking up the old theological figure of nature as the book of God. The interpreter attempts to explain the true meaning of the world as God's "text" through the "signs" of nature just as an interpreter of the Bible tries to discover God's meaning. Certainly this is how John Herschel uses the image in his cloying poem "Man the Interpreter of Nature." Whewell insists, however, that his statements on the hermeneutic nature of knowledge should not be understood as merely metaphorical or regarded as providing a rough, concrete analogy for the epistemology of the sciences: "The letters and symbols which are presented to the Interpreter are really objects of sensation: the notion of letters as signs of words, the notion of connexions among words by which they have meaning, really are among our Ideas;—*Signs* and *Meaning* are Ideas, supplied by the mind, and added to all that sensation can disclose in any collection of visible marks. The Sciences are not figuratively, but really, Interpretations of Nature" (*PI*, 1:37–38). Whewell here regards the work of science as a mode of textual interpretation. Not only does one have to bring meaning to the words in reading them, but the work of interpretation starts at a lower level; for it is an interpretive act that allows us to see the marks as letters to be read at all. Whewell writes: "We cannot read any of the inscriptions which nature presents to us, without interpreting them by means of some language which we ourselves are accustomed to speak" (*PI*, 2:31). As later theorists might put it, our knowledge is always an interpretation of an interpretation.

"Man," as Whewell says, "often interprets without being aware that he does so. Thus when we see the needle move towards the magnet, we assert that the magnet exercises an attractive force on the needle. But it is only by an interpretive act of our own minds that we can ascribe this motion to attraction" (*PI*, 1:41). When we are unconscious of the act of interpretation, we take our interpretations to be "facts." Whewell blurs the distinction between theory and observation. From the start, our observations are partly constituted by our ideas; data is not detachable from theory. On his view, "theory" and "fact" are two different ways of describing the same thing. "There are," he says, "no special attributes of Theory and Fact which distinguish one from another" (*PI*, 2:94). (F. H. Bradley echoes this view in his *Presuppositions of Critical Theory* [1874], writing that "in every case that which is called a fact is in reality a theory.")[16] Whewell's formulation precedes Nietzsche's famous fragment—"it is precisely facts that do not exist, only *interpretations*"—by many decades.[17]

In the *History of the Inductive Sciences,* Whewell examines scientific theory as a historical phenomenon (a central presumption of many of the postempirical views that are considered hermeneutic in philosophy of science). Science, Whewell argues, works by a process he calls the colligation of facts. Facts (or interpretations) are bound together by a conjecture or a hypothesis, which is then verified (or not) by the facts (considered facts for the purposes of the hypothesis, but theories on all other counts). He proposes a notion close to the hermeneutic circle, with the parts understood in relation to the whole, and the whole in relation to the parts. The history of science, he maintains (in an anti-Kuhnian view), involves a series of gradual developments or reinterpretations. "The earlier truths are not expelled but absorbed, not contradicted but extended; and the history of each science, which may thus appear like a succession of revolutions, is, in reality, a series of developments" (1.44–45). Whewell's description of the development of science in this passage is yet another form of the idea of progressive revelation in biblical exegesis. Further, Whewell appeals, like so many nineteenth-century hermeneuts, to those of special talent who can achieve "right interpretation."

If Whewell's methodology initially lost the battle with Mill's version of induction, interpretive paradigms became more common in scientific thought later in the period. W. B. Carpenter, the physician and physiologist (famous for his conception of "unconscious cerebration"), adopted the title "Man the Interpreter of Nature" for his Presidential address to the British Association for the Advancement of Science in 1872. (The address was considered an important popular scientific statement.) Science, for Carpenter, is "the Intellectual Representation of Nature."[18] He elaborates on the idea of science as a hermeneutic mode by associating the interpretations that it provides with those that the artist and the poet offer. The poet as "Interpreter of Nature" does not present a mimetic picture, Carpenter explains; rather the poet renders a unique vision: "*Nature is what he individually sees in her*" (418). The scientist's "interpretation" of nature may at first sight seem less individual. He may appear, Carpenter says, echoing Arnold's famous formulation about aesthetic interpretation, to get at nature "as she *really is*" (419). The scientific view, however, is actually also "*a representation framed by the Mind itself*"(419). Scientific interpretation does not afford a mimetic reconstruction of the facts any more than does poetic interpretation. Carpenter's conclusions take him beyond a version of Kantianism to the assertion that (and here he anticipates Wilde on aesthetic interpretation) "to each Man of Science, *Nature is what he individually believes her to be*" (419). "Our Scientific interpretations are clearly matters of *judgement,*" he ultimately claims.

The linkage of scientific and aesthetic interpretation is popular in late Victorian culture. Several years following Carpenter's address, J. C. Shairp, then chair of poetry at Oxford, published a book titled *The Poetic Interpretation of Nature* (1877). Shairp also conceives of science as an interpretation (and attacks a subjectivist hermeneutic): "It is not that Nature is a blank or unintelligible scroll, with no meaning of its own, save that which we put into it from the light of our own transient feelings. Each of the physical sciences attempts to explain the outer world in one of its aspects, to interpret it from one point of view."[19] Like Matthew Arnold, however, he is eager to assert that not the scientist, but rather "the poet is the highest, best, and truest interpreter of Nature."

For the positivist philosopher of science Karl Pearson, science remained the measure of truth, the best form of knowledge, but he also saw it as interpretation, comparable to aesthetic production.[20] We know only mental states, he believed, and can know nothing of any reality (if such exists) beyond the phenomenal. For Pearson too, scientific knowledge is understood as a mode of representation:

> Does not the beauty of the artist's work lie for us in the accuracy with which his symbols resume innumerable facts of our past emotional experience? The aesthetic judgment pronounces for or against the interpretation of the creative imagination according as that interpretation embodies or contradicts none of the emotional phenomena which it is intended to resume. If this account of the aesthetic judgment be at all a true one, the reader will have remarked how exactly parallel it is to the scientific judgment. But there is really more than mere parallelism between the two. The laws of science are, as we have seen, the products of the creative imagination. They are mental interpretations—the formula under which we resume wide ranges of phenomena, the results of observation on the part of ourselves or of our fellow-men. The scientific interpretation of phenomena, the scientific account of the universe, is therefore the only one which can permanently satisfy the aesthetic judgment.[21]

Combining an empiricist focus on sense data with idealism's notion of the mind's productive role, Pearson asserts that the mind constructs concepts that serve as a sort of shorthand and that are, in some sense, fictions, "mental interpretations," as he puts it. He holds on to the empiricist emphasis on "observation" as the basis of these constructs, but he also recognizes that "the scientific account" is creative and interpretative. Pearson sounds very close to both biblical exegetes and to Schleiermacher on meaning when he claims that science's aim is "the complete interpretation of the universe. . . . the *direction* in which we can move and strive, but never a stage we shall actually reach" (17).[22]

At the end of the century, the concept of science as interpretation became important to pragmatist theory as well. In an article of 1897 in *The Philosophical Review,* the American pragmatist J. H. Tufts explains that after Kant people have come to accept that there is an epistemological chasm between thought and the thing in itself. Thought is a representation of reality, not its direct perception. Tufts maintains that problems arise if one attempts to uphold a correspondence (what he calls a "copy") theory of knowledge, and his argument also relies on a comparison between the aesthetic and the scientific interpreter. "Just as realism in art has often insisted that the artist must copy nature without intruding any of his own interpretation or point of view, so this theory of knowledge, which might fittingly be called 'realism,' maintains that if the mind adds anything to its photograph," says Tufts—reminding us of the image making discussed by Daston and Galison—"it is spoiling the work and infecting the result with 'universality,' or 'relativity,' or 'subjectivity.'"[23] He then undercuts that position, suggesting that "we are not looking for a copy of an external reality, but for an interpretation of the reality which is present in experience" (588). He continues by offering a new criteria for "correct" interpretation of reality: "The question may arise: If knowledge is merely interpretation, how can I be sure that my interpretation is the right one? The only answer in my opinion is: 'Does it work?'" (589). Tufts has moved far from the idea that scientific knowledge is objective and certain. His paper ends with the claim that knowledge "is only an interpretation of reality, or better, reality interpreted. Nor is it even the only interpretation" (590). By the end of the period, the idea that there is no finality about scientific knowledge had become widespread. Like biblical exegesis, science does not offer infallible and final truths.

Hermeneutic strategies similar to those we have seen at work in textual interpretation are repeated in Victorian scientific theory. The arguments of Whewell, Carpenter, Pearson, and Jones demonstrate that the concept of interpretation played a significant role in accounts of scientific knowledge in the Victorian age. Given the way in which the empirical side of Victorian science has been emphasized, study of the alternative tradition that I have been tracing here is likely to repay us with a revised picture of the Victorian relation to fact. The view that science involves interpretation was also a recurring theme in George Henry Lewes's writing in the 1870s. Like Tufts, he believed that scientific knowledge is always provisional. Discussing the way in which the Copernican view had invalidated earlier and once-accepted theories, Lewes writes of Copernicus's model of the solar system, "Nor have we any grounds for supposing this interpretation to be final: it embodies present knowledge, that is all."[24] The notion that interpretations change over time, that any reading is never more than an approximation of meaning, should by now be very familiar. The aim of science for Lewes is the revelation of the real, yet he contends that "what we call Laws of Nature are not objective existences, but subjective abstractions" (273). For Lewes scientific laws are mental creations, "ideal constructions" as he called them (266), relations not independent of the observer, and words such as "force," and "matter," are "symbols of sensible experience" (32). Like Whewell, he regards facts as not separable from theory and expresses the view in linguistic terms: "Facts are mere letters which have their meaning only in the words they form; and these words again have their meaning, not in themselves alone, but in their positions in the sentence" (372). While Lewes was considering these questions in science, George Eliot was at work on her own theory of interpretation, which the next chapter investigates.

CHAPTER THREE

George Eliot's Hermeneutics of Sympathy

While it is true, in one sense, that the thoughts and feelings of others are inaccessible to us, in another sense it is inadmissible. . . . It is true that your subjective state can only be an objective fact to me, except in so far as I am able to interpret the objective fact in its subjective aspect. But this is true of all facts. . . . The psychologist interprets certain visible facts as signs of invisible feelings, just as he knows that sugar is sweet and dogs bite. The statement that "each individual is absolutely incapable of knowing any feeling but his own" is acceptable only on a very restricted definition of knowledge; and on this definition we must declare that man is incapable of knowing anything except his present feelings.

—George Henry Lewes

The statement that I dislike your pain becomes perverted into the assertion that I dislike something else; or, in other words, it is inferred that sympathy is a mere delusion.

—Leslie Stephen

Yet surely, surely the only true knowledge of our fellow-man is that which enables us to feel with him.

—George Eliot

If Carlyle offered a hermeneutic theory that was transitional, located somewhere in between the theological and the secular, George Eliot's thought on interpretation moved hermeneutics fully into the secular realm. As with Carlyle, hermeneutics was crucially important to all of her writing. Again like Carlyle, she was interested in large epistemological questions about the relationship between human knowledge and the act of interpretation. But whereas the latter issue was Carlyle's central problem, Eliot's primary concern was understanding others, and, especially, linguistic interpretation. Like the German Romantic hermeneuts, she believed that meaning was grounded in a speaker's intentions, although she was deeply aware of the problems attending an intentionalist account of meaning. Coming from an impressive grounding in religious hermeneutics and philosophy, George Eliot was well equipped to speculate on the complex issues involved in interpretation. In her view, theological exegesis had been for the most part a series of misguided distortions, usually prompted by personal need and rationalized by claims of infallibility or divine inspiration. Eliot attempted to shape a more viable and principled secular hermeneutic: a hermeneutics of sympathy.

In the last decades of the twentieth century, the view that Eliot's novels represent a proto-poststructuralist stance on interpretation, even if that stance works against some of her explicitly professed beliefs, has been a strong strain in literary criticism. More recently, critics, displaying Hobbesian tendencies, have reread sympathy in Eliot's works in analogous ways: sympathy, it turns out, is always disguised egoism, a form of narcissistic projection that subverts itself in the novels. Eliot begins chapter 29 of *Middlemarch* with a description of Dorothea, abruptly breaking off midsentence to ask, "—but why always Dorothea? Was her point of view the only possible one?"[1] This chapter similarly attempts to shift perspective to ask, "—but why always misunderstanding and appropriation? Is this mode of reading the only possible one?" The answer may have come to seem self-evident, as perhaps it does to some readers of *Middlemarch* when the contest is between Dorothea and Casaubon. Yet the view of Eliot as a, perhaps unconscious, representative of skeptical views on interpretation and sympathy needs to be reconsidered. Her novels have been able to support such readings because her inquiries into understanding and ethics are so sophisticated that she could incorporate into them most of the objections that later thought would raise. Granted, one might continue to regard Eliot's philosophical and hermeneutic arguments as covers for the subversion of sympathy that critics discern in her novels, even after recognizing the depth of her knowledge on the subjects. A close examination of her writing, however, in the context of the intellectual tradition to which she belongs (and helps form) ought to make it more difficult to accept that stance. To understand Eliot's perspective, we must shift from our contemporary orientation to the more solidly grounded historical recognition that Eliot's views are related to nineteenth-century Romantic hermeneutics.

Against the current view, I am not positing an Eliot who naively or stubbornly imagines that perfect sympathy is easily attained. The Eliot I am arguing for appreciates the obstacles in the way of understanding others, but judges that there are better and worse ways of getting around those obstacles and that there are pressing moral reasons for attempting to do so. She struggles against what she regards as the destructive effects of skepticism about understanding, even as she fully acknowledges the difficulties. Rather than valorizing the impossibility of understanding, or even resigning herself to it, Eliot dramatizes the cost of assuming the passivity of the object of interpretation.

I

Some critics who have regarded Eliot as a precursor of poststructuralist thought on interpretation have seen her as a proto-deconstructionist, proclaiming, or at least unwittingly demonstrating, indeterminacy. J. Hillis Miller has given the most sustained and influential reading of Eliot along these lines. The view that emerges in *Middlemarch*, he argues, is that "all interpretation of signs is false interpretation."[2] On Miller's reading, the novel willy-nilly enforces a relativistic view, even when it seems to be resisting that implication. Eliot's texts reveal an outlook that is essentially a version of Nietzsche's view in "On Truth and Lying in an Extra-Moral Sense." "If," Miller writes, "for Eliot all seeing is falsified by the limitations of point of view, it is an even more inevitable law, for her, that we make things what they are by naming them in one way or another. . . . The original naming was an act of interpretation which falsified. The reading of things into signs is necessarily a further falsification, an interpretation of an interpretation" (143).[3] In Miller's view, a consequence of Eliot's epistemology is that knowledge outside the self is impossible: "The terrible isolation of each person, for Eliot, lies in the way each goes through the world encountering only himself, his own image reflected back to him by the world because he (or she) has put it there in the first place, in the illusory interpretation of the world the person spontaneously makes" (142). Interpretations of others are inevitably solipsistic projections.

Miller vacillates on whether this view is demonstrated by the texts despite Eliot or whether she deliberately shows it to be true, but he has been followed by commentators who argue that Eliot explicitly professed these ideas. Daniel Cottom, for instance, connecting Eliot to Nietzsche, says of Miller's reading of *Middlemarch* in "Narrative and History": "This is not a subversive reading of the novel; rather, it falls in line with the understanding Eliot depicted herself."[4] If so, Eliot rejects truth in interpretation, having come to recognize that it is nonexistent and that given the impossibility of getting beyond our individual distorting perspectives and desire-driven projections, understanding between people is impossible.

Admittedly, for Eliot interpretation is a central paradigm, but her views are more akin to the Romantic hermeneutics of Friedrich Schleiermacher than to current understandings of Nietzsche. Nineteenth-century German hermeneutics, as we've seen, extended thought on interpretation from the attempt to determine interpretive procedures for disciplines such as theology to the establishment of general parameters for all acts of linguistic understanding. Postmodern hermeneutics, of course, challenges traditional hermeneutics, charging that it mistakenly seeks the true meaning of a text, an aim that rests on what are regarded as metaphysical beliefs in intentionality and truth.

But the latter are Eliot's beliefs (notwithstanding her own misgivings about metaphysics). It is not that Eliot is unaware of the role that projection plays in interpretation. She concedes that an interpreter's own situation is inextricably involved in the process of understanding. Yet her response is to insist that one should work against subjectivism. She enacts interpretive conflicts not to demonstrate indeterminacy, but to reveal the conditions needed for more accurate interpretation. Granted, Eliot is concerned with the limits of communication—her texts everywhere explore misunderstanding—but her aim is to overcome these limitations. She is committed to a hermeneutics that acknowledges the difficulties of understanding, and yet maintains it as a goal.

Distinctions must be made among interpretive questions that have sometimes been conflated in discussing Eliot's views. First, there are broad ontological and epistemological questions. Here the issue of whether grounds exist for adjudication among perspectives enters. Are there only differing perspectives, each equally valid, or are some false or distorting, others accurate representations of reality? Do interpretations construct "reality" or do they capture a mind-independent reality? In other words, does truth exist, is there a getting it right and can we get it right? A distinct question is how one correctly interprets an utterance or a text, the question central to nineteenth-century German Romantic hermeneutics. Eliot is concerned with both of these types of interpretive activity.

For Eliot, interpretation is through and through an ethical issue. As most of her readers agree, she promotes an ethics of sympathy, and self-lessness (even if these ideals are, according to some, challenged by the workings of her narratives).[5] The basic tenet of traditional morality is that one should respect others, that is, treat them as rational agents whose actions are guided by beliefs, desires, and intentions. To fail to consider those beliefs, desires, and intentions is to fail to respect the person in the way that morality demands. Eliot's narratives explicitly demonstrate how her moral views yield an interpretative method. She insists that there is an ethical imperative to try to understand others' words as they intend them. Eliot assumes, then, that the correct interpretation of any utterance is grounded in the intentions of the speaker. By striving to enter imagina-tively into the perspectives of others, one can work against the limitations of subjective perspective, and so more correctly "divine" (a favorite word of Eliot's) the meanings of their words.

Eliot is aware that meaning is in part conventional, the product of lin-guistic norms and shared public knowledge. The wedding scene in *Silas Marner,* in which the vows are misspoken, shows that she recognizes that intention (here "meanin'") is not a sufficient condition for meaning. Mr. Macey speculates on the workings of a speech act: "Is't the meanin' or the words as makes folks fast i' wedlock? For the parson meant right, and the bride and the bridegroom meant right. But then, when I come to think on it, meanin' goes but little way i' most things, for you may mean to stick things together and your glue may be bad, and then where are you? And so I says to mysen 'It isn't the meanin', it's the glue.'"[6] Meaning, in other words, requires more than intention; one also has to use words in accor-dance with agreed upon meanings. Eliot, then, knows that linguistic interpretation involves knowledge of social contexts, shared assumptions about the world, and linguistic norms, but it is finally the subjective dimensions of meaning that are of greatest interest to her.

This two-part system is comparable to Schleiermacher's, who also locates meaning in intention ("psychological" or "technical" interpreta-tion), while emphasizing its historical and grammatical dimensions. In brief, the psychological aspect of Schleiermacher's hermeneutic asks that one attempt to abandon one's own subjectivity in order to grasp the speaker's intention, or as Schleiermacher writes: "The divinatory method is the one in which one, so to speak, transforms oneself into the other person."[7] Since every utterance expresses the individuality of the speaker, a complete understanding requires an entering into the interiority of the speaker through a sort of divinatory process (or empathy). It is a hermeneutic ideal that requires the ability to see how another sees. This was not a naive view. Schleiermacher, as well as Romantic hermeneutics in general, was concerned with interpretation precisely because it reveals itself always to be a problem. He writes in his epigraph to *Confidential Letters:* "The talent for misunderstanding is infinite and it is really not possible to overcome it."[8] And that might well be an epigraph to any of Eliot's narratives.

It is important to recognize the degree to which Eliot works out of the tradition of nineteenth-century Romantic hermeneutics.[9] Placing her thought in this context allows us to better understand her approach to interpretation—and interpretation is a topic of more than just theoretical concern for Eliot; anxiety over whether she has been understood is a leitmotif that runs through her letters. More importantly, viewing her in this context allows us to see how Victorian writers struggled with the problems of interpretation in their own terms. We thus avoid the mistake of flouting Eliot's cardinal hermeneutic rule by recasting her struggles into our terms, doing, that is, exactly what Eliot's hermeneutic is designed to avoid.

II

Attending closely to the various strands that come together in Eliot's hermeneutic allows for a more precise understanding of her theory of interpretation. Her early translations of David Strauss (1846), Baruch Spinoza (1849), and Ludwig Feuerbach (1854), provided her with a solid foundation in theological hermeneutics. When Eliot encountered Charles Hennell's work, and through him, the work of Strauss, she found herself deeply involved in the writings of the Higher Critics. From Strauss, she received a systematic overview of biblical exegesis. The introductory chapter of his *Life of Jesus* surveys in detail various accounts of scriptural interpretation: allegorical, rationalist, and supernatural.[10] Strauss argues that the writer's intentions can only be understood in the context of the general consciousness of the time when the biblical narrative was written. He advocates a historicist approach, then, not believing that there is some kernel of historical truth to biblical narratives, which had been altered, either intentionally or through an erroneous understanding of the world. Rather, he believes that the stories were always to be understood metaphorically. In his view, supernatural or literal interpretations of the Bible should be replaced by an understanding of the stories as religious and moral myths attuned to their time. The painstaking work of translating Strauss's text acquainted Eliot with the central terminology and concepts associated with hermeneutic theory and introduced her to the historical-critical approach crucial to nineteenth-century thought.

Her translations of Spinoza further familiarized Eliot with historical approaches to interpretation.[11] In the *Tractatus Theologico-Politicus,* Spinoza aims to present "the true method of interpreting Scripture."[12] He is among the first to advocate a form of rationalist analysis, asserting that orthodox readings of Scripture are not necessarily right. He is skeptical about dogmatic claims and believes that the correct interpretation of a biblical text should be accessible to anyone who follows a number of rules for interpretation. For Spinoza, meaning is located in the author's intentions, and his exegetical principles are primarily historical. An interpreter must have some knowledge of the original language of the text and know something of the author's background, "who he was, what was the occasion and the epoch of his writing, whom did he write for, and in what language" (103). The interpreter should also be familiar with the cultural, political, and historical contexts in which the text was produced, for "narratives are in a great measure adapted to the prejudices of each age" (106). Spinoza argues that interpreters have made the Bible conform to assumptions that they have brought to it, rather than approaching it with impartiality, and he warns against the imposition of distorting interpretations: "We cannot wrest the meaning of texts to suit the dictates of our reason, or our preconceived opinions" (103). Here Spinoza makes a point that will be repeatedly echoed in Eliot's own comments: a critical aim of hermeneutics is the prevention of biased readings.

Spinoza makes two other points that will find resonance in Eliot's thought. First, he argues that meaning is not to be equated with truth. That is, the meaning of the text need not correspond to any real state of affairs or be in accord with verifiable facts. Eliot will adopt this viewpoint also, asserting that the initial and primary task of interpretation is the discovery of what a person means. The evaluation of that person's viewpoint, its correspondence to truth, is seen as a second-order consideration, which can be undertaken only after an understanding of meaning has been gained. Second, Spinoza emphasizes that interpretation must be independent of power relations. He thus (like Jowett) attempts to free interpretation from ecclesiastical control. It is not law or authority that determines meaning, but reason.[13] The nexus of concerns that Spinoza brings together in his inquiry into truth, interpretation, and meaning will be played out in Eliot's fiction as she works through a theory that she believes can resist grounding interpretation in power.

Feuerbach's rereading of Christianity is at the heart of Eliot's views on interpretation. I will return to the relationship between Feuerbach's and Eliot's hermeneutics in detail later in this chapter. Here I want only to briefly mention Feuerbach's remarks on textual exegesis in *The Essence of Christianity*. Like the other commentators on scriptural interpretation who influenced Eliot, Feuerbach noted the capricious and unconstrained nature of interpretations of the Bible and insisted that such interpretation does not elucidate the text's meaning, but instead bends it to the needs of the exegete. He believed his age to be particularly prone to twisting Scripture to preconceived ends. With an irony that often will be heard in Eliot's narrators, he comments on the ever-shifting meaning of Scripture: "And the Bible, as every one knows, has the valuable quality that everything may be found in it which it is desired to find."[14] Although he acknowledges that it is possible to make a text subservient to one's own ends, he regards such interpretation as neither legitimate nor unavoidable. Eliot also remonstrates against interpretations motivated by desire and need.

In the years that followed the early translations, before turning to fiction, Eliot wrote several essays that demonstrate that she remained at the forefront of nineteenth-century theological speculation on interpretation. Among these is her review of Mackay's *Progress of the Intellect* (1851).[15] Although she admires the historical aspects of Mackay's work, Eliot criticizes his system of interpretation. She protests against the tendency of allegorical interpretation to become fixed and mechanical and against the too indiscriminate application of this mode of criticism. She also denounces the opposite extreme, admonishing biblical literalists to succumb to the findings of history and science. "It would be wise in our theological teachers, instead of struggling to retain a footing for themselves and their doctrine on the crumbling structure of dogmatic interpretation, to cherish those more liberal views of biblical criticism" (*Essays*, 42).

In another review essay, "Introduction to Genesis" (1856), Eliot offers a taxonomy of various approaches to biblical criticism. She attacks accommodation (the theory that the transmission of God's word must be adapted to human language and understanding at a given time) and argues: "It is easy to see that this system of interpretation is very elastic, and that it may soon amount to little more than a theological formula for the history of human development" (*Essays*, 256). She also condemns "extreme orthodoxy." An adherent of this school is "not an inquirer, but an advocate. He has not to weigh evidence in order to arrive at a conclusion, but having arrived at a conclusion, he has to make it the standard by which he accepts or rejects evidence" (*Essays*, 256). In this, we see the now familiar challenge to biased interpretations, a challenge Eliot repeats in each of her essays on scriptural hermeneutics and throughout her fiction. Eliot's keen appraisals of various hermeneutic modes manifest a growing certainty in her sense of what is required for correct interpretation.

Eliot's critique of Dr. Cumming's interpretive stance in "Evangelical Teaching: Dr. Cumming" (1855) marks the emergence of her own distinctive hermeneutic. She charges that his scriptural exegesis is much like the misreadings that she will later attribute to Dorothea Brooke in her musings on Casaubon, a "filling up the outline of the record with an elaborate colouring quite undreamed of by more literal minds" (*Essays*, 164). To the historical-critical method and the condemnation of biased interpretations that she has found in her predecessors, Eliot brings an ethical basis to interpretation. She condemns Cumming for his "*unscrupulosity of statement*," his "moral distortion of view," and above all, "the moral spirit" (*Essays*, 165) of his interpretations, their lack of "truly human sympathies" (*Essays*, 183). Henceforth, the ethical attitude of the interpreter will be her primary consideration, overriding the still-relevant historical aspects of interpretation. Eliot, as before, urges the importance of evidence in support of interpretations, chastising Cummings for his upholding of dogma and his dishonesty, as she emphasizes the connections between knowledge and ethics: "A distinctive appreciation of the value of evidence—in other words, the intellectual perception of truth—is more closely allied to truthfulness of statement, or the moral quality of veracity, than is generally admitted. There is not a more pernicious fallacy afloat in common parlance, than the wide distinction between intellect and morality" (*Essays*, 166). The essay also introduces a somewhat puzzling notion about interpretation: ethical consequences are to be considered, at least when assessing a religious interpretation. She writes, referring to Dr. Cumming's fierce interpretations: "Quite apart from the critical basis of that interpretation . . . his use of prophecy must be a priori condemned in the judgment of right-minded persons, by its results as testified in the net moral effect of his sermons" (*Essays*, 180–81). Eliot again argues that ethical considerations are primary determinants of meaning, though here she moves from considering particular virtues in an interpreter to considering the ethical consequences of holding particular beliefs.

Eliot's emerging hermeneutic is evident also in her comments on historical interpretation, where she argues that only when extensive knowledge is supplemented by empathetic power can the past to some extent be regained. The passage makes clear that Eliot has been influenced by the tenets of Romantic hermeneutics: "Admitting that genius which has familiarized itself with all the relics of an ancient period can sometimes, by the force of its sympathetic divination restore the missing notes in the 'music of humanity' and reconstruct the fragments into a whole which will really bring the remote past nearer to us and interpret it to our duller apprehension—this form of imaginative power must always be among the very rarest, because it demands as much accurate and minute knowledge as creative vigour" (*Essays*, 320–21). In this remark, Eliot comes closest to spelling out the hermeneutic method that she will set in play in her novels. She distinguishes the two parts of her system, the attainment of "accurate and minute knowledge" and the capacity for an imaginative "sympathetic divination." She acknowledges that there are constraints on the project, as she later reminds her readers in her fiction: "Even the bare discernment of facts, much more their arrangement with a view to inferences, must carry a bias: human impartiality, whether judicial or not, can hardly escape being more or less loaded."[16] Yet the ideal stands.

III

This schooling in theological exegesis develops into a general hermeneutic as Eliot's widening investigations lead to the establishment of broader views on knowledge, language, and morals, which allow her to place her interpretive theory on a ground of philosophical reflection on epistemology and ethics.

Epistemological questions preoccupied Eliot from her first writings to her last.[17] All of her novels are centrally about the persistent problems of knowing the world and other minds. Her admiration for Feuerbach has sometimes been taken as evidence of her belief that certain knowledge is inaccessible, that all truth claims are illusory, but that view is based on a mistaken understanding of Feuerbach's ideas.[18] Feuerbach's central claim in *The Essence of Christianity* is that God is a fictitious creation of the human mind, a projection of human predicates, and hence that Christianity is not truth. Yet Feuerbach does not deny that there is any truth. He sees his project as the uncovering of an established, but erroneous, belief system in the pursuit of "unveiled, naked truth" (*EC*, xxxix). Things exist outside of human thought: "The object of the senses is in itself indifferent—independent of the disposition or of the judgment" (*EC*, 12), and certain knowledge is indeed possible through the senses. Feuerbach can be said to be a relativist only in a weak sense, in that he does not believe that we have access to a perfectly objective viewpoint, that is, a view outside of a human perspective. Nevertheless, he claims that truth is possible within this perspective: "It is true that I may have a merely subjective conception, i.e., one which does not arise out of the general constitution of my species; but if my conception is determined by the constitution of my species, the distinction between what an object is in itself, and what it is for me ceases; for this conception is itself an absolute one" (*EC*, 16). Feuerbach is committed to a version of perspectivism that does not entail the impossibility of human objectivity. He writes: "Not to invent, but to discover; 'to unveil existence' has been my sole object; to see correctly, my sole endeavor" (*EC*, xxxiv), and this might well stand as a statement of Eliot's own aim. We cannot attain absolute knowledge, Eliot believes, but that does not disqualify truth: "Approximate truth is the only truth attainable, but at least one must strive for that, and not wade off into arbitrary falsehood."[19]

Feuerbach provided Eliot with a model of hermeneutics primarily concerned with understanding the world rather than interpreting texts and utterances. He regards Christianity as projection, a product of desire, emerging from an unchecked subjectivity. It is this realization that many critics of Eliot have seized on, claiming that she too, as much as she may resist it, sees that projection is the paradigm and limit of human knowledge. But Feuerbach understands projection as delusion, imagination unrestrained by reality. His hermeneutic, then, like much rationalist biblical criticism, seeks to demystify. But at the same time that it reaches for more accurate explanation, it also tries to understand religion from its own point of view. He describes his approach in this way: "Speculation makes religion say only what it *itself* thought. . . . I, on the contrary, let religion itself speak; I constitute myself only its listener and interpreter, not its prompter" (*EC*, xxxv). The method that Feuerbach outlines here is essential to Eliot's hermeneutic as well. Like Feuerbach, one of her starting points is that much human belief is projection; she aims to reveal the distortions of understanding because she believes that more accurate interpretation is possible. Again like Feuerbach, she insists on the necessity of entering into the point of view of the interpreted. She learns from him to fuse two hermeneutic modes, the sympathetic and the critical.

It has also been common to align Eliot's views on knowledge with Lewes's professed "relativism." (Precisely what Lewes means by the term relativism, and the ways in which it differs from many later uses has often been overlooked.) Even if we suppose her to be in agreement with Lewes's views, we cannot infer that she was a radical subjectivist. It is, in any case, a mistake to regard Lewes as holding a view that undercuts traditional understandings of objective knowledge and truth.[20] Lewes, like many Victorians, believes that we cannot attain a pure objectivity: "Consciousness can never transcend its own sphere, we cannot possibly have a test of Objective truth."[21] He continues by qualifying this view: "In one sense this is correct. We can never know more than states of consciousness, we cannot know objects except through these states. But to reach the Truth we have no need for deeper knowledge, since truth is simply *correspondence* between the internal and external orders" (*HP,* 1:lxv). In *Problems of Life and Mind,* Lewes discusses the difficulties of attaining an objective viewpoint. "How," he asks, "do we distinguish the Certitude of Truth" from hallucination or false convictions? In the latter cases, he explains, "my conviction . . . turns out to be a subjective feeling without objective validity,—it is mine, and true for me; it is not true for others, therefore cannot be used as knowledge."[22] He then points to cases in which certainty is possible: "No such failure can exist when a conviction is objectively confirmed, and the equivalence of the sign and the thing signified is proved, by the ability to use the one in lieu of the other. The Certitude in that case is absolute" (69). Like Feuerbach, Lewes claims that we are limited to the human point of view, so our perspective is relative in that sense, but this counts as truth for us. Lewes's "relativism," in other words, is a version of the all-knowledge-is-conditioned position that we have encountered many times already.

The realism and empiricism characteristic of her early fiction have also encouraged critics to connect Eliot with Auguste Comte. But Comte's work falls into two periods, the true empiricism of the *Cours de philosophie positive* (and it was to this early work that Lewes subscribed so enthusiastically), which was systematically committed to establishing a realist and objectivist account of knowledge, and the tempered positivism of the *System of Positive Polity,* which Lewes, among many others, found unpersuasive.[23] Eliot appears to have been more drawn toward the later work in which Comte begins to dilute his empiricism.

In the *System,* Comte takes a more overt interest in moral questions than he does in his earlier work. Here he allows a larger place for feeling, placing the "affective" over the "intellectual" and conceding that it is possible to attain some knowledge through this more emotional, less rational means. Eliot kept two notebooks (1875) in which she selected passages from the *System* which show Comte's attempts to combine objective and subjective methods. Like Comte, she was drawn toward an objective view of knowledge, though for her this always meant more than a purely empirical mode of investigation. What she found most compelling in Comte's epistemology were his efforts to connect a theory of knowledge to a theory of morality and his efforts to reconcile subjective and objective ways of knowing.

Ultimately, Eliot believes that morality is a necessary condition for full knowledge. In a chapter epigraph in *Daniel Deronda,* she identifies ignorance with false perspective. Ignorance is "like the falsity of eyesight which over-looks the gradations of distance, seeing that which is afar off as if it were within a step or a grasp." Knowledge, on the other hand, is "power reigned by scruple, having a conscience," the prerogative of those "having a prac-ticed vision."[24] Knowledge is aligned with correct perspective and we see again the convergence of moral character and accurate knowledge.

Just as critics have misinterpreted Eliot by misinterpreting Feuerbach, so they misunderstand her views on language by starting from an oversim-plified understanding of Comte. A number of critics have regarded her as moving from a Comtean realism and a concomitant, naive theory of lan-guage in her early fiction to a more sophisticated antirealist position in her final works. Eliot never held either of these views. She was familiar with the debates among Victorian philologists on the origins and nature of language. She read Mill's *Logic* as well as J. W. Donaldson's *New Cratylus* and Max Muller's "great and delightful book" *Lectures on the Science of Language* (1862), among others. From the first she recognized the com-plexities of language.[25]

Critics have ascribed to Comte a simple reference theory of meaning and then connected this to Eliot's early views on language.[26] Comte makes many statements that suggest that a word gains its meaning by directly hooking on to an object in the extralinguistic world. The value of signs, he argues, "depends entirely on their fixity, a thing which would be impossi-ble, but for permanence in the system of nature."[27] Although he conceives of reference on such a model and connects this feature of language with its usefulness as a tool for the acquisition of objective knowledge of the exter-nal world, he attributes a second and more central purpose to language, that of communication between humans: "We must steadily keep in view the social purpose, the special mark of Language, the communication from man to man of Feelings and thoughts" (*System*, 203). He maintains that clarity of understanding requires more than a perfect system of reference. In order for language to be most effective in its aim of allowing "mutual communication" (188), a certain ethical disposition is required of lan-guage users: "Its first function being to communicate emotions, Language, like Religion, has most natural affinity with the sympathetic instincts which alone are capable of complete transmission" (*System*, 183). Comte specu-lates that language will function ideally only when the achievement of his social vision results in a certain ethical character, when people have begun to practice "the habitual cultivation of the active instincts of Benevolence" (*System*, 184). Commentators have overlooked this ethical aspect of Comte's thought on language, yet it is here that we find the connection between Eliot's views on language and Comte's.

Even before Eliot began to write fiction, she recognized that language is not a scientific instrument and that understanding is always a potential problem. In an essay written in 1856 (the period during which she was most interested in the Comte of the *Cours*), Eliot comments on the imperfections of language: "It must be admitted that the language of cultivated nations is in anything but a rational state; . . . one word stands for many things, and many words for one thing. The subtle shades of meaning, and still subtler echoes of association, make language an instrument which scarcely anything short of genius can wield with definiteness and certainty" (*Essays*, 287). It might be expected, given the premise that she subscribes to a naive view of language at this time, that Eliot would suggest that these deficiencies should be remedied through an improved system of reference. These putative improvements might include eliminating all ambiguities from language, promoting literal meaning, and excluding emotive meaning. She goes on, however, to propose that no perfect scientific system of language will serve to improve communication:

> Suppose, then, that the effort which has been again and again made to construct a universal language on a rational basis has at length succeeded, and that you have a language which has no uncertainty, no whims of idiom, no cumbrous forms, no fitful shimmer of many-hued significance . . . —a patent de-odorized and non resonant language, which effects the purpose of communication as perfectly and rapidly as algebraic signs. Your language may be a perfect medium of expression to science, but will never express life, which is a great deal more than science. With the anomalies and inconveniences of historical language, you will have parted with its music and its passion, with its vital qualities as an expression of individual character, with its subtle capabilities of wit, with everything that gives it power over the imagination. (*Essays*, 288)

Eliot clearly recognizes that it is its complicated, nonliteral features that allow language to do what we want it to do. Her solution to the problem of language is not, then, a simplification of the system of language. Instead, it is a matter of character and growth. Like Comte, Eliot argues that successful communication will require a change in the humans who use language: "Language must be left to grow in precision, completeness, and unity, as minds grow in clearness, comprehensiveness, and sympathy" (*Essays*, 287–88).

Though Eliot does not hold to a naive view of language, neither does she adopt an antirealist position. In some recently published essays from the period during which, it has been argued, her notion of language changed radically, Eliot discusses the development of language. She argues that there are limits to the ways in which humans can develop and think and express themselves, claiming that "different groups of human beings, though in the very beginning of their existence sundered from each other, must inevitably fall upon the same devices for . . . communication and analogical representation."[28] Eliot believes that language is not developed solely through cultural and social means, but that humans by their nature are constrained to think in certain ways: "They might have in no single case the same name for the same thing, but . . . they would of necessity have much agreement in the metaphorical development of their speech: above & below, light & dark, fast & slow, warm & cold, sweet & sour, hard & soft, smooth & rough, heavy & light, noisy & still, cloudy & clear, wet & dry, far & near, & so on, would be the same qualities for each group, & the words expressing them would be transferred from the external to the internal, from the visible and palpable to the invisible and imaginary" (388). The ways in which humans can conceive of the world, the range of possible conceptual schemes are necessary and limited. Eliot argues that the world is inevitably to be carved up in certain ways, that language does not create these divisions but instead reflects them: "In short, their languages would be to a good extent translatable. They would be different media of ideas held in common. Their grammar must have corresponding elements, however differently rendered, since the main elements of grammar are simply indispensable facts of human existence; that I am not you, that He is neither of us, that the sky is still the sky though it may be either bright & sunny or dark & starry, that my hand is still my hand though it may be hot or cold" (388). Rather than supporting a radical subjectivism, Eliot insists on the constraints on human thought and so argues indirectly against the notion that language creates reality.

Worries about linguistic communication are not for Eliot solely abstract intellectual matters. Eliot's anxiety about the reception of her novels is notorious. As a public figure, she is convinced that she is likely to be misconstrued. She is unwilling to allow one of her letters to be made public, for instance, because of her fear of being "served up in a work of commentary" and "misinterpreted" (*GEL*, 6:89). She worries, even with close friends, that they have failed to comprehend one another: "There is always an after-sadness belonging to brief and interrupted intercourse between friends—the sadness of feeling that the blundering efforts we have made towards mutual understanding have only made a new veil between us" (*GEL*, 3:90). In a letter to Harriet Beecher Stowe, however, she suggests that certain qualities in an interpreter can help with these problems: "But I have little anxiety of that kind in writing to you, dear friend. . . . I trust your quick and long-taught mind as an interpreter little liable to mistake me" (*GEL,* 5:31).

In another letter, drawing on the eighteenth-century theory that sympathy occurs through an exchange of physical vibrations between people, Eliot imagines successful understanding as the reproduction of one's consciousness in another's, words serving as the transmitter of thought, as the telephone was to transmit the vibrations of the voice over a wire: "It is necessary to me not simply to *be* but to *utter,* and I require utterance of my friends. . . . It is like a diffusion or expansion of one's own life to be assured that its vibrations are repeated in another, and words are the media of those vibrations" (*GEL,* 1:255). But Eliot rarely expresses such confidence in unobstructed understanding, and success is always dependent upon the ethical character of the interpreter. This is underscored in her essay on the art of translation, in which she emphasizes "the moral qualities especially demanded in the translator—the patience, the rigid fidelity, and the sense of responsibility in interpreting another man's mind" (*Essays,* 211).

IV

The complexity of Eliot's moral theory needs to be understood if we are to do justice to her claims about sympathetic understanding. Eliot's fundamental moral principle is that the capacity for sympathy is necessary for a moral agent, since morality grows from the ability to imagine another's state of mind. Her presiding position is clearly expressed in an often quoted passage from her letters: "My own experience and development deepen every day my conviction that our moral progress may be measured by the degree in which we sympathize with individual suffering and individual joy" (*GEL,* 2:403).

Critics have ascribed a variety of meta-ethical views to Eliot, but finally she holds an intuitionist account of morality, despite her attempts to explain her ethics on other grounds. Her moral theory is not relativist as some critics have argued.[29] She speaks, for instance, of "moral facts" and in a late notebook entry writes: "The fundamental conceptions of morality seem as stationary through ages as the laws of life."[30] She worried about the justification for her moral principles, and may, in part, be seen as an ethical naturalist, that is, one who believes it possible to establish empirical means for deriving ethical truths. Both Lewes and Comte attempted to demonstrate that morality is physiologically grounded, arguing that moral sentiments are inherited through a directed evolution, a process that moves humans from egoistic tendencies to altruistic ones.[31] Lewes's account of morality is close to Eliot's, for he argues that "moral life is based on sympathy. It is feeling for others."[32] George Eliot was amenable to Lewes's (and Spencer's) goal of founding ethics on science, but Lewes, Comte, and Eliot run into the same stumbling block: they begin by *assuming* that certain traits are inherently moral. In Eliot's thought, sympathy and altruism are unquestioned goods.

Two general ideas are pervasive in her view: first, the stress on sympathy, and second, an emphasis on intuition as the method of making moral judgments. These ideas are articulated in the well-known passage from *The Mill on the Floss* in which Eliot is vehement in her assertion of the core idea of ethical intuitionism, that no general rules for how to act in every practical situation can be established:

> All people of broad, strong sense have an instinctive repugnance to the men of maxims because such people early discern that the mysterious complexity of our life is not to be embraced by maxims and that to lace ourselves up in formulas of that sort is to repress all the divine promptings and inspirations that spring from growing insight and sympathy. And the men of maxims are the popular representative of the minds that are guided in their moral judgment solely by general rules, thinking that these will lead them to justice by ready-made patent method, without the trouble of exerting patience, discrimination, impartiality, without any care to assure themselves whether they have the insight that comes from a hardly-earned estimate of temptation or from a life vivid and intense enough to have created a wide, fellow feeling with all that is human.[33]

In this passage, Eliot rejects rationalist, rule-based moral systems such as Kantian or Utilitarian ethics, arguing that moral behavior should emerge not from the application of exceptionless moral principles but instead from attentive response to the complex particularities of a situation (such as those which a novel can portray). Above all, moral judgments must be rooted in feeling.

A similar idea is articulated in an essay in which Eliot discusses "deficiency in moral, *i.e.*, in sympathetic emotion" (note the full identification of the two terms): "In its theoretic and preceptive side, morality touches Science; on its emotional side poetic Art. Now the products of poetic Art are great in proportion as they result from the immediate promptings of innate power, and not from laboured obedience to a theory or rule. . . . In the same way, in proportion as morality is emotional, it will exhibit itself in direct sympathetic feeling and action, and not as the recognition of a rule" (*Essays*, 379). She acknowledges the "scientific" or rule-bound aspect of ethics, the cognitive, along with what she calls the "poetic" aspect of morality: intuitive and affective. But whereas Mill and many of his contemporaries focus on the science, Eliot emphasizes the poetry.

Sympathy as a motive for action is always a moral good for Eliot. She urges that we try to sympathize even with actions and states of mind that we would not condone. Sympathy is not, however, a medium of moral judgment, nor is it a form of emotional infection. This is not to suggest that sympathy precludes moral judgment in her view. Eliot's narrator urges readers to try to understand what motivates Rosamond's selfishness, Bulstrode's hypocrisy, and Casaubon's egoism and to see that we too might have similar motives and act in similar ways. But we are not asked to approve of Rosamond's desire for power nor Bulstrode's and Casaubon's bad faith.

Eliot's novels and essays think through the theoretical and practical issues to which an ethics of sympathy give rise in such detail that they demonstrate that she is aware of the problems attending her account. The view that sympathy should be the foundation of ethics is often criticized because sympathy is not impartial. It is difficult to feel the same sort of sympathy for those far away and unknown as for people one loves. Eliot is aware of the problem of extending sympathetic morality to those one does not know: "Through my union and fellowship with the men and women I *have* seen, I feel a like, though fainter, sympathy with those I have *not seen;* and I am able to live in imagination with the generations to come, that their good is not alien to me, and is a stimulus to me to labour for ends which may not benefit myself, but will benefit them" (*Essays,* 201). As I'll show in more detail later, Eliot is concerned with the extent to which impartiality is required by morality, and she works through that issue both dramatically and discursively in her novels.

It is not surprising that Eliot dramatizes sympathy in virtual dialogue with philosophical discussions of it. Sympathy played a central role in the thought of those she identified as her primary influences: Rousseau, whose belief that sympathy is innate greatly influenced the Romantics; Feuerbach, for whom sympathy is a key concept in his anthropology of religion; and Comte, to whom her model of sympathy is especially indebted. These connections suggest a loose genealogy for Eliot's view, but a concern with the workings of sympathy was widespread in Victorian culture.

Sympathy as an ethical force was much discussed in the eighteenth century, and that thought continued to influence the Victorians. Moral philosophers countered the pessimistic view of humans as purely egotistic with the claim that sympathy is innate, a position that received its most influential treatments from David Hume and his follower Adam Smith.

On Hume's account in *A Treatise of Human Nature*, sympathy is mechanical and mimetic, largely an involuntary process, a transference of affect that results in a faint copy of another's feelings. Only occasionally does he connect it with compassion as later theorists—and particularly George Eliot—would do. Smith, following Hume's lead, produced an account on which sympathy involves "changing places in fancy with the sufferer," a view that comes closer to Eliot's than does Hume's.[34] Bishop Butler famously opposed Thomas Hobbes's belief that the object of pity is in fact oneself rather than another, and Butler's arguments were repeatedly invoked throughout the Victorian period. Versions of the current skeptical arguments were resisted in Matthew Arnold's objection to "Hobbes's resolution of all benevolence into a mere love of power" or in Lewes's claim that Comte's account of altruism defeated the view that "reduced all our emotive actions to a principle of Selfishness."[35]

The concept of sympathy came to be of widespread importance in Victorian writings on ethics, psychology, and science.[36] Debates centered on the question of whether sympathy is instinctual and innate or developed through experience and over time. Most Victorian discussions of sympathy focused on its workings and its origins: few doubted that it existed. Often Victorian philosophical texts take sympathy to be innate. James Martineau, for instance, writes: "The Impulse to abate the sufferings and share the joys of one's fellow man is rooted in an original endowment of the human mind."[37] Even Darwin regarded sympathy as instinctual.

Among the Victorians, then, Eliot was far from alone in believing that sympathy was crucial to morality. We have already seen Carlyle's thought on these matters. John Ruskin claimed that "the Imaginative understanding of the natures of others, and the power of putting ourselves in their place, is the faculty on which the virtue depends."[38] Pater wrote: "As sympathy alone can discover that which really is in matters of feeling and thought, true justice is in its essence a finer knowledge through love."[39] And even Wilde, who at times critiqued the Victorian fixation on sympathy, could assert: "His morality is all sympathy, just what morality should be."[40] The preoccupation with sympathy that manifests itself in Eliot registers a widespread cultural conviction.

As I've indicated, though, much recent criticism regards sympathy in Eliot as always in fact a hidden manifestation of self-interest and connects it with appropriation and even sadism or masochism. Those readings have tried to show how sympathy is undermined in the novels in order to prove that the texts portray (and that Eliot may well have come to recognize) its impossibility. Such approaches are consonant with

Foucauldian approaches or Nietzschean unmasking (though Nietzsche's own frequent attacks on sympathy charge not that it is false or a form of shrouded self-interest but instead a sign of decadence and a promotion of weakness).[41] As we've seen, however, versions of the self-interest argument have long currency, the most influential rendition being Hobbes's claim that "pity is *imagination* or *fiction* of *future* calamity to *ourselves*."[42]

Such Hobbesian perspectives on Eliot were first suggested in examinations of the theme of interpretation in the novels.[43] Later criticism has focused more exclusively on the concept of sympathy.[44] Marc Redfield, for example, discussing Eliot's ethics of sympathy, writes that "a certain violence will always qualify sympathy's occurrence" and that a consequence of Eliot's moral view is that "ethical judgment becomes flavored with voyeurism and sadomasochism, since sympathy requires for its existence the spectacle of another's suffering."[45] Similarly, Ann Cvetkovich reads Eliot's "Sympathy as Benevolent Sadism,"[46] while Michael Heyns argues that although "the plot [of *Adam Bede*] claims to be propelled by sympathy," it is really about persecution.[47]

A tendency of many of these readings is to collapse distinctions. If Eliot dramatizes cases in which interpretation or sympathy goes awry, then she has undermined sympathy altogether. *Any* failure of sympathy is read as a questioning of the very possibility of sympathy. If Deronda is not perfectly sympathetic, then he is revealed to be self-interested and appropriating. If he is sympathetic, on the other hand, then he enjoys his own or others' pain. To see all sympathy in Eliot's novels as a form of self-interest or as the enactment of neurosis is a misinterpretation. Although such critiques illuminate aspects of the novels, ultimately they fall short of grasping Eliot's complex, deeply informed thought on the relations between sympathy and knowledge.

The view that Eliot's "sympathy" can never be anything more than imaginary—a form of representation—is often linked to the belief that Adam Smith's model of sympathy is the basis for Eliot's. David Marshall, whose account of the complications of Eliot's view is very good, was the first to connect her theory with Smith's. According to Marshall, on Eliot's view (following Smith) sympathy requires that "we imagine that we are persons who can be only representations to us."[48] J. Jeffrey Franklin maintains that for Eliot sympathy "is identification not with a real object or referent external to the self, but with a representation within the self of that object that is generated by the imagination."[49] More recently, Audre Jaffe in *Scenes of Sympathy* has taken Smith's account as the model for Victorian novelistic depictions of sympathy. In Smith, she contends, "sympathy 'does away' with bodies in order to produce representations, replacing persons with mental pictures." It follows that sympathy "is fictional, in the sense that it is fundamentally involved with representation."[50]

I want to take a critical look at the logic of these arguments to unpack some of their assumptions and in so doing explain more precisely how Eliot can coherently link understanding, that is, knowledge of others, with moral action. There is a slippage in Jaffe's move from "representation" to "fiction." She assumes that representation ("imagination" in Smith's terms) is to be equated with fiction. Our knowledge of others' mental states requires representing them in our own minds (in Smith's view, we do this by calling on our own analogous experiences) and is thus "fiction." That claim seems to involve the supposition that we can directly know the external world and our own states of mind, that is, that some thinking—ordinary perception and introspection—is possible apart from mental representation. The view pervasive in Victorian philosophy and in current psychology as well is that *all* thinking is representational: apprehension of events, objects, and even our own states of mind is not possible without mental representation. (Experiments in psychology strongly suggest that imagination and sensory perception may share the same representational forms and mechanisms.) Further, most mental activity depends on "imagination," that is, the ability to represent in one's mind things that are not actually present. Such representation or "imagination" allows us to think about objects that are absent—hence, to have any thought about the past, the present, or anything beyond the contents of our immediate perceptual field. Certainly all abstract thought and any form of writing requires mental representation. To link, then, *all* mental representation with fiction is in some sense to make everything fiction.

Lewes, whose work in psychology was at the forefront of the developing field and whose five-volume *Problems of Life and Mind* made significant contributions to the view that the mental supervenes on the physical, regarded mental representation as fundamental to human mentality. Leslie Stephen also emphasized the centrality of the human ability to mentally represent what is not there: the only way we can make up an image of the objective world, he argues, is by summoning perceptions we are not currently experiencing. We must call up sensations in consciousness that are "regarded as representative of others not actually present."[51] Against objections that it is impossible to know the minds of others, Stephen contends that all knowledge of the world involves similar mental representation: "The actual sensations of every moment are completed and held together in the mind by a whole system of ideal perceptions"

(229). To fill out representations in this way is, in Stephen's view, no different than affixing emotions to a person: "I do not really think of a man till I have interpreted the external signs by the emotions which they signify. . . . I must put myself in his place, feel what he feels. . . . I imagine a state of consciousness not actually present" (229). If representation is involved in all thought, then its involvement in sympathy is hardly a compelling threat to its legitimacy.

It is nevertheless clear that we cannot know another's state of mind in the same way that we know our own, since we cannot gain access to another's internal states. The question is whether that is enough to impugn all knowledge of other minds. For Eliot, Lewes, and many other Victorians, the answer was no. Many critiques of sympathy implicitly adopt Hobbes' dubious picture of the subject: a self who is a fully formed individual and whose internal states preexist his/her relations with others. That is not Feuerbach's picture. In his view, any knowledge depends on the recognition of other minds. One cannot have a concept of an "I" without the concept of an other: "Where there is no *thou,* there is no *I*" (*EC,* 92). The understanding of self and other develops simultaneously.

Leslie Stephen developed a similar account. Sounding much like Eliot, Stephen begins his section on "Sympathy" in *The Science of Ethics* with the claim, "In the first place, the recognition that there are other centres of consciousness besides my own is bound up in the closest way with the recognition of what is called an objective world" (228). Knowledge of the objective world, he asserts, depends on shared understanding with others. Concepts—that is, abstract ideas—are needed for any knowledge, and these emerge through "sympathy" or through knowledge of other minds: "It would appear that sympathy is not an additional instinct, a faculty which is added when the mind has reached a certain stage of development, a mere incident of intellectual growth, but something implied from the first in the very structure of knowledge. I must be capable of representative ideas in order to think coherently or to draw the essential distinction between object and subject. I must be able to regard certain modes of thought and feeling as symbolic of modes present in other minds, and to my own in other positions" (230).

On this account, entirely consistent with George Eliot's, sympathy is essential to the ability to know anything at all. "'Put yourself in his place,'" Stephen claims, "is not merely a moral precept; it is a logical rule implied in the earliest germs of reason, as a description of reasoning itself, so far as it deals with other sentient beings" (230). Here Victorian debate manifests a complexity that anticipates the twentieth-century rejection of the Cartesian model, on which we can know our own states of mind incorrigibly but cannot be certain of anything about others' internal states.[52] Such an account of human mental activity calls to mind free indirect discourse, the narrative technique that Eliot so exploited.[53]

V

The most comprehensive and nuanced version of Eliot's hermeneutics of sympathy is enacted in her final novels. There, concrete situations provide a rich context in which to explore her views. Notwithstanding her forceful dramatization of the difficulties of moving beyond one's own subjective viewpoint, Eliot never abandons the idea that there are correct ways of interpreting. Aware of the difficulties involved in a hermeneutics of sympathy, she develops an increasingly complex picture of its workings in narratives that represent what is at stake in understanding others.

Eliot's preoccupation with interpretation has been discussed primarily in the context of *Middlemarch*, in which the narrator famously asserts that "signs are small measurable things, but interpretations are illimitable" (23). The above quotation and the now familiar parable of the scratched pier glass have often been cited as demonstrating Eliot's relativistic understanding. While Eliot does acknowledge that things look different from varying subject positions, her aim is to find a way to correct for these differences. Repeatedly, she demonstrates that holding on to an ego-centered perspective and operating without sympathy are moral failings and result in misinterpretation.

In these terms, Eliot's concern in *Middlemarch* is to lead Dorothea from her "moral stupidity" (198) to a position in which she is able to enter imaginatively into others' viewpoints. Dorothea is initially a poor hermeneut; rather than trying to enter another's perspective, she creates meaning that, like Fred Vincy's, is "no more than the reflex of [her] own inclinations" (111). This is seemingly the error of all inaccurate readers in Eliot, the inability to prevent their own desires or preconceptions from distorting perceptions of the world and others. Projection is rife, Eliot grants; Lydgate "interpreted [Rosamond's beauty] as the sign of a ready intelligent sensitiveness" (556) because he wished to. The narrator remarks in relation to Casaubon that "manners must be very marked indeed before they cease to be interpreted by preconceptions either confident or distrustful" (20). Eliot knows the patterns of cognition, the ways in which understanding is shaped by predisposition. Dorothea likewise projects her desires onto Casaubon, seeing in him "every quality she herself brought" (22). The narrator comments, echoing Feuerbach, that "the text, whether of prophet or of poet, expands for whatever we can put into it" (46). Dorothea's mode of exegesis assures that she will find what she is predisposed to see: "She filled up all the blanks with unmanifested perfections, interpreting him as she interpreted the works of Providence, and accounting for seeming discords by her own deafness to the higher harmonies" (68). Eliot's allusion to scriptural interpretation reveals that she recognizes the same mistaken modes of exegesis that she has dismissed in theological hermeneutics carried over into secular understanding.

As Dorothea progresses she comes to understand that Mr. Casaubon has "an equivalent centre of self" (198). By achieving impartiality and imaginatively entering into the perspectives of others, she corrects her own distorting perspective. In the climactic scene in which Dorothea looks down from her window after her night of misery and resolves to put aside her own desires for Rosamond's sake, she has accepted the morality that grounds proper interpretation. She succeeds in her self-imposed goal of "the reaching forward of the whole consciousness towards the fullest truth, the least partial good" (190). Eliot's wording here is significant. Understanding is a goal to be approached, yet never quite attained. Yet Dorothea's new moral state renders her a more accurate interpreter: "She was no longer struggling against the perception of facts, but adjusting herself to their clearest perception" (343). Eliot is doing more here than implying that there are ethical consequences to the choices we make. She is insisting on a method that makes an interpretation true or false.

Here, then, we have a straightforward assertion of Eliot's hermeneutic, and the view that contemporary criticism has challenged. *Daniel Deronda,* however, adds new complexity to this model of sympathetic hermeneutics. The book brings interpretation to the forefront even more than does *Middlemarch.* Eliot emphasizes the difficulty of interpretation on every level, in questions of epistemology, in textual and scriptural interpretation, in everyday encounters with others in the world, and in knowing another culture. She thus keeps in view the formal exegetical debates of her time, while simultaneously giving us her own wider-ranging, secularized hermeneutics.

Eliot's intense study of Torah interpretation in preparation for writing *Daniel Deronda* is recorded in her notebooks for the novel. Carefully distinguishing between modes of Jewish hermeneutics in her notes, she remarks on the interpretive principles driving particular approaches to the Torah. This contextual material makes its way into the Philosopher's Club scene at The Hand and Banner; there Eliot rehearses exegetical debates that were central to both Torah interpretation as well as to the

Christian hermeneutics of the period. Mordecai promotes a developmental theory of interpretation, according to which meaning unfolds and expands over time: "The native spirit of our tradition was not to stand still, but to use records as a seed, and draw out the compressed virtues of law and prophecy" (453). Even when the texts were appropriated by Christianity, he argues, "our Masters were still enlarging and illuminating with fresh-fed interpretation" (454). Although Eliot's portrait of Mordecai is largely sympathetic, she had earlier been highly critical of the idea of development. Gideon, sounding much closer to Eliot in her early essays on scriptural interpretation, insists that "the most learned and liberal men among us who are attached to our religion are for clearing our liturgy of all such notions as a literal fulfillment of the prophecies about restoration, and so on" (455). Exegesis, the novel suggests, is far from being a topic only for theologians. Scriptural hermeneutics is central to Mordecai's vision, and Daniel's vocation, like Bardo's in *Romola,* will also depend on textual interpretation. The novel ends, after all, not with Deronda in Palestine but instead "reading and sifting old manuscripts" (635) found in his grandfather's chest.

The opening chapters of the novel turn emphatically on the process and problems of arriving at knowledge of others. From the opening paragraph's depiction of Daniel's uncertainty about Gwendolen, through chapter epigraphs on incomprehension ("The beginning of an acquaintance whether with persons or things is to get a definite outline for our ignorance" [91]), to narrative commentary ("what construction of another's mind is not strong wishing equal to?" [289]), the text reminds readers of the complications involved in knowing. Eliot makes many direct statements on the problem of perspective in interpretation in *Daniel Deronda:* "Often the grand meanings of faces as well as of written words may lie chiefly in the impressions of those who look on them" (158). As in *Middlemarch,* she underscores the pervasiveness of misinterpretation. The young clergyman, Mr. Middleton entirely misinterprets Gwendolen according to his desire. Eliot writes: "Indeed he occasionally felt that her more formal treatment of himself was such a sign of favor as to warrant making advances. . . . for all meanings we know, depend on the key of interpretation" (46). Eliot, however, assures us that this is no more than faulty exegesis. Gwendolen simply finds him comic.

From the very start the novel plays with point of view and shifting perspective. Using free indirect discourse, moving between internal and external views, shifting sometimes almost imperceptibly from one character's thoughts into another's, the narrative both enacts and thematizes the human mind's capacity to move between third-person and first-person representations. Deronda is skilled at achieving "a quick change of mental light, shifting his point of view to that" of another (421). Gwendolen, on the other hand, regards others as "ghosts," beings who are not quite full individuals themselves, and she knows them only as they reflect upon her. She attempts to shift point of view only as a way of gaining an external perspective on *herself*. In the archery scene, the narrative underscores its quick shifts from internal to external, third-person to first person representations, in its parenthetical renderings of Gwendolen's thoughts. At the same time, Gwendolen's unspoken thoughts demonstrate the ways in which she seeks views that are essentially third-person representations of herself. "(Pause, during which she imagined various degrees and modes of opinion about herself that might be entertained by Grandcourt)" (92). "(Pause, during which Gwendolen made several interpretations of her own speech)" (92). She wonders about others' internal states only as they are directed at her, and the novel shows that this is her central moral deficiency.

Only by reading Eliot's novels as dramatizing an ethics of sympathy can one adequately register Gwendolen's narrative: her moral education from a girl unable to see beyond her "own little core of egoistic sensibility" (13) through a sharp punishment, to an awakening to the reality of others. She rarely considers the desires of others except as they impinge on her own. As she confesses, "I have never thought much of anyone's feelings" (387). Because she is completely unconcerned with what others might think or feel—except about her—she misinterprets almost everyone around her, and is brought down to her acknowledgment in the final pages that she deserves everything she gets because, "I only thought of myself" (695). Having been "dislodged from her supremacy in her own world" (689) she can at last feel for others in the altruistic abnegation of her own desires. This pattern of growth and critique of egoism is familiar from all of Eliot's novels.

Despite a long history of readings from Henry James, to F. R. Leavis, to postcolonial critics who condemned Daniel's vapid, abstract qualities, his role in the novel is also essential to this moral narrative. Daniel, in clear antithesis to Gwendolen, because of his "habit of thinking himself imaginatively into the experience of others" (436) has a wonderful capacity to "divine" their intentions. We are told of his "sympathetic interest," his "answering depth of sympathy" (352), his "ready sympathy" (354). Deronda is the paradigm of the moral sensibility that Eliot presents to us, the embodiment of the ethics of antiegoism: "Daniel had the stamp of rarity in a subdued fervour of sympathy, an activity of imagination on behalf of others" (151). What comes to Dorothea at the end of *Middlemarch* as a hard-won lesson, Daniel has known since childhood. He is so little egoistic as often to lose his sense of self. He attempts escape

from his own subjectivity, taking on the position of an "impartial spectator": "He was forgetting everything else in a half-speculative, half-involun-
tary identification of himself with the objects he was looking at, thinking
how far it might be possible habitually to shift his centre till his own personality would be no less outside him than the landscape" (160). The
closest Gwendolen can come to something like selflessness through most
of the novel, conversely, is "a desperate indifference to her own doings, or
at least a determination to get a superiority over them by laughing at
them as if they belonged to someone else" (40).

But despite the alignment between moral disposition and adeptness at
interpretation, key episodes of the novel challenge this convergence.
Romantic relations are of course central to Eliot's novels, and it is these
relationships that put the greatest pressure on her hermeneutic of sympathy. Granted, Eliot had a novelistic tradition of misunderstandings
between lovers to influence her, but her narratives go beyond that tradition in explicitly bringing the act of interpretation to the forefront.
Often, the actors in these episodes of muddled understanding are her
moral characters, those who understand the need to overcome their own
perspectives and desires. Further, they have all the will in the world to
enter into the other's perspective, and yet they fail dismally.

Let us return briefly to *Middlemarch,* to the scene in which Will believes
he has revealed to Dorothea his feelings for her. Despite the full engagement of her sympathy, Dorothea completely misconstrues Will's feelings
and words, and the text presents a series of misinterpretations of the
other's utterances. When Will admits: "What I care for more than I can
ever care for anything else is absolutely forbidden me" (*MM,* 594), he
believes he has made an unmistakable confession. Eliot writes: "Will
paused, imagining that it would be impossible for Dorothea not to understand this" (595). But even in this case Dorothea fails to interpret his
words properly, thinking instead that he refers to Rosamond Vincy.

Similar misunderstandings occur in *Daniel Deronda,* in ways that help
explain some of the interpretive problems that Eliot works through in the
novels. Gwendolen, of course, regularly misinterprets Grandcourt.
According to the moral scheme of the novel, misinterpretation is inevitable
given these characters' egoism. Gwendolen enjoys playing on the tendency
of language to be misconstrued; she endeavors to be enigmatic and difficult to interpret. Never does she actively attempt to understand
Grandcourt's words; she is not interested in what he might mean, desire,
feel, but only in the possibilities of meaning to be found in her own utterances. She shows an awareness of the capacity of language to express multiple meanings and to mask rather than to reveal, but is surprisingly blind to

the likelihood that another's real intentions may be equally as difficult to discern as her own. This is primarily because she rarely considers that others have intentions. It is only with Deronda that Gwendolen first attempts to imagine the possibility of shifting perspectives, asking: "What should you do—what should you feel, if you were in my place?" (386). Only to him does she urgently insist, "I understand what you mean" (388).

But even Deronda and Mirah, the characters who most surely have the moral disposition the novel praises, confront interpretive impasses which suggest that a hermeneutics of sympathy is very difficult to attain. Again, in a scene offering a fully detailed series of misinterpretations, Mirah and Deronda misconstrue each other, "each of them interpreting mistakenly the increased reserve and diffidence of the other" (670). Mirah mistakes Deronda's feelings, believing he is in love with Gwendolen. Deronda believes that his perceptible love for Mirah pains her. Even when Deronda makes a full declaration, Mirah persists in her misinterpretation to the final moment, initially understanding Deronda's words to be a sign of his regard for her brother. In Gwendolen's case, the narrator repeatedly underscores her misreadings, connecting them to her inability to see beyond herself. But these characters similarly misread each other, though their mistake is not a too-confident prejudgment in their favor, but instead a too-hasty acceptance of their insignificance.

If these characters have achieved the moral sensibility, the sympathetic capacity, the antiegoism that Eliot prescribes, why is interpretation still such a problem for them? I don't intend to show in my turn that Eliot's texts subvert her professed ideas, but rather to demonstrate that Eliot—too smart to accept an overly simple view—plays out the complications involved in a hermeneutics of sympathy. The recognition of the difficulties does not lead her to a resignation to indeterminacy, nor do her texts make the case for such a view. To understand how she avoids the slip into skepticism, it is important to see the precise nature of the complications she represents. In what follows, I analyze particular moments in *Daniel Deronda* that help us to see the ways in which Eliot thinks through central hermeneutic problems as she shifts the ground to an ethical orientation.

The scenes of romantic encounter demonstrate that Eliot has not overlooked the unconscious dimensions of meaning. Through Lewes she was familiar with work at the forefront of the new field of psychology, and she read, in addition to Lewes's texts, other important works in psychology. Eliot recognized that a great deal of mental activity goes on below the level of consciousness. As the narratives show, her characters are not always fully aware of what they mean by what they say or do. "Watch your own speech," Eliot writes, "and notice how it is guided by your less conscious purposes"

(*MF,* 459). Dorothea in Will's confession scene discussed above has not yet acknowledged the extent of her feelings for Will. Sympathetically entering into another's viewpoint, if that viewpoint is equated with what is consciously present in a speaker's mind, is an inadequate method of understanding an utterance when the speaker herself is not wholly conscious of her own meaning. Schleiermacher (following Kant) takes this into account in his hermeneutic, asserting that it is an interpreter's task to understand an author's words better than he himself has understood them.

This problem, however, cannot account for everything that goes wrong when Eliot represents her hermeneutic at work in her novels. Complete misinterpretation occurs between the characters, even when they are more fully conscious of their meanings. Will, in the scene above, has acknowledged his feelings toward Dorothea, yet she fails to understand him. Certainly Eliot repeatedly demonstrates that the ideal is hard to attain: "To shift one's point of view beyond certain limits is impossible to the most liberal and expansive mind; we are none of us aware of the impression we produce on Brazilian monkeys of feeble understanding."[54] But why is it that the characters depicted as the best interpreters because of their sympathetic capacities have such difficulties in certain situations?

As we have seen, Eliot's model of sympathetic divination requires that one separate oneself from one's own desires, interests, and perspective in order to enter into another's point of view. One's habitual state should be a comparative selflessness, as the contrast between Gwendolen and Deronda tells us, a state that will easily allow one to disengage from one's own viewpoint to sympathetically enter the other's. Eliot, however, is alert to the problems of negotiating claims between self and other and aware that it is not always easy to distinguish between selflessness and self-affirmation.

Although the ideal of two consciousnesses merged into one is a model of romantic love that fits well with Eliot's regard for selflessness, *Daniel Deronda* repeatedly points to its difficulties. The narrator does express this Fichtean notion in her description of Deronda's attitude toward Mirah: "Our self is a not-self for whose sake we become virtuous" (319). When Mirah and Deronda finally do come to comprehend each other, they are described as "meeting so fully in their new consciousness that all signs would have seemed to throw them further apart" (679). Here, then, is the complete sympathetic joining of minds. But most of the narrative explores the difficulties of any such complete mutuality.

Elsewhere, Eliot, despite her ethic, depicts romantic love as a condition that makes it difficult to shift from one's own perspective to another's as a hermeneutics of sympathy asks one to do. The narrative suggests that "being in love" demands that one be intensely conscious of one's own desires and self. Still, Daniel's and Mirah's misreadings are surprisingly unlike the examples of misinterpretation that Eliot typically depicts. Her paradigmatic case of bad interpretation is that which results from the projection of one's own desires. These romantic misinterpretations, however, are not in accordance with the characters' wishes, but rather in opposition to them. Their mistakes take the form of pessimism about possibilities for self rather than self-aggrandizement, and the selflessness of these characters gets in the way of successful understanding.

The ideal of a selfless romantic love is displaced and played out in the relationship between Deronda and Mordecai, where it is recast as the spiritual aspiration to overcome human finitude. It is Ezra's desire to merge with Deronda, to break down the boundaries between the self and the other so that Deronda can pursue Ezra's Zionist vision. Their relationship, as has been noted, is repeatedly described in terms of romantic love. It is, according to Mordecai, "a marriage of our souls" (424). Eliot seems to value this ideal of the merging of selves, comparing it to the maternal love that she so highly regards: "The sense of spiritual perpetuation in another resembles that maternal transference of self" (425).

And yet, the narrative also questions this ideal. Mordecai wants to merge with another self, but it is his vision that is to be central: "All his passionate desire had concentrated itself in the yearning for some young ear into which he could pour his mind as a testament" (404). Although Ezra employs a rhetoric of selflessness, we might see a form of appropriation in his conduct. Deronda feels himself to be "half-dominated" (434). (Mordecai's desires, however, are for the good of a larger community, something that Eliot along with many Victorian social theorists understood as involving selflessness.)

Mirah and Deronda seem to accept Ezra's vision, especially in the closing tableau where they kneel with arms around the dead Ezra. Yet Deronda describes Mordecai as interpreting reality as he would have it, charging that his zeal "turned his wishes into overmastering impressions, and made him read outward facts as fulfillment" (438). Although Deronda eventually enters into Ezra's plans, it is not in fact through a complete identification with Mordecai, but rather through a reconceptualization of the mission brought about by the receipt of family records, documents that present another hermeneutic task for Deronda.

Mirah also refuses complete selflessness. In the one piece of explicit textual exegesis in the novel, Mirah, who has just admitted obliquely that she really is not able to grasp Mordecai's ideas, interprets a story differently than he does. Mordecai recites the following: "Somewhere in the later *Midrash,* I think, is the story of a Jewish maiden who loved a Gentile king so well, that this is what she did:—she entered into prison and changed clothes with the woman who was beloved by the king, that she might deliver that woman from death by dying in her stead, and leave the king to be happy in his love which was not for her" (629). Mordecai's summation of the story's meaning is that "this is the surpassing love, that loses self in the object of love" (629). Mirah, who now realizes that she loves Deronda, instead insists on the woman's longing for recognition of self: "No, Ezra, no . . . that was not it. She wanted the king when she was dead to know what she had done, and feel that she was better than the other. It was her strong self, wanting to conquer, that made her die" (629). Mirah's resistance does not go so far as to allow the heroine to remain alive, but she does insist on claims for the self.

In this way, the narrative stages a conflict between the ideal of sympathetic coalescence and the desire to maintain an autonomous self.[55] The merging of consciousnesses is alternatively represented as double-edged, as a force for good, "our virtue in the making" (833), and as a form of domination. Daniel's mother, the artist who has refused to sacrifice desire and self, even for her child, best articulates the latter view: "I know very well what love makes of men and women—it is subjection; it takes another for a larger self, enclosing this one . . . I was never willingly subject to any man" (571). While according to the novel's central ethic, the Princess's perspective should be rejected, the contradictions in the narrative suggest that Eliot vacillates. As a result of this apparent ambivalence, the novel is taken, despite itself, to recognize that appropriation is the norm.

There are many places in Eliot's work that might encourage this reading, the most obvious being her early story, "The Lifted Veil," in which a man named Latimer is able to enter into others' minds. He finds this "diseased participation in other people's consciousness" to be an affliction, so much so that he shrinks from the company of others, becoming alienated and despondent.[56] Latimer is barred only from entering into the thoughts of Bertha, the woman he loves, and it is because he is forced to interpret her from small signs that his desire for her remains strong. The story renders the idea of shared consciousness as the destruction of love. Terry Eagleton, in an influential early essay on the story, argues that Eliot here reveals that sympathy is not a viable means to knowledge, that one gains "knowledge" only through power and appropriation: "consciousness greedily or wearily absorbs consciousness."[57]

Other critics have followed Eagleton in reading the story as a representation of Eliot's anxieties about the impossibility or at least undesirability of knowledge of others. An equally plausible interpretation is that

"The Lifted Veil" is not a story about the impossibility of distinguishing between projection and empathy, but instead an account of knowledge devoid of sympathy. On this reading, it is Latimer's lack of sympathy that makes his clairvoyance a hell for him (and the name "Latimer" means "interpreter"). Latimer reacts to, as he puts it, "the obtrusion of" other minds, with disgust rather than with compassion (13). Eliot, in other words, leaves no room to imagine that Latimer's mind reading is to be identified with sympathetic understanding. That the ideas Latimer expresses are in opposition to the ones that Eliot typically promotes has encouraged critics to regard the story as a mask behind which she can break from the too-demanding morality that she imposes on herself and others. Yet it is a commonplace that first-person narrators are not representatives of their authors "real selves," and Latimer can easily be taken as an example of the distortion in moral view that Eliot has elsewhere discussed. My point is that we should expect Eliot to be aware of the difficulties involved in her interpretive theory. She can show that she has fully considered the range of objections to a hermeneutics of sympathy, and yet still maintain that her interpretive account is correct.

Yet if Eliot's sympathy is not really a form of sadism or masochism, why does she torture Gwendolen? According to the readings that assert that sympathy subverts itself, Deronda's connection to Gwendolen is more accurately described as exploitative than sympathetic and is not really very different from her relation with Grandcourt. Cvetkovich, for instance, finds "a peculiar complicity between Daniel's and the narrator's politics of sympathy and Grandcourt's emotional terrorism" (129). The themes of domination and appropriation are not by any means absent from Eliot's dramatizations of human relationships. We've seen that one could read aspects of Daniel's relationship with Mordecai in these terms, and Grandcourt's interpretations of Gwendolen certainly issue from "the courage and confidence that belonged to domination" (582). Although repeatedly described as wanting in sympathy, Grandcourt has a puzzling ability to "divine" certain of Gwendolen's thoughts: "Grandcourt could not indeed fully imagine how things affected Gwendolen: he had no imagination of anything in her but what affected the gratification of his own will; but on that point he had the sensibility which seems like divination" (474). What Grandcourt does understand neither arises from nor results in fellow feeling. His powers of interpretation are an extension of his relentless domination—his "mastery" as the narrator puts it—of Gwendolen.

Let us consider the argument that Deronda's "sympathy" might be taken as a form of domination as well. The narrator does refer to "the coercion he had exercised over [Gwendolen's] thought" (278). Recall also that Gwendolen's quite unwonted feeling toward Deronda is submission, and she is described as having taken on a double-consciousness in seeing all her acts as he would see them. On such a reading, Daniel's options are either to choose Mordecai (and so be eclipsed by another) or Gwendolen (and so in turn become the dominator of another's consciousness). But to erase the distinction between Deronda and Grandcourt or to make all understanding a form of domination is to obliterate some crucial differences. As Eliot writes in another context: "Heat is a great agent and a useful word, but considered as a means of explaining the universe it requires an extensive knowledge of differences" (52). Granted, Deronda does not achieve perfect sympathy at every moment, and Grandcourt, despite his sadism, is at times a successful interpreter of Gwendolen's feelings. Yet this is entirely consistent with Eliot's ethics of sympathy. Max Scheler's *The Nature of Sympathy*, a significant twentieth-century treatment of the subject, helps us see why Grandcourt is not Deronda, why sympathy must be distinguished from sadism. Scheler explains that sympathy cannot be merely equivalent to understanding what another feels, since one can have knowledge of another's state of mind without wishing them well.[58] As Scheler writes, the "delight in the suffering of others in which cruelty consists" depends "on the capacity to realize those sufferings in imagination." That some cases of understanding another can be connected to cruelty, however, does not mean that *all* understanding is inextricable from domination or sadism.

In her revisions to the last volume of Lewes's *Problems of Life and Mind*, Eliot, discussing the development of altruism, admits that increased mental capacity does not necessarily result in greater benevolence: "True, the same enlargement of perception and imagination brings with it more elaborate forms of egoism, and civilised man is still a beast of prey directing murderous artillery for the satisfaction of his more highly differentiated greed."[59] But if, as she grants, "appetite is the ancestor of tyranny," "it is also the ancestor of love" (5:492). Eliot provides a taxonomy of various capacities for sympathetic understanding in her portraits of various psychologies, depicting the "extensive knowledge of differences" that she has called for. Lush, to take one example, is set in clear contrast to Grandcourt: "With no active compassion or goodwill, he had just as little active malevolence" (511). And despite Grandcourt's occasional successes, Eliot is insistent on the limitations of his understanding: "In dog fashion, Grandcourt discerned the signs of Gwendolen's expectation, interpreting them with the narrow correctness which leaves a world of unknown feeling behind" (580).

Deronda's sympathy, however, is explicitly challenged by his mother's denial of his ability to understand her. To his statement, "I enter into the painfulness of your struggle" (541), she replies: "You may try—but you can never imagine what it is to have a man's force of genius in you, and yet to suffer the slavery of being a girl" (541). The Princess's words are frequently read as representing Eliot's recognition of the limits of under-standing. Yet it is not so easy to say where the narrative positions itself in relation to the Princess's claims. Although Deronda cannot achieve full understanding or sympathy, he does do what Eliot enjoins: he tries to put aside his own feelings and see from the Princess's point of view. Eliot is too sophisticated to insist that perfect sympathy is required or attainable; and when she notes a failing in her "good" characters or a success in her "bad" ones, she complicates but does not compromise her views.

Most importantly, Eliot does not qualify her sympathetic ideal, but comes to recognize the problems of demanding too much impartiality of a morality. She writes in one of her notebook entries that morality should not demand unattainable standards—"impossible prescriptions" as she puts it.[60] As in the Princess's case, to charge that Daniel does not sympa-thize with Gwendolen is to ignore the abundant narrative evidence that he does. In dramatizing these dynamics, Eliot works through one of the central problems associated with an ethics based in sympathy: apart from Deronda's own inclinations (wanting to marry Mirah rather than Gwendolen), sympathizing with Mirah precludes fully accommodating himself to Gwendolen's needs. The accusation that he does not sympa-thize with her presumes that sympathy requires complete surrender to another and that that is possible in a densely realistic world in which char-acters must respond to multiple and conflicting claims. Given that read-ers typically find Gwendolen a more attractive and a more fully represented character than Mirah, it is not surprising that they want to see Deronda choose Gwendolen. That he does not cannot be taken as evi-dence of the failure of sympathy.

Daniel arrives at exactly what is to be expected of an ethics of sympathy: partiality. What the novel comes to is not a subversion of sympathy, but a recognition that a too selfless morality is untenable. Eliot finds fault not with sympathy, but with the ideals of rationalism, according to which one can extend the same impartial morality to everyone. This critique is pres-ent in Eliot's depiction of Daniel from the novel's start. Too detached from his own needs, desires, and judgments, Daniel is ineffectual exactly because he tries to enter into all points of view. Daniel's "imagination had so wrought itself to seeing things as they probably appeared to others, that a strong partisanship" is rendered unlikely. Such impartiality, the narrator explains, "tends to neutralise sympathy" (307) and threatens to render Deronda passive.

At the end of the novel, Daniel is required to reel in his "many-sided sympathy," to choose between sympathies. In a suggestive formulation, Eliot elucidates the dynamics of her ethic of sympathy when she describes Daniel with "his judgement no longer wandering in the mazes of impartial sympathy, but choosing, with the noble partiality which is man's best strength, the closer fellowship that makes sympathy practical—exchanging the bird's eye reasonableness which soars to avoid preference and loses all sense of quality" (638). John Stuart Mill has described his ideal ethics in *Utilitarianism* in this way: "As between his own happiness and that of others, utilitarianism requires [the agent] to be as strictly impartial as a disinterested and benevolent spectator."[61] This is the morality that Eliot comes to reject in the novel. As much as he seeks it at the novel's start, Daniel's is not a disembodied view from nowhere. If Gwendolen's progress is toward greater selflessness, Deronda's trajectory is the opposite.

Daniel's choice, however, has also come in for its share of critique in the arguments that discredit sympathy. Eliot, it is argued, closes down the possibilities of understanding people different from oneself by showing that "sympathy" is reduced to racial connection.[62] Yet through Deronda's adaptation of Mordecai's project, the novel in fact provides one more site for an exploration of sympathetic understanding. The narrative underscores that Daniel finds it uncharacteristically difficult to sympathize with Mordecai: "That keenly perceptive sympathetic emotiveness . . . was never more thoroughly tested" (425). Putting aside the sleight-of-hand plotting that at the last reveals Daniel to be a Jew (and that might be taken to symbolically represent that success is possible even in difficult acts of sympathy), by the novel's end, Deronda has deliberated and chosen. Eliot affirms her commitment to the notion that one must ultimately be able to separate oneself from others' viewpoints in order to judge the perspectives that one has come to understand through sympathetic identification. The problem of how to choose one project over another, how to make judgments, remains. Eliot never ceases to disparage "the interpretations of ignorance" (*MM*, 422). Daniel insists on "valid evidence" (440), taking from Ezra's vision only what he can believe and finding in it what is valuable, "however erratic some of his interpretations might be" (465). This is Feuerbach's hermeneutic, critical yet sympathetic.

I am aware that it is impossible to decisively defeat the argument against Eliot's hermeneutics of sympathy simply by showing how complex and subtle and critical her treatment of it was. Even this might be regarded as her sophisticated way to avoid confronting her own preoccupations with self-interest, power, and domination. But, as Eliot says: "Skepticism, as we know, can never be thoroughly applied, else life would come to a standstill" (*MM,* 225). And, finally, there is no reason to believe that a skeptical explanation—one that claims to expose "real" motivations: self-interest, egoism, power, domination—is always deeper, more persuasive, and more correct than a nonskeptical one. In her novels, Eliot recognizes the mode and attributes it to those figures who are locked hopelessly in their own egos, one fragilely, one tyrannically. It is Casaubon, on the one hand, who practices "suspicious interpretation" (*MM,* 392) and Grandcourt, on the other, who hones his "power of suspicious divination" (*DD,* 519). It may have come to seem naive to take Eliot at her word: "The only effect I ardently long to produce by my writings is that those who read them should be better able to *imagine* and to *feel* the pains and joys of those who differ from themselves in everything but the broad fact of being struggling, erring, human creatures" (*GEL,* 3:111). But when her novels demonstrate so complex a grasp of the workings and problems of intentionalist hermeneutics, it seems preferable to take seriously her commitment to the value of sympathetic understanding. In doing so, we recognize the crucial role Eliot played in moving hermeneutics to the center of secular culture in the Victorian period.

2

Victorian Literary Criticism

The members of the Browning Society, like the theologians of the Broad
Church Party, or the authors of Mr. Walter Scott's Great Writers Series,
seem to me to spend their time in trying to explain their divinity away.
— Oscar Wilde, "The Critic as Artist"

Victorian literary criticism, a much richer and more complex activity than
has sometimes been allowed, is a subject that deserves at least several
books of its own. I want here to discuss briefly a few of the key issues that
arose when in the late nineteenth century the focus of criticism began to
shift from evaluation and judgment to the principles of interpreting literature. I will not be attending to the interesting varieties of criticism whose
primary concern is merit or appreciation; nor will I treat criticism interested in formal, generic, and aesthetic properties, for example, J. A.
Symonds's important essay "The Application of Evolutionary Principles to
Art and Literature" (1890). My subject is rather the revolution in critical
approach that led to a new emphasis on interpretation, so I will not be
examining specific interpretations of texts to determine the underlying if
unexpressed methodologies on which they rely. Instead I will be looking
at the ways in which British critics began to theorize explicitly the interpretation of literary texts in the last decades of the century. Widespread,
conscious attention to the workings and principles of the interpretation
of secular literature was, as I've demonstrated, largely new in modern
British culture and followed upon the development in hermeneutics that

this book has been tracing. Coming into its own at the end of the Victorian period, literary interpretation struggled to define both its rationale and its procedures.

Scholarly attention to the institutionalization of English literature has reminded us that the academic study of literature has a short history, with literature entering the universities as a subject only at the end of the nineteenth century. Extensive theorizing on the interpretation of literary texts has an equally short history in modern culture, though its development does not exactly parallel the establishment of the discipline of literary study in the universities. Of course, earlier cultures had been concerned with the interpretation of texts other than the Bible, as we can see, for instance, in Plato's *Ion* or in the Stoics' interpretations of Homer's epics.[1] But an extensive and specifically literary hermeneutics emerges in modern British culture only after it had absorbed German Romantic hermeneutics' attempts to formulate general theories of linguistic understanding, and only after the reconception of the Bible as literary text had been accomplished. Only then did literary texts widely attract the methodologically self-conscious theorizing that had long been reserved for sacred or legal texts. The history of this development makes apparent how closely current literary interpretation is modeled on late nineteenth-century literary studies, itself in many ways shaped by biblical exegesis. In the literature of the late Victorian period, we can watch literary interpretation as we practice it today develop in debates on English literature among literary societies and in the texts of the first professors of literature.

The abundant criticism that preceded this methodological turn—sufficiently abundant, indeed, to induce Carlyle to remark in 1831 that "by and by it will be found that all Literature has become one boundless selfdevouring Review"[2]—was primarily concerned with questions of literary merit and standards of taste. Much of the literary criticism that Carlyle was complaining about in the early nineteenth century followed an eighteenthcentury model and was not concerned with the interpretive processes that underlay critical judgments. Statements on the principles of interpretation were infrequent and usually made only in passing. A number of critics adopted in an offhand way the historicist principles that informed Romantic hermeneutics, philology, and the new criticism of the Bible; so George Henry Lewes (who was surprisingly unconcerned with the problems of textual interpretation, considering George Eliot's preoccupation with the topic) wrote that the critic must rid himself of "all personal predilection," since this "enables him to transport himself into the peculiarities of other ages and nations, and to feel them as it were from their central point."[3] Others accepted just as casually that the aim of criticism was to understand the great writer's mind and heart. (Both aims are somewhat vulgarized versions of Schleiermacher's grammatical and psychological interpretation.) But these were largely unexamined assumptions. Further, one finds only rarely the sort of close readings that we have come to expect in current literary analysis. Ruskin's well-known interpretation of a passage from Milton's *Lycidas* is one exception, but Ruskin, in that instance, discusses a text with theological content. He had also written much close exegesis of biblical texts, and he does with the Milton passage what interpreters generally thought of doing only with the Bible (recall Jowett's comment from 1859 on the absurdity of anyone constructing elaborate systems of interpretation for secular texts).

Late in the century, a confluence of conditions led to a more widespread interest in the interpretation of literary texts. Most importantly, the rereading of the Bible as literature that Matthew Arnold had championed had taken hold, and the methods and concerns of theological interpretation were transferred from the Bible to secular literature. Popular studies in etymology and philology had led to greater interest in the workings of language. Finally and crucially, the formation of a number of learned societies (basically the models for what academics in literature do more than one hundred years later) fostered interpretive debate over meaning, and the movement to make English literature a subject of study in the universities played an important role as well.

One of the crucial arenas in which close attention to the principles of the interpretation of literature first emerged was in the debates and activities of the literary societies that were founded in the later decades of the nineteenth century.[4] These societies preceded and helped facilitate the establishment of English studies in the universities. The first societies of the Victorian period were devoted to older literature: Shakespeare and Chaucer as well as old English texts. In these cases, the issues that had been of concern in the study of the classics and in much biblical criticism—problems of textual corruption, manuscript transmission, translation, and diachronic linguistics—were still important. Shakespeare had of course long been considered the great national literary genius, and had received critical attention for many years.[5] Much late Victorian Shakespeare criticism shifted toward approaches such as Edward Dowden's in *Shakspere: His Mind and Art;* biographical and speculative approaches that aimed to reveal the personality of the poet through the examination of his works. The work becomes a bridge to the author. The New Shakspere Society, formed in 1873 by the energetic founder of many literary societies, F. J. Furnivall (Browning was the honorary "president"), was the second of two important Victorian Shakespeare societies, and its members conceived of their work as different from that of the earlier society. They were not interested in emendation and other textual work; rather they wanted to understand the evolution of Shakespeare's thought and the interconnections between the plays; like Dowden, they sought to know the great mind through a study of his works.

As the issue of how authority was to be secured for a literary interpretation became increasingly significant, a concomitant interest in method and procedure grew up, and as a consequence, by the late century, a well-established movement for scientific literary criticism had developed. Furnivall advocated scientific criticism and pursued a statistical approach to interpretation (although his criticism did not always hold to this). Literary studies ought largely to concern itself, he contended, with factual scholarship and such matters as the establishment of chronologies and metrical tests.[6] Criticism, he hoped, would become "entirely objective."[7] In the transactions of the New Shakspere Society for 1874, Frederick Fleay, a prominent member of the society and a Shakespeare scholar at Cambridge, advocates a new method of explication: "Our analysis, which has hitherto been qualitative, must become quantitative; . . . the test . . . is this: can you say, not only of what kind, but how much? If you cannot weigh, measure, number your results, however you may be convinced yourself, you must not hope to convince others, or claim the position of an investigator; you are merely a guesser, a propounder of hypotheses."[8]

Criticism of this sort was to leave subjective and affective response behind. A prominent example of the interpretive battles that arose in Shakespeare studies is the fervent and hostile public controversy between Furnivall and Algernon Swinburne in periodicals during the 1870s. Swinburne, who regarded his own criticism as "aesthetic" or "intuitive," condemned and virulently satirized the society's focus on chronology in his *Study of Shakespeare,* declaring that "it is not, so to speak, the literal but the spiritual order which I have studied to observe and indicate."[9]

Records of the proceedings of Furnivall's and Emily Hickey's Robert Browning society (founded in 1881) even more clearly reveal the growing emphasis on the theory of interpretation in literary study. In his thorough account of the society and its published transactions, *Interpreting the Oracle: A History of the London Browning Society,* William S. Peterson notes that the society was the first founded to study the works of a living author. The aim of the society was "to learn more of the meaning of the poet's utterances" (*BSP,* 1881:19). According to Furnivall, Browning "needed interpreting" and "this interpreting must be done during his life-time, or the key to it might be lost."[10]

A group of largely middle-class men and women met to discuss Browning's poetry. They offered interpretations of what many took to be Browning's cryptic utterances, and brought theories—for instance, the philosophy of Hegel—to bear on the poems. By and large, Furnivall was overly sanguine about problems of meaning, writing at one point: "As to the interpretation of difficult poems, our society will soon make all clear."[11] As the transactions of the society show, however, examining the works of a living author raised questions about meaning that had not been quite so practically foregrounded in biblical exegesis or classics, where there was no opportunity to simply go and ask an author what he had meant. Moreover, there were no questions about manuscripts, translations, or historical philology for the group to examine. Problems of historical distance were eliminated, leaving the society free to focus solely on interpretation and its aims.

That careful exegesis of literary texts was still closely connected to the project of biblical exegesis is apparent in the society's concern with determining Browning's theological opinions through the study of his poems. That close attention to literary interpretation was new in the culture is revealed in the immediate and relentless satirizing of the society's activities in the periodicals. To many it seemed simply foolish to scrutinize the words of a living author with the same intensity as those of the Bible. Questions of interpretative methodology emerge in transactions recounting the often-critical reactions to the papers. One member, for instance, complains that a presenter "chooses a certain number of passages from Browning's texts, having divorced them utterly from their connection either as links in an argument or as the expressions of opinions of individual characters" (Peterson, 65). Another cautions that the group must "be careful not to father upon Browning by way of interpreting him, the bantlings born of our own ignorance and conceit" (*BSP*, 1881:22). The transactions show the society in the process of determining what it was doing in closely examining literary texts, and how one ought to proceed.

The attempt to establish principles for valid interpretation of literary texts has been regarded, in some recent treatments of the institutionalization of literary studies, as arising from the profession's need for authority. Institutionalized literary study sought to create its own autonomous domain of specialization and knowledge in order to justify its continued existence. It is important to point out, then, that this work in fact went on prior to the profession's establishment, among a group of amateur enthusiasts. This is particularly visible in the debates that arose over intention and the locus of textual meaning. As Furnivall's statements on the aims of the society show, he assumed that meaning is found in the author's intentions.

So whenever an interpretive conflict arose, he simply wrote to Browning. In response to allegorical readings of "Childe Roland," for instance, Furnivall insisted that "he had asked Browning if it was an allegory, and in answer, on three separate occasions, received an emphatic 'no'" (*BSP* 1881:25). Whether the group ought to turn to the living author to adjudicate such conflicts became a point of contention. In another incident a presenter argued that one of Browning's characters is meant to represent the ideal woman. When disagreements arose, the group voted that Furnivall should contact Browning to ask him "whether his poem was an allegory only, or meant to represent any type of woman present or past." The proceedings go on to explain: "This has accordingly been done; and as the author's own interpretation follows, the printing of the discussion becomes needless. So (it may be said) is the printing of the paper. But as that was set before the meeting, and contains a view that may be fairly taken in the absence of authoritative exposition, the paper is not cancelled" (Peterson, 109).

The obvious problem with the ask-the-author method of proceeding is that if you go with what he says, you simply shut down the interpretive activity that the society is set up to do, since one can no longer legitimately claim that the poem means anything outside of Browning's expressed intentions. If one wants to continue interpreting but also maintain that meaning is found in authorial intention, then it is more convenient if the author is not available for questioning. One member "deprecated Mr. Furnivall asking Mr. Browning the meaning of his poems, and remarked that by doing so, there would be no need of the Browning society" (*BSP,* 1881:26). Others suggested that if meaning is found in intention, one need not assume that the author was conscious of all his intentions. So the early founders of literary studies assailed the problems about meaning that had been at the center of theological hermeneutics for many years.

Although in the last years of the century the greatest number of publications with the word "interpretation" in the title continued to be concerned with biblical exegesis, this use was no longer nearly exclusive. Dowden's "The Interpretation of Literature" (1886), for example, conceives of interpretation as "finding the author's secret." And William Henry Hudson's *Studies in Interpretation* (1896) is also entirely devoted to literary studies.[12] As emphasis began to shift toward secular literature, the question of subjectivity, central also to biblical interpretation, emerged importantly. John Addington Symonds, for instance, writes: "Owing to this intrusion of subjectivity, one of the prime difficulties of criticism is correct interpretation."[13] "The chief danger of criticism in its present stage is," he claims, "that the critic should be insufficiently upon his guard against subjective fancies, paradoxes of opinion, and super-sub-tleties of ingenuity" (71). In a much earlier consideration of literary hermeneutics, Ruskin had likewise warned readers against the intrusion of subjectivity, following his reading of "Lycidas":

> We have got something out of the lines, I think, and much more is yet to be found in them; but we have done enough by way of example of the kind of word-by-word examination of your author which is rightly called "reading"; watching every accent and expression, and putting ourselves always in the author's place, annihilating our own personality, and seeking to enter into his, so as to be able to say, "Thus Milton thought," not "Thus I thought, in mis-reading Milton."[14]

These worries about subjectivity in literary interpretation can be seen as another manifestation of the general unease about subjectivity in Victorian scientific culture that critics have noted, leading to the interest in "scientific criticism" and methodology.[15] As I've already argued, many Victorians accepted subjectivity as the necessary starting point for inquiry, but sought to limit and temper what is *always* avowed to be subjective and interpretive by attempting to establish methods for getting things right. Late-century scientific theory of literary interpretation attempted to give interpretation validity, by adopting empirical methods and resting inter-pretation on "facts" instead of the vague critical "tact" of Arnold, Jowett, and others.

As the century proceeded, the interest in the interpretation of litera-ture shifted into organized pedagogy, as is evidenced in John Churchton Collins's vastly popular lectures on English literature for the Society for the Extension of University Teaching. The clearest sign of this interest, however, developed in the last third of the century, when the question of whether English studies should enter into the university was hotly debated. English literature first appeared in the B. A. exams in 1873 at Oxford (although there was no one to teach it), and the first chair of English literature was established, after much struggle, at Oxford in 1885.[16] In 1893 Oxford established its English Honours school.

A sustained attempt to theorize interpretation within the terms of the recognition of the subjectivity of literary response was found in the work of another promoter of extension education, Richard Green Moulton (also a teacher of English literature at Cambridge University).[17] In *Shakespeare as Dramatic Artist* (1885), Moulton considered questions of literary interpreta-tion in surprisingly detailed ways, and his views seem to have provided the ground for the New Criticism of the next century. He notes that while most literary criticism had been interested in judging works and founding "canons of taste," he seeks to support scientific, or what he calls "inductive," interpretation.[18] Despite his frequent appeal to scientific analogies, he can still make the George Eliot-like claim that "it is a foundation principle in art-culture, as well as in human intercourse, that *sympathy is the grand interpreter:* secrets of beauty will unfold themselves to the sunshine of sympathy" (7). Moulton is concerned with the question of how critics might come to agreement on interpretive questions when literary response is necessarily subjective. Although he begins by suggesting that there is a radical split between science and literature, he attempts immediately to break it down: "Science deals only with ascertained facts: but the details of literature and art are open to the most diverse interpretation. They leave conflicting impressions on different observers, impressions both subjective and variable in themselves. . . . Where in the treatment of literature is to be found the positiveness of subject-matter which is the first condition of science?" (23). His theory, designed to answer this question, acknowledges that subjectivity is central to literary interpretation, but at the same time seeks to constrain interpretation by an appeal to fixed properties of the text. The critic, he says, "quite recognizes that it is not the objective details but the subjective impressions they produce that make literary effect, but the objective details are the *limit* on the variability of the subjective impressions" (24). The argument leads him to his "foundation axiom of inductive literary criticism" through which he tries to show how what is necessarily subjective response (an interpretation) can seek verification in the objective features of the text: "*Interpretation in literature is of the nature of a scientific hypothesis, the truth of which is tested by the degree of completeness with which it explains the details of a literary work as they actually stand*" (25). The explanatory power of an interpretation is a measure of its confirmation.

Moulton's next move in essence does away with the conception of authorial intention as the locus of meaning: "I have often found that such positive analysis raises in the popular mind a very practical objection: that the scientific interpretation seems to discover in literary works much more in the way of purpose and design than the authors themselves can be supposed to have dreamed of. Would not Chaucer and Shakespeare, it is asked, if they could come to life now, be greatly astonished to hear themselves lectured upon? To find critics knowing their purposes better than they had known them themselves?"(26). His solution to the problem is to cut "intention" from conscious purposes. Intention takes on a scientific meaning for Moulton; just as science analyzes a substance to understand its makeup and "purpose," so the critic analyzes a text to discover its "intention." Intention is redefined; it is found not in the authority of the creator, but instead inheres in the text.

In an indication of how fully the discourse of interpretation was coming into its own, Moulton became "Professor of Literary Theory and Interpretation" at the University of Chicago in 1915, and his essentially New Critical ideas were crystallized in *The Modern Study of Literature: An Introduction to Literary Theory and Interpretation* (1915). In this book, which expands on the ideas he formulated in his earlier text, inductive criticism becomes "the criticism of interpretation."[19] Moulton attempts to determine "what constitutes evidence in literary interpretation" and investigates methodological issues: should interpretation consider the author's biography? Should it consider other literary works? What sort of context is involved in interpretation? He also sets out a number of "fallacies" of interpretation, such as the *"author fallacy"* (the basis for Wimsatt and Beardsley's "intentional fallacy"?): "It is safe to lay down the position that the best evidence as to what an author has meant is what he actually said [in the work]. . . . The concern of criticism is with the art product itself, irrespective of the author who has produced it." The "poet is not a final authority as to his own poem" (293–94). Similarly, he also opposes what he refers to as the fallacy of the "infallibility of the reader" (Wimsatt and Beardsley's "affective fallacy" of 1949?), an interpretive principle whose name announces its roots in biblical interpretation. "Inductive interpretation," Moulton insists, "makes its appeal neither to the reader nor to the critic, but always to the literature itself" (301). Finally, "interpreting a poem resolves itself, ultimately, into grasping its unity" (107).

In the Victorian critic Moulton's now forgotten works we find the principles of New Criticism originally and brilliantly introduced. In his redefinition of intention as a property of the text, Moulton shifts the locus of textual meaning from the inner state of the author to the fixed properties of an autonomous text. While on the one hand he attempts to retain the concept of intention as a ground for objective meaning, on the other, he essentially erases it. In locating meaning in semantics, he opens the way to a range of anti-intentionalist arguments to follow, from Oscar Wilde through the New Critics, and ultimately to structuralist and poststructuralist theory.

When the question of getting the meaning right is transferred from religious to secular texts, one might well wonder what could possibly be at stake. Correct meaning in biblical exegesis obviously mattered to religious practice and to one's spiritual life; but what difference did it make if one interpreted a Browning poem incorrectly? Some critics have suggested that the institutionalization of literature was an effort at universalizing middle-class values. While this may be right, the desire to get the meaning of the text right seems also for these Victorians most immediately tied to the practical need to assign value to literary study in order to justify it as an activity. If one were to devote attention to its interpretation, then literature must have some value that resided in itself. In more recent thought, the value of the study of literature has shifted to the act of interpretation itself for many. Although such views evolve from the nineteenth-century emphasis on interpretation, rarely did Victorian critics conceive of interpretation in this way. That is, not until Oscar Wilde began to write about literary interpretation in the last decade of the period.

❧

CHAPTER FOUR

Subjectivism, Intersubjectivity, and Intention

Oscar Wilde and Literary Hermeneutics

Who, again, cares whether Mr Pater has put into the portrait of the Mona Lisa something that Leonardo never dreamed of?

> —Oscar Wilde

I noticed it because it made a suggestion about the intention of the author in writing the book, which needed correction.

> —Oscar Wilde

If a man approaches a work of art with any desire to exercise authority over it and the artist, he approaches it in such a spirit that he cannot receive any artistic impression from it at all. The work of art is to dominate the spectator: the spectator is not to dominate the work of art. The spectator is to be receptive. He is to be the violin on which the master is to play. And the more completely he can suppress his own silly views, his own foolish prejudices, his own absurd ideas of what Art should be, or should not be, the more likely he is to understand and appreciate the work of art in question.

> —Oscar Wilde

Unlike most of the earlier commentators on hermeneutics that this book has discussed, Oscar Wilde comes to interpretation from an early background in literary studies. He was introduced to literary interpretation at Trinity College in Ireland and at Oxford University, where he studied classics along with the philosophy that informs his theoretical writing. In a letter on his course of study, he wrote: "Greats is the only sphere of thought where one can be, simultaneously, brilliant and unreasonable, speculative and well-informed, creative as well as critical."[1] Wilde carries these ideals into all of his insightful but unsettled writing on literary interpretation. He is also the first of the authors treated in this study whose writings on interpretation are almost exclusively concerned with literary hermeneutics, and in this way his work is the exemplar of one of the nineteenth-century hermeneutic narratives I have been tracing. Although the secular and the aesthetic are his provinces, he concentrates on the same problems of textual interpretation that consumed the biblical exegetes—albeit with a levity that is rarely found in theological hermeneutics. In Wilde, we see the transformation this book has been following, in which literary criticism displaces biblical exegesis as the central site of interpretive activity and speculation. As the culmination of that Victorian transformation, Wilde clearly recognized (and satirized) the theological sources of literary interpretation.

In parallel with (or rivalry with?) those theologians who had argued that theological exegesis required its own specialized hermeneutics because of the Bible's unique status, Wilde attempts to carve out a distinctive hermeneutics for the aesthetic sphere alone. By the end of the century, interpretive discourse had become pervasive in many disciplines, as we've seen, and as a result the universality that Schleiermacher had advocated was once again challenged. Wilde reinstates the belief that different disciplines require their own particular hermeneutic rules, and in the dialogues and in "Mr. W. H.," he is concerned with a specifically literary hermeneutics. In the autonomous aesthetic sphere that Wilde envisions, a unique literary hermeneutics can operate that would not be feasible in practical spheres.

As the above chapter epigraphs (all composed in 1890) show—and as he readily acknowledged—Wilde was not consistent in his views. While Wilde's capriciousness made it impossible for some earlier critics to take him seriously as a theorist, others have largely overlooked the inconsistencies to identify him as holding a consistently subjectivist theory of interpretation. Wilde's inconsistency should not be ignored; yet neither does it detract from his importance for hermeneutic speculation. The range of views Wilde explores and the ways in which his writing explicitly engages with the work of others demonstrate that his criticism is deeply involved in the hermeneutic speculation I have been discussing throughout this book, and his complex and unstable relation to those arguments should significantly modify conventional understandings of Wilde's project. Rather than offering a single account of meaning, Wilde stages a particularly rich exploration of the interpretive problems that have continued to be central to literary theory. His thought on interpretation makes his work unusually useful for theoretical discussion because, as we shall see, even the most obviously modern and seemingly amoral of writers in the development of the Victorian hermeneutic tradition founds his theories on the ethical.

To make the case for Wilde's seriousness as a student of hermeneutics (and Philip Smith and Michael Hefland have shown Wilde's engagement with philosophy in their examination of his Oxford notebooks), the pages that follow begin by examining the theories presented in the dialogues in relation to Wilde's nearly contemporaneous essay "The Soul of Man under Socialism," to establish the ethical grounding of Wilde's interpretive theory. I look next at "The Portrait of Mr. W. H.," Wilde's story about literary interpretation, in the context of late-Victorian Shakespeare criticism. "Mr. W. H." manifests a hermeneutic principle that is never explicitly articulated by his speakers: Wilde's portrayal of interpretive praxis in that story represents interpretation on an intersubjective model. I want finally to show that at the time of *De Profundis* Wilde turns to an intentionalist account of meaning, as he reassesses the beliefs that there can be an aesthetic sphere apart from the practical and that a distinction is to be made between literary and practical language. It will be possible, by considering these various texts, not only to emphasize how deeply involved Wilde was in hermeneutic speculation but also to show that the range of theories he adopts requires a reconsideration of his subjectivism and a recognition of a much more unsettled understanding of the questions than critics usually allow.

I

Wilde has commonly been placed in a line of thought running from Arnold through Pater to Wilde. On this account, the subjectivist position that Wilde advocates is seen as a reversal of Arnold's claim that the critic's aim is to "see the object as in itself it really is."[2] Influenced by Pater's reformulation of this aim in his "Preface" to *The Renaissance*—"In aesthetic criticism the first step is to know one's own impression as it really is"[3]—Wilde again revises the critic's project, claiming that "the primary aim of the artist is to see the object as in itself it really is not."[4] Through Pater, Wilde seems to lead us to a complete reversal of Arnold's foundational critical claim, and this reversal is seen as a motto for a subjectivist theory of interpretation.[5]

Wilde's interpretive speculation is most fully presented in his two dialogues, "The Decay of Lying" and "The Critic as Artist." If we take Gilbert and Vivian to represent Wilde's views in the dialogues, then Wilde rejects conventional notions of truth, dismisses intentionalism, and, further, denies that a critical judgment should be disinterested, as Arnold famously insisted it should be. Instead, Wilde emphasizes the role of the interpreter in meaning and argues that good criticism is subjective and biased, an outgrowth of the personality, needs, and desires of the reader. In the more extreme formulations, Wilde's speakers maintain that an interpreter creates the world or a text's meaning, that there is no distinction between interpretation and invention. Consequently, critics have widely regarded Wilde as advocating an extreme interpretive subjectivism and, more recently, as anticipating postmodernism.[6]

Because Wilde presents his critical views so often in the form of a dialogue, it is difficult to disentangle his own thoughts from those of his characters, and what might have been a declarative essay becomes instead a complex narrative. Yet commentators have sometimes overlooked the structure of Wilde's criticism, distilling from it a position that ignores his far from straightforward presentation; thus, what is an exploration of the issues in a dialogue has been taken as the promotion of an established account of interpretation.[7] Most critics have accepted that Gilbert and Vivian stand in for Wilde in the dialogues. On this reading, those characters, like the Socrates of Plato's late dialogues, use the conversations not to discuss ideas but rather as an occasion to expound their theories, and bring their interlocutors around to their views of the matter.[8] The dialogue form matters, however, and the view that emerges should be regarded as a product of the interaction between the two speakers, rather than as the fully formed theory of one speaker.[9] In any case, the obvious inconsistencies in even a single speaker's claims make it hard to say that Wilde advocates any one position through a single character.

We might take Wilde to be simply turning on its head Arnold's objectivist stance or the intentionalist account of linguistic meaning advocated by Romantic hermeneuts; but in fact his project is more complex and speculative than that. Wilde explores in more detail than any other Victorian writer a subjectivist theory of interpretation, but he also considers a range of alternative theories. Gilbert says of an author's use of the dialogue form that "by its means he can exhibit the object from each point of view and show it to us in the round, as a sculptor shows us things, gaining in this manner all the richness and reality of effect that comes from those side issues that are suddenly suggested by the central idea in its progress, and really illumine the idea more completely" (1046). "The

Critic as Artist," as Wilde suggests, succeeds in showing all sides of the debate far more than it does in advocating a single view.

I want to begin by looking closely at the subjectivist position, since this is the theory most frequently ascribed to Wilde, before examining the alternative interpretive theories that are considered in the dialogue. In the discussion on aesthetics in the "Decay of Lying" (1888), Vivian advances a position that can be seen as providing an epistemological foundation for Gilbert's anti-intentionalist theory of meaning. With his well-known pronouncement that "Life imitates Art far more than Art imitates Life" (992), Vivian contends that our perceptions are always colored by our perspectives, and that the way we talk about things has much to do with the way we see them. "Things are because we see them, and what we see, and how we see it, depends on the Arts that have influenced us" (986). The formulation may sound shocking, but when the substance is considered, it turns out to be a version of the recognizable idealist epistemology of the sort this book has been considering throughout, according to which objects are not independent of cognizing minds. Vivian is, of course, attacking realism in art and mimetic theories of creation, but he is also arguing for our basically interpretive relation toward the world. His central claim, with clear roots in Romantic epistemology, is that the perceiver discovers what he has in fact partially created. If this view were carried into interpretive theory, it would follow that an interpreter at least partially creates the text she reads.

"The Critic as Artist" concentrates primarily on the narrower topic of literary criticism, and, apparently, the most striking feature of the dialogue is Wilde's subjectivism. Gilbert begins by arguing that "criticism is itself an art" (1027) and therefore not subordinate to creation: "Criticism is, in fact, both creative and independent. Criticism is not more to be judged by any low standard of imitation or resemblance than is the work of a poet or sculptor" (1027). Here is Wilde's well-known formulation of creative criticism, as he admired it in Pater and Ruskin, where an artwork becomes the occasion for a critic's own dazzling performance. Rejecting mimesis in criticism (as Vivian rejects it in art), Gilbert dismisses the conception of interpretation as reproduction: "The critic will indeed be an interpreter, but he will not be an interpreter in the sense of one who simply repeats in another form a message that has been put into his lips to say" (1033). Instead, he says, echoing Pater, the critic's "sole aim is to chronicle his own impressions" (1028).

Denying the notion that the artist's intention determines meaning, Gilbert asserts that a work "whispers of a thousand different things which were not present in the mind of" the creator (1030). The locus of meaning is, at least to a good extent, in the interpreter. The best criticism, Gilbert says "does not confine itself—let us at least suppose so for the moment—to discovering the real intention of the artist and accepting that as final. And in this it is right, for the meaning of any beautiful created thing is, at least, as much in the soul of him who looks at it as it was in his soul who wrought it. Nay, it is rather the beholder who lends to the beautiful thing its myriad meanings, and makes it marvellous for us, and sets it in some new relation to the age, so that it becomes a vital portion of our lives" (1029).

Gilbert's theory sounds much like a variety of reader-response criticism in these formulations, with meaning sometimes residing somewhere in between text and reader, sometimes almost wholly in the reader. (One has to attend, however, to Gilbert's interjection—"let us suppose so at least for the moment"—since such attention to temporality and provisionality is crucial to Wilde's strategy in the dialogues.) Gilbert acknowledges the author's intentions, but claims that "when the work is finished, it has, as it were, an independent life of its own, and may deliver a message far other than that which was put into its lips to say" (1029).[10] It is crucial to note that the question, as Wilde poses it through Gilbert, is not whether it is *possible* to determine the author's intentions, but rather whether one *ought* to do that. If we did know (putting aside the question of accessibility) the author's intended meaning, it would not, according to Gilbert, override alternative interpretations.

Along with intentionalism, Gilbert jettisons the popular nineteenth-century contention that history can provide authority in interpretation. Rather than attempting to reconstruct the historical context in which a work was produced, the critic revitalizes a work of art for his own time: "He will be always showing us the work of art in some new relation to our age. He will always be reminding us that great works of art are living things" (1034). Gilbert's views fall into the Newman (vs. Jowett) side of the division within hermeneutic theory, as I've explained it, with textual meaning understood as either evolving or changing in history.

Gilbert's rejection, then, of Arnold's dictum that "the proper aim of Criticism is to see the object as in itself it really is" (1028) also involves the denial that criticism should discover some other standard for determinate meaning that does not involve authorial intention, such as a theory of semantic autonomy would provide (as the New Critics were to argue). The best "modes of art" "by their imaginative beauty make all interpretations true, and no interpretation final" (1031). Arnold's formulation of the critic's task, Gilbert argues, "takes no cognizance of criticism's most perfect form, which is in its essence purely subjective, and seeks to reveal its own secret and not the secret of another" (1028). With this claim he

reverses one of the most common critical assertions of his age, found in
any number of reviews (including Wilde's own on occasion), that is, that
the critic's aim is to reveal the author's secret. Gilbert contends, on the
other hand, that interpretation is a form of self-revelation. Interpreting a
text, one self-interprets.

Gilbert's subjectivism thus carries with it the repudiation of Arnold's
belief that a critic must approach a work of art in the spirit of disinterested inquiry.[11] Against the persistent worries about subjectivism and
how to avoid it that we have seen in other discussions of literary interpretation, Gilbert asserts that the critic must bring his own personality
to bear on a text: "It is only by intensifying his own personality that the
critic can interpret the personality and work of others; and the more
strongly this personality enters into the interpretation, the more real
the interpretation becomes, the more satisfying, the more convincing,
the more true" (1033). An interpretation not only is, but should be—
and this is where Wilde's account most differs from those of his predecessors—a reflection of the responder's own personality, needs,
desires, and biases.[12] Criticism is always inevitably, Gilbert says, "the
record of one's own soul" (1027).[13] Wilde, then, consciously reverses
the Romantic hermeneut's attempt to rid himself of his own biases and
perspectives. We are now far from George Eliot's injunctions against
mistaking one's own subjectivity as the limits of the world. While much
Victorian interpretive theory, as we've seen, sought to escape arbitrary
readings and the imposition of the self into the text, Gilbert instead
endorses the reading of one's own interests onto the text. He sees this
as the best possible way to increase the aesthetic satisfaction that art
can provide.

There we have the outlines of the subjectivist theory that Gilbert
offers. But although this is the dominant interpretive theory discussed
in the dialogue, it is far from being the only one. Ernest asks at the close
of part 1 of the dialogue, in response to Gilbert's lengthy description of
the creative critic: "Will not the critic be sometimes a real interpreter?"
(1032). Gilbert replies that the critic "can pass from the synthetic
impression of the work of art as a whole, to an analysis or exposition of
the work itself" (1032), although he designates the latter as the lower
sphere of criticism. Gilbert makes a clear distinction between aesthetic
impressionism, which he here calls "synthetic" criticism, and textual
analysis. Both activities are called "interpretation" in the dialogue and
both are said to yield the "meaning" of the text, yet they call for very different methods. Gilbert's understanding of the work of synthetic—or
creative—criticism is expansive. It involves the broad ways in which a

work of art affects a responder: the train of personal associations it initiates, the series of private impressions and feelings it induces. As we have seen, these aspects of response are explicitly cut from the concept of "interpretation" in the thought of theorists such as Chladenius or Jowett, who believe that private associations connected with one's own experience cannot be said to be the *meaning* of the work, but rather peripheral considerations, or digressions, suggested by the content of the work. Similarly, E. D. Hirsch in his well-known essay "Objective Interpretation" refers to these changing aspects as the text's "relevance" rather than its "meaning."[14] (Much reader-response criticism, of course, considers personal response and experience to be unavoidably the basis of interpretation.)

The constraints on the interpreter are upgraded considerably once Gilbert begins to discuss analysis, the second type of "interpretation" (the work of Ernest's "real interpreter"), and this shift is distinctly marked by the move into the second part of the dialogue. Yet in considering Wilde's theoretical views, commentators have by and large ignored the theories discussed in part 2. It is there that Wilde fleshes out the other terms of his "Greats" description: not the creative, but the "well informed" and the "critical." Wilde's inconstant admiration for method and historiography reenters with interpretive requirements echoing the demands for historical contextualization and background knowledge called for by critics such as George Eliot and Jowett. In a long passage on literary hermeneutics, Gilbert sets out a number of interpretive principles:

> He who desires to understand Shakespeare truly must understand the relations in which Shakespeare stood to the Renaissance and the Reformation, to the age of Elizabeth and the age of James; he must be familiar with the history of the struggle for the supremacy between the old classical forms and the new spirit of romance, between the school of Sidney, and Daniel, and Johnson, and the school of Marlowe and Marlowe's greater son; he must know the materials that were at Shakespeare's disposal, and the method in which he used them, and the conditions of theatric presentation in the sixteenth and seventeenth centuries, their limitations and their opportunities for freedom, and the literary criticism of Shakespeare's day, its aims and modes and canons; he must study the English language in its progress, and blank or rhymed verse in its various developments; he must study the Greek drama, and the connection between the art of the creator of the Agamemnon and the art of the creator of Macbeth; in a word, he must be able to bind Elizabethan London to the Athens of Pericles. (1033)

This is a tall order for the interpreter, who in order to "truly" understand Shakespeare, must, among other things, know all of literary history, be acquainted with the historical context of the work, have read all relevant contemporary texts, and in addition be an expert in philology. Following this account, an interpreter goes outside the artwork in order to discover its meaning, placing the work in its historical and literary contexts.

Gilbert's earlier subjectivist claims are also unsettled by an increasingly elitist portrait of the ideal interpreter. Good interpretation requires detailed and knowledgeable scholarship, but more importantly, it will be the product of a person who possesses what Gilbert refers to as an "artistic sensibility." Gilbert endorses the idea, so pervasive in hermeneutic theory, that special qualities are required in an interpreter, qualities that go beyond method: tact, as Arnold called it, intuition in Schleiermacher's terms. The tendency to see criticism as an exclusive pursuit is obvious as well in Wilde's own reviews, written prior to and simultaneously with the dialogues. "When criticism," Wilde writes, "becomes in England a real art, as it should be, and when none but those of artistic instinct and artistic cultivation is allowed to write about works of art, artists will no doubt read criticisms with a certain amount of intellectual interest."[15] (What exactly it means to have an artistic sensibility, however, is never made clear. Wilde's definition so far as it goes is tautological.) The reviews, in general, are far from confirming Gilbert's pronouncement that all interpretations are true. Wilde takes swipes at subjectivism, commenting that "indeed, there is something very flattering in being told that one's own emotions are the ultimate test of literature" (*Reviews,* 17), and he makes many caustic comments on other critics' readings of texts, repeatedly claiming that only a select few have the proficiencies necessary to produce good interpretations. (In fact, Wilde is committed to the notion that many people will not be able to understand his works). Here, as elsewhere, reading the dialogues against the reviews forces qualifications of the positions normally inferred from the dialogues.

Gilbert demands so many qualities of the critic in part 2 of "The Critic as Artist" that the range of interpretation is considerably narrowed, and he ultimately arrives at a description of the critic that is purely Arnoldian and so directly contradicts Gilbert's claims in part 1:

> And who the true man of culture, if not he who by fine scholarship and fastidious rejection has made instinct self-conscious and intelligent, and can separate the work that has distinction from the work that has it not, and so by contact and comparison makes himself master of the secrets of style and

school, and understands their meanings, and listens to their voices, and develops that spirit of disinterested curiosity which is the real root, as it is the real flower, of the intellectual life, and thus attains to intellectual clarity, and, having learned "the best that is known and thought in the world," lives—it is not fanciful to say so—with those who are the Immortals. (1041)

Here Gilbert dismisses the critic who creates the text through his interpretation and turns to the depiction of the critic as a knowledgeable, dispassionate, and even objective (if we take disinterestedness as a synonym for objectivity) evaluator, who discerns the value that inheres in a work: the Arnoldian critic as arbiter of the literary canon.

Beyond the demand for a learned and gifted interpreter, Gilbert offers a number of other interpretive principles that conflict with the subjectivist ones explored in part 1. For instance, he makes claims that sound suspiciously close to supporting the notion that one attempts to understand an artwork by understanding the author's point of view. Thus of a poem by Baudelaire, Gilbert says: "Let its subtle music steal into your brain and colour your thoughts, and you will become for a moment what he was who wrote it" (1037). This familiar emphasis on entering into an author's consciousness is obviously a wholly different picture of interpretation than he has hitherto promoted. Also in contradiction to his earlier claims, he discusses artworks in a way that suggests that response is largely uniform among interpreters and that the work of art itself is responsible for this likeness of response. He says that if we desire to experience a particular emotion or feeling, we can simply go to texts that will induce this experience in us (which would also imply that response stays fairly uniform in an interpreter over time). And he uses the first-person plural to describe these reactions, suggesting that all readers will react in a like way: "Our blood quickens . . . wild tears of anguish break from us" (1036). Here it seems that at least our initial understanding of the work is a product of our vicarious experiencing of its subject matter, and hence that a text has an independent status apart from the various interpretive strategies that are brought to bear on it.

In a similar vein, Gilbert's introduction of the hereditary soul works to overturn the view that aesthetic response is entirely unique to the individual.[16] Gilbert abruptly turns to a discussion of the Victorian belief in "organic memory" (a concept clearly related to Darwinian development), arguing that the imagination is the product of collective experience, a form of memory passed on through evolution: "The imagination is the result of heredity. It is simply concentrated race-experience" (1041). Bringing in this scientific theory allows Gilbert to offer a cultural aim for criticism, in tension with his claims of art as pure contemplation. The critic's self-development will perfect not only his own life, but ultimately "the collective life of the race" (1040) through "the transmission of racial experiences" (1041). That view leads Gilbert to assert fairly conventional nineteenth-century hermeneutic aims. The hereditary soul "can help us to leave the age in which we were born, and to pass into other ages, and find ourselves not exiled from their air. It can teach us how to escape from our experience, and to realise the experiences of those who are greater than we are" (1041).

This close look at the dialogue ought to make it clear that Wilde does not offer only one theoretical position. Yet Ernest takes none of these counter-assertions into consideration in his summation of Gilbert's subjectivist position at the end of the dialogue (which is perhaps a reason why commentators have ascribed that theory to Wilde). Wilde, of course, often defends inconsistency, and the overall movement of the dialogue reflects his irresolution as the conversation moves from subjectivist to objectivist views without marking the shifts. As Wilde writes, in part borrowing from Pater again but also echoing language familiar from Romantic hermeneutics: "It is Criticism that, recognising no position as final, and refusing to bind itself by the shallow shibboleths of any sect or school, creates that serene philosophic temper which loves truth for its own sake, and loves it not the less because it knows it to be unattainable" (1057). Wilde's inconsistencies and his refusal to commit to any one hermeneutic theory leave us with a brilliant and provocative exploration of the crucial issues in literary interpretation that would be important for the century and more of speculation to follow.

II

Although he had some background in philology (he worked briefly with Max Mueller at Oxford), Wilde is much less concerned with the specifically linguistic aspects of meaning and interpretation than are other hermeneutic theorists that this book has discussed. He instead begins with the assumption that language can support a wide range of meanings, moving immediately to consider the psychological grounds of indeterminacy.

It is not surprising that his explorations of subjectivist theory have received much attention in critical discussion, given that Wilde was among the first in English letters to present such a theory positively. As we've seen, most Victorian theorists of interpretation saw subjectivist response as something to be worked against, and although some theologians developed what must be seen as theories of indeterminacy—theories that undoubtedly influenced Wilde, as I've already argued—most of those retained at least a faint hold on the idea of a determining, if for all practical purposes unattainable, intention. Wilde's Gilbert, while never denying that such a meaning does exists, is willing (at times) to completely eliminate it from consideration in aesthetic interpretation. It also makes sense that later criticism would take great interest in Wilde's subjectivist criticism, given that in it he introduced views that have affinities with theories predominantly committed to indeterminacy, which became pervasive in the second half of the twentieth century. It is crucial to recognize, however, that the subjectivist theory that Wilde presents through Gilbert is not—as most poststructuralist theory is—founded on the idea that language by its very nature makes determinacy impossible. Wilde (insofar as we can take Gilbert to express his views on the question) does not reject intentionalist method because he believes the discovery of intention to be impossible. Rather, Gilbert submits a case for the aesthetic and ethical benefits of ignoring intention. He is primarily interested in what we *can* do when interpreting—the "uses" of criticism, as the original title planned for the dialogue had it—not with what we *must* do. Just as the artist creates beautiful things because he brings his own viewpoint to bear on experience, so should the interpreter approach an artwork in a like way, for the enrichment of the artwork and, more importantly, for the interpreter's own enrichment. In unrestrained personal response to a text, Gilbert argues, the reader discovers and hence is able to develop his true self.

As I suggested earlier, the subjectivist theory that Gilbert proposes in "The Critic as Artist" is specifically intended for the interpretation of artworks and, primarily, literature. For Wilde, at the time of the dialogues, literary texts have a special ontological status. Gilbert does not present a theory that applies to all linguistic interpretation. Wilde, like the New Critics who were to follow, believed (at least sometimes) that "practical" language—the language of law, for instance—was to be treated in ways different from literary language.

This special aesthetic sphere is famously carved out in the "Decay of Lying," in which Vivian rejects moral criticism and literary realism in favor of aestheticism and the autonomy of art. Vivian adopts an antiethical stance and challenges utilitarian evaluation of art, going so far as to claim that "as long as a thing is useful or necessary to us, or affects us in any way, either for pain or pleasure, or appeals strongly to our sympathies, or is a vital part of the environment in which we live, it is outside the proper sphere of art" (976). Once again, the view is expressed in hyperbolic terms, but the force of the position is that Vivian (and later

Gilbert and Wilde himself in his correspondence and in the "Preface" to *Dorian Gray*) wants to allow art its own autonomous domain separate from and untouched by the spheres of ethics and action. The aesthetic domain should offer unrestrained freedom, and art should be allowed to escape authoritarianism.

If taken seriously, however, the necessary corollaries of these claims are that art can have no ethical, political, or concrete effect of any kind in the world—a consequence that, as readers of Wilde have noted, obviously stands in direct contradiction to Vivian's claim that life imitates art and, as we've already seen, to some of Gilbert's shifting views. More importantly, Wilde is obviously far from uninterested in ethical and political questions, as is manifest in his contemporaneous essay, "The Soul of Man under Socialism" (1890), where his political views are most fully developed. There Wilde advocates a form of socialism, contending that each individual's interests must be protected so that he can most fully develop his innate capacities. Wilde argues in his own voice for individualism and the absence of restraint in art, but the essay makes clear that he supports these views not because art has no consequences in the world, but because it is only when people are allowed to freely create that they will be able to develop what Wilde refers to as their "ideal" selves. While he certainly criticizes moral commentary concerned with judging and limiting the content of a literary work, Wilde's aim in demanding freedom for art is explicitly ethical.[17]

In the essay on socialism, Wilde argues that the most important thing in life is that a person "realises the perfection of soul that is within him" (1087). The unfettered development of an individual's "nature" will lead to the greater good of society as a whole. Accordingly, Wilde dismisses traditional moral requirements such as altruism and self-sacrifice (so crucial to George Eliot), asserting that we must be relieved from the "necessity of living for others" (1079). The few perfect individuals, he argues, have been those who have managed to keep themselves "out of reach of the clamorous claims of others" (1079) and have thus been able "to realise the perfection of what was in" them (1079). Wilde here endorses a perfectionist ethics, although as it is outlined in the essay, it does not rest on the nonegalitarian assumptions that typically inform perfectionist moralities. (Perfectionist moralities, such as Nietzsche's or Carlyle's, notoriously emphasize the development of a select few.) Wilde instead demands that each individual have an equal opportunity for self-development.

Interestingly, the theory of self upon which the "Soul of Man" depends (and the theory that underlies Gilbert's subjectivist theory) is, perhaps surprisingly, rigorously essentialist. Wilde maintains that the self is wholly autonomous, that personality comes entirely from within, and that the highest aim for humans is the perfection of this essential self: "It is within you, and not outside of you, that you will find what you really are, and what you really want" (1086). Although Wilde, with his characteristic inconsistency, elsewhere introduces the ideas of masks and the impermanence of character, he frequently relies upon the notion of a deep, unitary, and fixed individuality: "The things people say do not alter a man. He is what he is" (1086). Some critics have argued that Wilde denies that the self is autonomous and essential, linking Wilde's thought to postmodern conceptions of self.[18] On the contrary, Wilde's arguments in this essay and elsewhere rest on the belief that human beings have innate capacities, and that a more tolerant and equitable society is required so that these already existent capacities can reach their fullest potential.

It is important to recognize that the views on self-development expressed in the "Soul" also underlie Wilde's theories of aesthetic creation. In the essay, Wilde sets freedom in creation against "the extraordinary tyranny of authority" (1101) that he sees in society. Because "art is the most intense mode of Individualism that the world has known," he argues, people have tried "to exercise over it an authority that is as immoral as it is ridiculous" (1090). The free expression of personality in creation, Wilde believes, is crucial to the development and perfection of the individual. While Wilde's overt interests in "The Critic as Artist" are in criticism and personal psychology rather than politics, Gilbert's subjectivist theory of interpretation is inseparably connected to its social and ethical consequences. Gilbert links subjectivism in textual interpretation—that is, creative criticism—with individualism and freedom for self-perfection, just as Wilde connects them with unrestrained artistic creation. As Gilbert says of the critic: "You must not ask of him to have any aim other than the perfecting of himself" (1053). Many of Gilbert's claims are motivated by this partially expressed assumption, and it is only by making distinct these expressly ethical and political concerns that we can fully understand Wilde's subjectivism or make sense of the long portions of the dialogue which concern the utopian effects of criticism, and which many critics have dismissed as being bewilderingly in contradiction to Wilde's frequent descriptions of art's inhabitation of a purely aesthetic domain of contemplation.

That Wilde does not take indeterminacy to be necessary given the working of language, but rather contends that it is beneficial to interpret language in the aesthetic sphere differently than one does in other areas of life, is underscored by one of the few comments that he makes on the problem of signification. In "The Soul of Man," Wilde argues in passing that the despotic nature of current society has led to general linguistic distortion and a deficient system of communication: "One of the results of the extraordinary tyranny of authority is that words are absolutely distorted from their proper and simple meaning, and are used to express the obverse of their right signification" (1101). A more liberal social arrangement, he suggests, would rectify this: "Under Individualism people will be quite natural and absolutely unselfish, and will know the meanings of the words, and realise them in their free, beautiful lives" (1101). Interestingly, he calls upon "proper and simple" meaning (the sense in which Jowett argued the text of the Bible should be taken, that is, in a sense close to what legal theorists referred to as the "plain" meaning of the text). Wilde does not in this case assume that freedom in society is connected to a free play of interpretation; rather he connects individualism and a freer society with "right signification." These comments echo arguments in Victorian scriptural exegesis and legal interpretation. As we've seen, liberal exegetes, such as Jowett, and legal theorists, such as Lieber, contended that tortured interpretations had become commonplace and that those in authority distorted the meaning of texts for their own ends. Wilde similarly does not believe all interpretations to be true in practical life.

III

The force of Wilde's writing on interpretation becomes clearer if we see its connections to the emerging literary theory of the final decades of the nineteenth century. His postuniversity career as a reviewer for journals meant that he knew thoroughly the tendencies of contemporary criticism. Many of Wilde's comments are in implicit dialogue with periodical criticism, while others respond to the new views on scholarship and interpretation arising in the universities.

Wilde's remarkable story about hermeneutics, "The Portrait of Mr. W. H."—part fiction, part critical essay, and first published in a short version between the two dialogues—manifests his engagement in this burgeoning literary critical milieu. The larger context of the story is the late-century debate on methodology and interpretation that I have discussed in the intertext preceding this chapter. In "Mr. W. H." Wilde plays with the theoretical controversies important to contemporary Shakespeare studies.[19] In so doing, he dramatizes a unique view of interpretation that can help clarify aspects of the dialogues. Interpretive activity is represented in the story as a medium of relations between people, relations that Wilde represents as erotically charged.[20]

The story concerns a young man, an unnamed narrator, who hears from an older friend, Erskine, a theory on Shakespeare's sonnets put forth a number of years earlier by his close friend Cyril Graham. The theory is that the sonnets were addressed to a beautiful boy actor whom Shakespeare loved. The frame story encloses the narrator's carefully worked out interpretation of the sonnets in support of that theory. Beyond the fictional frame and the accounts of the interactions between the men, the interpretation presented does not look very different from other contemporary accounts of the sonnets. Its methods and procedures are a fairly standard mixture of historical scholarship and close reading.

In the scholarly portions of the narrative, Wilde demonstrates how deeply grounded in current Shakespearean criticism he is.[21] Horst Schroeder has shown that in fact much of the scholarship attributed to Wilde's narrator came directly from the works of others, a move that if perhaps unscrupulous, at least shows that he followed the controversies.[22] The story commences with the narrator's defense of Chatterton's "so-called forgeries." In beginning the story with a discussion of forgery, Wilde may be writing into it justification against charges of plagiarism, but the attention to forgery does more work than that. As in the dialogues, Wilde tries to carve out an unregulated aesthetic sphere that will permit self-realization: "All Art being to a certain degree an attempt to realise one's own personality on some imaginative plane out of reach of the trammeling accidents and limitations of real life, to censure an artist for forgery was to confuse an ethical with an aesthetical problem" (1150). The allusion to forgery would certainly have had topical resonance for Wilde's readers, in that Shakespeare studies had been rife with literary crime in the recent past. Shakespearean scholar John Payne Collier, the founder of the original Shakespeare society, had been accused of forging documents, which he alleged to be written by Shakespeare. William Henry Ireland had written plays under Shakespeare's name and forged a number of documents to support his version of Shakespeare's life. Additionally, in the heated controversy over the authorship of the plays that were attributed to Shakespeare, the theory that they were in fact authored by Sir Francis Bacon, and plagiarized by Shakespeare, had a good deal of support.

What is most significant about the discussion is the questions it raises about intentionalism and interpretation. The defense of forgery suggests that knowing the identity of the author or the actual historical period in which a work was produced is unnecessary to the understanding, enjoyment, or value of an artwork. The narrator, nevertheless, insists that using a forgery to support a literary theory is unacceptable. It may initially seem surprising that the narrator rejects the forgery that figures in the story. Like Chatterton's forgeries, it is a painting that fraudulently passes itself off as dating from the Renaissance, although it is in fact of recent date. As is also the case with Chatterton's work, the narrator makes clear that the painting is an admirable artwork on its own, regardless of the period of its production. The narrator, however, rejects the forgery because it is used as a piece of evidence to support an interpretation, and interpretations should not require external evidence in their support—the logic apparently being that requiring outside corroborating evidence for an interpretation is to bring the standards of the practical sphere into the aesthetic domain. Wilde's presentation calls up a contemporary trend in the interpretation of the classics among academics, where in the later decades of the century, textual interpretations were increasingly supported by an appeal to archeological findings, a practice that some felt diminished the status of the ancient texts.[23]

The forgery also attempts to validate the interpretation by supplying facts about Shakespeare's personal life, a practice that Gilbert (at least mostly) repudiates. In the tradition of Dowsen's criticism, the interpretation of the work *seems* to attempt to reveal something about the experiences and mind of the great author. The narrator contends, though, that the claims are evident in the sonnets themselves and, further, do not pretend to the status of objective truth or verifiable fact. Yet the reading is not one that would normally be regarded as largely internal to the text. Cyril's interpretation rests upon the positing of a flesh and blood figure that existed outside the text, a referent to which the text points. The implication is, however, that although the theory offers an account of Shakespeare's life, both the frame story and the personal nature of the interpretation mark it out as a piece of creative criticism, a historical fiction about the "author" "Shakespeare."

Treatments of the story have taken several forms. Wilde's contemporaries largely ignored the narrative aspects, concentrating instead on the theory either as genuine Shakespearean criticism or as ingenious farce.[24] Later commentaries focused on the importance of the frame story, through which Wilde is able to represent his attitudes on the inevitably biased, personal, and unstable nature of interpretation. Still more recent accounts have seen the piece as Wilde's not-so-covert revelation of his own secret (his sexuality) to his public.[25] It is no surprise that for Wilde's contemporaries the interpretation itself dominated their response, since, as I've said, the theory is clearly the work of someone thoroughly at home in the current critical milieu. The frame narrative, however, is essential to the piece. There Wilde supplies highly specific details about the interrelations of the three men, and in these we find a different theory of interpretation than any that Wilde or his speakers have explicitly discussed. This story is not "homosexual romance disguised as literary quest," as Gerhard Joseph puts it, for the literary endeavor is far from incidental to the narrative and could have been replaced by no other activity.[26]

The frame story works to subordinate the theory to the characters and the relationships between them and sets the theory in a temporal mode, thereby underscoring the relational nature of intellectual activity. The various permutations that the theory takes in the course of the story exhibit Gilbert's notion that an interpreter always has something personal at stake in any interpretation. The theory that Shakespeare's sonnets and plays emanate from his love for the beautiful young actor who plays the female roles in his plays is originally put forth by Cyril, a beautiful young man who plays the female roles in Oxford productions of Shakespeare's plays. Wilde is at pains to show how very far Cyril's interpretation is from the impartiality Cyril claims. Cyril's interpretation is clearly based on his own need to conceive of himself as an object of desire, capable of inspiring a great work of art. The narrator's own passionate espousal of the theory is aroused by "his strange fascination" with "the wonderful portrait" of the young man of "quite extraordinary personal beauty" (1151) (actually a portrait of Cyril). In his adoption of the theory, the narrator casts himself in the role of the enamored genius Shakespeare.

The story provides a tour of late-Victorian literary interpretation, surveying its various methods, approaches, and orientations. Cyril wants to believe that his interpretation is definitive, telling Erskine that "working purely by internal evidence," "he had at last discovered the true secret of Shakespeare's sonnets; that all the scholars and critics had been entirely on the wrong track" (1153). With this brief comment, Wilde characterizes a number of the common moves of the criticism of his day. He emphasizes the growing necessity of positioning a critical text in relation to the work of other professional critics. He refers to the Victorian practice of dividing literary evidence into two main types, external and internal (a distinction that is still invoked by Wimsatt and Beardsley in the mid-twentieth century). Finally, he conceives of interpretation on the model of a literary puzzle or a coaxing forth of hidden meaning; once some vital "secret" has been revealed, a final understanding of the text will have been reached.

Cyril and Erskine agree that an essential requirement for an interpretation is that it be capable of rendering difficult passages intelligible and clarifying puzzling references: "According to his new explanation of their meaning, things that had seemed obscure, or evil, or exaggerated, became clear and rational, and of high artistic import" (1157). The reading must exhaustively account for every aspect of the work, making all its parts cohere. Cyril, though, plays the role of the Swinburne-like aesthetic critic, the critic who possesses the mysterious artistic temperament required for successful interpretation. His theory, he claims, grows "purely from the Sonnets themselves, depending for its acceptance not so much on demonstrated proof or formal evidence, but on a kind of spiritual and artistic sense, by which alone he claimed could the true meaning of the poems be discerned" (1156). Erskine, on the contrary, represents the scientific critic. He immediately begins to discover holes in the theory and demands verification, "some independent evidence about the existence of this young actor" (1159).

Recounting the theory a number of years after Cyril has proposed it, Erskine assumes that he is unlikely to convince the narrator of its merits because he no longer believes it to be true. Yet the narrator is unexpectedly swept up by it, declaring that "it is the only perfect key to Shakespeare's sonnets that has ever been made" (1160). In response, Erskine raises the image of a body of critics who are fast becoming the new authorities on interpretation. The interpretation, he says, is "a thing that no Shakespearean scholar would accept for a moment. The theory would be laughed at" (1161). (Certainly there is more than a trace of satire here, since theories that ought to have been laughed at, such as that the plays were extended cryptograms that revealed Bacon's authorship, were supported by prominent Shakespeareans.)[27]

The newly convinced narrator's exegesis of the sonnets brings together the two aspects that Wilde has praised in his "Greats" description, the speculative and the informed. The narrator's reading is highly personal and imaginative, and yet he attempts "to place the new interpretation of the Sonnets on something like a secure historical basis" (1189). He brings in extensive historical evidence to support his case, such as studies of boy actors in the Renaissance, and demonstrates his expertise in literary history. The analysis alludes to other Shakespeare experts and also calls for a reordering of the sonnets, a common move in late-Victorian Shakespeare criticism with its concern for chronology and dating.

And, yet, despite this "scholarly" work, it is evident that a literary theory has been transformed into a consuming infatuation, the narrator dwelling on descriptions of Willie Hughes's "delicate mobile limbs," and confessing that "his very name fascinated me" (1169). As he works he comes to recognize that, although he has been using the language of intention, he has in fact been telling his own story. "Art," he says, "can never really show us the external world. All that it shows us is our own soul, the one world of which we have any real cognizance" (1194). Literary interpretation, as Gilbert would have it, is always a form of autobiography.

Wilde, as a number of critics of the story have noted, emphasizes the transitory nature of belief. Even an interpretation once emphatically subscribed to comes to look unpersuasive. After weeks of impassioned enthusiasm, the narrator abruptly ceases to find his interpretation believable. Although he is no longer convinced, however, his arguments have succeeded in reanimating Erskine's belief.[28] The two now change roles, the narrator attempting to convince Erskine that the theory is groundless, Erskine passionately supporting it, each trotting out the arguments that the other had previously used. Erskine's claims for objective procedure and his use of scientific language, however, are now in support of a theory that can claim no more empirical proof than when he rejected it.

The point is that Erskine now has a reason to believe in the theory since in narrating its story and watching the narrator's response to it, his former desire for Cyril has been resurrected and in part transferred to the narrator. Erskine's repetition of the tale is a form of seduction; it is the story of an older man's passion for a younger one, and in telling it, he makes plain his former desire for Cyril. Erskine shifts this desire from Cyril to the narrator with the narrator's adoption of the theory, while the narrator adopts Erskine's passion for Cyril, though displaced onto the (representation of Cyril as the) young man in the portrait.

The narrative, in fact, insistently links up the theory with the dealings of the three men. The forms that it takes in the course of the story are concrete manifestations of their interrelations. Wilde's carefully selected details in his representations of their interpretive play underscore this. Cyril responds to Erskine's desire for evidence by commissioning a portrait of "Willie Hughes," which he passes off as a Renaissance painting that he has found "by mere chance" in an attic trunk. Erskine's willingness to accept this implausible account perhaps reveals his excessive faith in hard evidence, but it also throws us back on the details of the characters' relationship. For Erskine's demand for evidence is not the result of a reasoned adoption of empiricism. With a few phrases, Wilde presents a revealing portrait of Cyril. Cyril was "wonderfully handsome" (1152), spoiled, willful, petulant, insincere, and charming; he "fascinated everybody," yet had "an inordinate desire to please" (1153). Erskine, conversely, was "an awkward, weakly lad, with huge feet, and horribly freckled," "very jealous" of Cyril's acting, and "absurdly devoted to him" (1152). Erskine is cast as the desiring one, while Cyril desires not Erskine, but his desire.

Wilde takes care to mention that Cyril, each time the two meet, summons Erskine with the promise of some important revelation and then for no apparent reason delays his disclosure. Given the concision of the narrative, this repetition of a small detail seems gratuitous unless we take it to reveal something that Wilde sees as crucial to understanding the characters and their relation to the theory. Cyril has a power of attraction and deferral that Erskine lacks, yet it is vital for Cyril's own self-conception as an object of desire that he be able to convince Erskine that just such a young man as he was responsible for the creation of Shakespeare's sonnets. Recognizing this, Erskine takes on the role of an ardent believer in empirical evidence, and in so doing gains some control: Cyril "used to go over the whole question again and again, entreating me to believe" (1158).

Likewise, the narrator's version of the theory reflects his interactions with Erskine. The picture of Willie Hughes's character that emerges in the narrator's interpretation is almost indistinguishable from Erskine's portrayal of Cyril: Willie is beautiful, weak, and fascinating; he loves praise and desires to please. Where Erskine would like the narrator to play Cyril for him so that he can rewrite his past, the narrator instead adopts Erskine's desire, but recasts it as the idealistic and inspirational love of a great genius.

The text portrays interpretation not as the product of one's own subjective response, as Gilbert would have it. It is not, as the narrator has said, that "all that [art] shows us is our own soul." Instead interpretation is intersubjective, dependent on an interpreter's relations with others. The aim of the act of interpreting is shown to be not an interpretation per se; the emphasis instead falls on interpretation as a medium of interaction. This is a version of Gilbert's claim that the personal always informs interpretation, yet with a crucially important difference. Wilde's depictions of interpretation in the story take us beyond the condition of interpretation as always only a form of self-replication. Meaning turns out to be not the projection of one's self onto the text, but instead a contextual and intersubjective construction. The story also helps us to see that the same situation is at work in both of Wilde's dialogues. Although it may appear that in the dialogues one of the figures dominates the conversation, in fact the cumulative effect of the dialogue as theory is ultimately relational.

Importantly, the interactions depicted by Wilde in the story are erotically charged ones. (His view differs from Roland Barthes' in that for Wilde the erotic is not a product of the interaction of reader and text; interpretation is an erotically charged activity between interpreters.) Nor is the conflation of erotics and aesthetics merely a way of obscuring the desire that Wilde wants to reveal, but cannot.[29] Rather, for Wilde interpretation is an activity that can best be modeled on erotic/romantic exchange. Constructing Shakespeare's imaginary biography, the narrator of "Mr. W. H." comments on the ways in which "what in its origin had been mere aesthetic impulse, and desire of art" can be transformed for those "exquisitely susceptible to the influences of language" into "a strange sensuous energy" (1186). This formulation explains the trajectory of the theory; it becomes an almost physical force in the encounters between the three, marking out their interrelations. The allusion is made more explicit when the narrator in his discussion of Platonic love praises Plato's *Symposium* for "the curious analogies it draws between intellectual enthusiasm and the physical passion of love" (1174). In the story, the intellectual is clearly infused with romantic passion.

Wilde seems to satirize extreme interpretive ardency, particularly when he represents Cyril as having taken his own life to show his support of the theory. Certainly the levels of exhilaration and despondency that the characters experience over a literary interpretation seem exaggerated; the narrator, for instance, claiming that his loss of belief in the theory caused him "a sorrow greater than any I had felt since boyhood" (1197). Yet the Furnivall-Swinburne controversy had been carried to equally impassioned lengths. Note the similarity between Furnivall's quite genuine account of his analysis of Shakespeare and those of Wilde's characters: "I worked it all out, and I had the most exciting fortnight of my life on discovering how the plays grew one into the other. . . . I was in a state of exaltation all the time I was working on this."[30] Wilde pokes fun at these tendencies and at the same time accepts that such ardor is vital to intellectual endeavor. Wilde's paralleling of intellectual enthusiasm and romantic love may help to shed light on why critics continue to worry about seemingly irresolvable questions of interpretation. It is perhaps not so much the answers we seek—as Wilde's own shifting interpretive views indicate—but the experience of impassioned argument.

IV

Some months after leaving prison, Wilde wrote to Reggie Turner, apropos an attempt to block his income and control his relationship with Alfred Douglas, in words that contradict Gilbert's statements on aesthetic interpretation: "Would you some day inform them that in a legal document words have to be interpreted in a legal sense: and not by private feelings of whatever kind they may be. . . . They do not understand that legal documents are things that have to be carefully, rightfully, interpreted"

(*Letters,* 990). This comment might suggest that Wilde continues to maintain a distinction between non-literary and literary language. It certainly shows that he does not see subjectivist interpretation as inevitable, as he must if he believes language by its very nature to be indeterminate. As I've argued, aesthetic interpretation that leaves authorial intention to one side represents a choice for Wilde.

Given Wilde's refusal to commit to any one position, we should not expect him to submit a final and completed theory of interpretation, and he does not. *De Profundis* signals a change in Wilde's views on literary interpretation. He comes to question his earlier commitment to an autonomous aesthetic sphere in a move that opens the way for a reconsideration of the importance of intention in construing literary meaning. When Wilde writes his letter from prison, his sense of the consequences of interpretation has changed, and whereas earlier his characters had investigated the problems of a determinate account of meaning, Wilde now turns his attention to the problems of indeterminacy. In *De Profundis,* the emphasis shifts to an intentionalist view, which like the subjectivist view that Wilde has explored earlier, is grounded in ethics.

As we've seen, Gilbert argued that the meaning of a text should not be limited by authorial intention, primarily because this would be to constrain an interpreter's own self-development. And yet, Wilde has been unwilling to give up the notion that his own artworks express himself, as his words to Douglas in *De Profundis* reassert: "You know what my Art was to me, the great primal note by which I had revealed, first myself to myself, and then myself to the world" (895). Gilbert's subjectivist theory of interpretation, however, entailed that the artist's self-revelation to others ("to the world") was impossible, since interpretation only reveals the interpreter's own subjectivity. This conflict between an expressivist view of artistic creation and an impressionist view of interpretation was always a source of tension in Wilde's thought, and, at least in his own case, the assertion that his art expressed his self had overridden claims of interpretive freedom.

Gilbert rejected an intentionalist account of literary meaning because he implicitly connected it to an authoritarianism involved in the assertion of one right meaning, as my juxtaposition of "The Soul of Man" and Wilde's concurrently written dialogues has demonstrated. Events leading to his imprisonment, however, gave him cause to question whether the distinction between literary language and more practical forms of communication, between the aesthetic sphere and the practical realm, could be maintained. Wilde's literary texts were used as evidence to support an interpretation of his actions that would result in his conviction. The course his trial took demonstrated that freeing aesthetic interpretation from the constraints of authorial intention would not necessarily foster the less authoritarian society that he had envisioned in "The Soul of Man." Cutting his intentions from the determination of meaning led instead to the conditions that Wilde had decried in the essay, in a statement quoted earlier in the chapter: "One of the results of the extraordinary tyranny of authority is that words are absolutely distorted from their proper and simple meaning, and are used to express the obverse of their right signification" (1101).

Throughout *De Profundis* Wilde defends his intentions. He insists that he has written the letter in such a way that his intentions are made clear: "As for the corrections and *errata,* I have made them in order that my words should be an absolute expression of my thoughts. . . . my letter has its definite meaning behind every phrase" (948). Discussing an early letter to Alfred Douglas that made an appearance in his trial and was submitted as evidence of his indecency, Wilde writes that no attempt was made "to interpret rightly its fantastic phrases" (889). Instead "every construction but the right one is put on it" (889).[31] Wilde suggests in his final writing that considering authorial intention (for ethical reasons) may outweigh the ethical benefits of aesthetic free play. As he writes to Frank Harris: "Words, now, to me signify things, actualities, real emotions, realised thoughts" (*Letters,* 894). Whereas in "Mr. W. H.," Wilde had an interpretation arise dialogically among interpreters, in his final writing, authorial intention enters into the mix.

Wilde called on the image of Christ as a paradigm for individualism in "The Soul of Man," but the figure becomes central in *De Profundis* as the model for correct understanding through sympathy. Wilde's conception of Christ is based on Renan's *Life of Jesus* (and is thus a product of a certain mode of interpretation—the Higher Criticism). In his letter to Douglas, Wilde connects Christ with the artist, no longer identified by his will to self-development achieved by disregarding the claims of others, but instead by a capacity for imaginative sympathy. Wilde writes that Christ "realised in the entire sphere of human relations that imaginative sympathy which in the sphere of Art is the sole secret of creation. He understood the leprosy of the leper, the darkness of the blind, the fierce misery of those who live for pleasure" (923). Asserting a view surprisingly like George Eliot's, Wilde ties understanding to an ethics of sympathy.

A year after his release from prison, he wrote to a friend that people often "make the harsh error of judging another person's life without understanding it. . . . Charity is not a sentimental emotion: it is the only method by which the soul can attain to any knowledge" (*Letters,* 1081). Whereas he has earlier ridiculed the Victorian valorization of altruism, sympathy, and charity, he now argues that those qualities lead to a greater capacity for understanding. Some of Wilde's commentators have suggested that the turnabout in his views during and after his imprisonment is to be seen as the inevitable result of coercion.[32] It would be a mistake, however, to read *De Profundis* as nothing more than a manifestation of oppression. A change in views is, of course, nothing new for Wilde. More importantly, he has always connected interpretation and ethics. Earlier, through Gilbert, Wilde had turned his attention to the interests of the interpreter. In his later writing, he continues to maintain that interpretation has moral consequences. But now these consequences are not only the interpreter's, but the author's as well.

In adopting interpretive constraints that ground meaning in a speaker's intentions and in arguing that understanding is tied to ethics, Wilde returns to characteristics pervasive in Victorian hermeneutic theory. For Wilde in his later writing, literary interpretations have consequences that go beyond aesthetic enrichment and the opportunity for personal development through imaginative play; the aesthetic/practical distinction has broken down. Wilde comes to question whether because we can show a literary text to mean many things, it follows that this is what we should do—a question that criticism has repeatedly returned to. Late-twentieth-century interpretation will, like the later Wilde, largely refuse to recognize a distinction between aesthetic and practical language. But while Wilde's trajectory is the extension of his views on nonaesthetic language into what he once considered the autonomous realm of the aesthetic, twentieth century criticism will follow the opposite trajectory, extending to all language the indeterminacy that Wilde once regarded as limited to the aesthetic realm.

Yeats commented in 1891 that Wilde writes "some of the most subtle literary criticism we are likely to see for many a long day."[33] Subsequent discussion has proven this to be right. Wilde's work allows us to trace the course of hermeneutics from its break with theology and the Church through its reinstitutionalization as literary study at the end of the Victorian period. His explorations of subjectivism, intersubjectivity, and intention open the way to almost every prominent interpretive position in twentieth-century literary theory. In Wilde we see the history of hermeneutic speculation in the nineteenth century culminating in questions that remain at the center of current literary theory's impassioned speculation.

❧

Hermeneutics and the Self

If the superior psycho-physical mechanism of vision can in dream life seize upon what is really nothing but rows of meaningless blackish spots upon the retina and can convert them into imagined pages of print which may be read with great satisfaction off-hand in a dream, what is it not capable of achieving? That it can cut all manner of capers in hermeneutics I know by abundant experience.

—George Trumball Ladd

By the end of the nineteenth century, the hermeneutic strategies borrowed from biblical exegesis had made the move into secular literary criticism, but also into a wide range of Victorian disciplines. In this epilogue, I conclude by looking briefly at a Victorian phenomenon in which hermeneutics plays a crucial role without any direct allusion to its biblical ancestry: the new field of psychology and in particular the study of memory. The workings of the mind were understood as hermeneutic by many late Victorians. For interpretation, as we now can recognize, moved from texts into our very imaginations of ourselves, in the new discipline of psychology.

Although as it was developing in the nineteenth century, psychology was subject, like the other Victorian sciences, to the requirements of "observation" that accompanied the growth of laboratory studies, it was subject also to another imperative: that it rely on interpretive methods. George Henry Lewes, for instance, in *The Study of Psychology*, maintained that our methods of understanding mental processes always involve interpretation. "We have no microscope, balance, and reagent, to see what is too minute for the unassisted eye, to measure what is quantitative, to test what is compound in mental processes: our closest observation is *interpretation*. . . . Nay, even the observations of external data have all to be interpreted, and their value lies wholly in interpretation."[1] Lewes uses "interpretation" here in the sense that theorizing must always go beyond the already theory-laden observation.

Sigmund Freud, at the end of the period, was to conceive of psychology as involving interpretation in ways closer to the process of textual interpretation. In the *Interpretation of Dreams,* writing that "the aim which I have set before myself is that dreams are capable of being interpreted," Freud proceeds to show that dream psychology involves a double process of interpretation, the unconscious interpretive activity of the dreaming mind and the interpretive deciphering of the analyst.[2] But Victorian writers had themselves already been figuring mental activity as a mode of interpretation, and the self as requiring interpretation. James Sully, whose *Illusions: A Psychological Study* treats all forms of human cognition as interpretive, described a dream as a "palimpsest" some years before Freud's work appeared, in an essay whose influence Freud acknowledged: "Like some letter in cipher," Sully wrote, "the dream-inscription when scrutinized closely loses its first look of balderdash and takes on the aspect of a serious, intelligible message."[3]

This interpretive model of human psychology is particularly apparent in Victorian writing on memory. Toward the end of the period, psychological and philosophical theory began to conceive of memory in ways that relied upon models borrowed from hermeneutics. With the development of the experimental study of memory in the nineteenth century, theoretical work on memory came to focus on fallibilities, distortions, and illusions of memory, and this research reads very much like current literary theory on autobiographical texts, with its interest in the construction of the self and time in memory, and, especially, on the interpretive aspects of retrospection. Victorian theorists suggested that memory—and thus identity—belongs in the sphere of hermeneutics. Underscoring the unreliability of reminiscence, they argued that memory was a constructed narrative, at the best distorted, partially imaginary, a mode of interpretation that almost always threatens to become misinterpretation.

In the last decades of the century physiological research led to increased knowledge of brain functioning: neurological research provided insights into cerebral localization; experimental psychology, relying on statistics, was introduced in Hermann Ebbinghaus's laboratory investigations of memory. Even those who most fervently held to memory's spiritual nature began to accept that memory is in part dependent on physical processes.[4] The move away from introspection as the primary means of studying memory that came with developments in physiology led to an increasing emphasis in the research on the pervasiveness of forgetting, on the ways in which memory goes wrong, and rarely succeeds in accurately representing what really happened. This emphasis was new to the Victorians, a subject that W. H. Burnham in his important four-article series, "Memory, Historically and Experimentally Considered" (1882), claimed "has until recently been neglected."[5]

If earlier philosophers had been able to view the "fidelity" of memory as a self-evident truth, late nineteenth-century scientific study of memory was to undo that conception.[6] Previously, it had been argued that every experience was recorded somewhere in the mind, although the record might not be easily retrievable.[7] New research overturned the belief in the permanence of memory traces. It may seem surprising that strong argumentation would be needed to establish the fallibility of memory. Laboratory experiments would seem unneeded to prove what experience surely shows. Yet this late-Victorian literature was intent on convincing its readers of memory's unreliability.

Sully's 1881 "Illusions of Memory," the lengthiest treatment of the subject in late Victorian psychological literature, argues that memory is far from a thorough and passive recording of images. Sully (a friend of George Henry Lewes), begins with the widely accepted opinion that each person is infallible in the arena of personal memories, that access to a person's past is available only through introspection, and that individuals are the sole authorities over their memories. We take the past in memory to be "a faithful imitation," and believe that when we "fix our retrospective glance on it" it "start[s] anew into life."[8] Likewise, R. Verdon's article "Forgetfulness" (published in *Mind*, 1877) begins by quoting many recent texts on physiology that accept the hypothesis that "total forgetfulness does not occur," "that nothing of which we have had experience can be absolutely forgotten."[9] Both Verdon and Sully go on to argue vigorously against this—as they see it—entirely misguided view. As in other spheres, the person who would seem to hold the key to meaning is dislodged as interpretive authority.

Sully depicts an illusion of memory as "a wrong interpretation of a special kind of mental image" (242) With a George Eliot-like emphasis on the propensity for misreading (and he greatly admired her novels) Sully writes that memory is often a "semi-voluntary process of self-delusion" (259); and "active errors" of memory are likened to "'interpreting' an old manuscript which has got partially obliterated" (267). He underscores the near impossibility of an objective rendering of the past. "In trying to reconstruct the remote past, we are constantly in danger of importing our present selves into our past selves" (267), he says, "reading back a present preconception into the past" (292). In memory, every event is taken to contribute to a plot that is cast back retrospectively from the present self, and like any reader, the one who remembers finds it difficult to avoid bringing present context to bear on the text from the past.

A recurring note in the literature is the idea that memory is selective; much goes unrecorded. "One who selects things, rejects, ignores, and forgets things" (443), says Verdon. Sully confronts the importance of selectivity for conceptions of the self: "The consciousness of personal identity is said to be bound up with memory. . . . If this is so, it would seem to follow from the very fragmentary character of our recollections that our sense of identity is very incomplete" (241). We are left, he argues, to fill in "the numberless and often huge lacunae of the past left by memory" (241). Like Iser, he emphasizes the constant "process of filling in the gaps" (282). Such gaps are "filled up, and the sense of identity restored by a kind of retrospective 'skipping'" (289). John Stuart Mill had written some years earlier that "the phenomena of Self and that of memory, are two sides of the same fact, or two different modes of seeing the same fact. . . . We may say, in treating of Identity, that the meaning of Self is the memory of certain past sensations."[10] Sully's analysis of memory raises the question: What happens to identity if our memories are not fixed, if the construction of our pasts is basically interpretive, subjective rather than objective, changing rather than fixed?

As Sully proceeds, he accelerates his delineation of memory's deficiencies, repeatedly using terms such as "fragmentary," "defective," "illusory," "misrepresentation," and "arbitrary." "Our minds" he writes, "are refracting media, and the past reappears to us not as it actually was when it was close to us, but in numerous ways altered and disguised by the intervening spaces of our conscious experience" (262). Like the study of the historical past, the understanding of the self is reliant on the fragments that remain. "Our idea of any stage of our past history," Sully writes, "is built up out of a few fragmentary intellectual relics" and "that which we seem to see in the act of recollection is thus very different from the reality" (262). The representation of an individual's past, even in the mind of the very person who experienced it, gives rise to the same epistemological problems that worried the Victorians about the representation of the historical past.

Sully and Verdon are not alone in this emphasis on the pervasiveness of forgetting; late Victorian accounts of mind are often preoccupied with what goes wrong in memory. Frances Power Cobbe is not referred to in Burnham's or any other psychological study, her writing being literary rather than scientific. Yet her essay "Fallacies of Memory," written in 1866, fifteen years before Sully's, and at a time when science held strongly to the permanence of memory traces, comes to many of the same conclusions. "Our remembrance," she writes, "is habitually, not merely fallible, but faulty."[11] Despite experience, we go on acting as though memory were reliable. She argues, in a striking passage, that "memory is neither an impression made, once for all, like an engraving on a tablet, nor yet safe for an hour from obliteration or modification. . . . Rather is memory a finger-mark traced on shifting sand, ever exposed to obliteration when left unrenewed; and if renewed, then modified, and made, not the same, but a fresh and different mark" (104). What we have remembered remains, paradoxically, only through what Cobbe calls "the fixing process of revision" (105), a fixity that is clearly not fixed. Memory is not stable, but dynamic and evolving, a text constantly modified.

The pages of professional journals such as *Brain* and the *British Medical Journal* in the last few decades of the century present numerous case studies of amnesia: the young woman who woke from a brief nap with all of her memories wiped out, the injured man who repeatedly tells his wife that he must now return home to his wife. It is easy to read the pervasive representation of such cases as indicative of anxieties about the instability of identity. If every memory is full of gaps, if continuity is only an illusion, then these extreme cases of memory loss are not of a different order, but point to the tenuous nature of identity.

All of this might evoke a Derridean world of traces, interpretations of interpretation, without origin. "The failure of memory is," Derrida writes, "not a failure; we can interpret its apparent negativity, its very finitude, what affects its experience of discontinuity and distance, as a power, as the very opening of difference."[12] The Victorian reaction to the failures of memory, however, was far more anxious. Coupled with the emphasis on memory's deficiencies is the frequently articulated belief that there is (or was) a real way that things happened and that we must learn how to counter memory's misinterpretations in order to get it right. For some, this involves recourse to documents, letters, and other fixed and "objective" records of the past. Burnham invokes character, arguing that "strong . . . critical judgment" will guard against error. Sully's final appeal is to evolution. These last moves are typical of a common belief about the aim of interpretation among many Victorians, as we have seen. In their sophisticated examinations of hermeneutics, they recognized the problems involved in interpretation, yet continued to believe that one could approximate to correct meaning.

The Victorian study of psychology suggests still further the pervasiveness of hermeneutics in the period, and its continuity with our own. This book has sought to show that hermeneutics penetrated every aspect of Victorian culture and that contemporary thought is deeply indebted to that Victorian development of hermeneutics. Our histories of the Victorians need to be modified to come to terms with a theoretical sophistication with which they are rarely credited. Viewing literary theory in the wider perspective afforded by Victorian hermeneutics, we have come to see an important Victorian presence in current thinking about meaning and interpretation, while also gaining ways to step outside our own perspectives. As the brilliant nineteenth-century hermeneutic theorist Nietzsche advises: "The *more* eyes, different eyes, we can use to observe one thing, the more complete will our 'concept' of this thing, our 'objectivity,' be."[13]

❦

Notes

An Overview

1. Henry Jones, *Browning as Philosophical Thinker* (New York: Macmillan, 1891), 275.

2. K. M. Newton, *Interpreting the Text: A Critical Introduction to the Theory and Practice of Literary Interpretation* (New York: St. Martin's Press, 1990), 1–2.

3. James Engell, *Forming the Critical Mind: Dryden to Coleridge* (Cambridge: Harvard University Press, 1989), xi.

4. For overviews of the hermeneutic tradition see Jean Grondin, *Introduction to Philosophical Hermeneutics,* trans. Joel Weinsheimer (New Haven: Yale University Press, 1997); Kurt Mueller-Vollmer ed., *The Hermeneutics Reader* (New York: Continuum: 1988); and Richard Palmer, *Hermeneutics* (Evanston: Northwestern University Press, 1969).

5. Although many historians of hermeneutics consider Schleiermacher to be the founder of modern universal hermeneutics, some argue that the origins of Romantic hermeneutics are in fact in Friedrich Schlegel's early (though unpublished) work. See, for instance, Ernst Behler, "The New Hermeneutics and Comparative Literature," *Neohelicon: Acta Comparationis Litterarum* 10.2 (1983): 25–45; and René Wellek, *History of Modern Criticism: 1750–1950,* vol. 2 (New Haven: Yale University Press, 1955). Schlegel was part of a literary circle in the 1790s that included Schleiermacher and Novalis. See Jack Forstman, *A Romantic Triangle: Schleiermacher and Early German Romanticism* (Missoula, MT: Scholars Press, 1977) for an account of this circle. Still others have argued that universalist hermeneutics in fact emerges during the Enlightenment, in the work of the eighteenth-century rationalist investigators of interpretation such as Meier and Chladenius, and that the emphasis on Schleiermacher's work as constituting something entirely new in hermeneutic thought has caused these important thinkers to be overlooked. See, for instance, Peter Szondi, *Introduction to Literary Hermeneutics,* trans. Martha Woodmansee (New York: Cambridge University Press, 1995).

6. F. D. E. Schleiermacher, *Hermeneutics: The Handwritten Manuscripts,* ed. Heinze Kimmerle, trans. James Duke and Jack Forstman (Missoula, MT: Scholar's Press, 1977), 95. August Boeckh similarly claims: "The task of interpretation is to reach as close an approximation as possible by gradual step-by-step progression: it cannot hope to reach the limit." Philip August Boeckh, "Theory of Hermeneutics," in *The Hermeneutics Reader,* 138.

7. Schleiermacher was taken by his followers, particularly Dilthey, to be advocating an empathetic understanding of the author's creative personality. There has been much debate about the extent of Schleiermacher's psychologism.

8. Boeckh writes: "Aside from quality of training, not everyone can be equally good as an expositor; and above all an original talent belongs to interpretation. . . . Some naturally have penetration into understanding." "Theory of Hermeneutics," 139.

9. Hans-Georg Gadamer, *Truth and Method,* 2nd ed., trans. Joel Weinsheimer and Donald G. Marshall (New York: Crossroad, 1990), xxi.

10. Jacques Derrida, "Limited Inc abc . . . ," in *Limited Inc,* trans. Samuel Weber (Evanston, IL: Northwestern University Press, 1988), 61.

11. William K. Wimsatt Jr. and Monroe C. Beardsley, *The Verbal Icon: Studies in Meaning and Poetry* (Lexington: University Press of Kentucky, 1954), 3.

12. E. D. Hirsch, *Validity in Interpretation* (New Haven: Yale University Press, 1967), 5.

13. Roland Barthes, "The Death of the Author," in *Image, Music, Text,* trans. Stephen Heath (New York: Noonday Press, 1977), 146.

14. Michel Foucault, *The Birth of the Clinic: An Archeology of Medical Perception,* trans. A. W. Sheridan Smith (New York: Vintage, 1975), xvii.

15. Jacques Derrida, *Of Grammatology,* trans. Gayatri Spivak (Baltimore: Johns Hopkins University Press, 1976), 13.

16. Jacques Derrida, *Spurs: Nietzsche's Styles,* trans. Barbara Harlow (Chicago: University of Chicago Press, 1979), 107.

17. Jacques Derrida, "Structure, Sign, and Play in the Discourse of the Human Sciences," in *The Structuralist Controversy,* ed. Richard Macksey and Eugene Donato (Baltimore: Johns Hopkins University Press, 1972), 264.

18. Friedrich Nietzsche, *On the Genealogy of Morals* in *On the Genealogy of Morals and Ecce Homo,* trans. Walter Kaufmann and R. J. Hollingdale (New York: Vintage, 1967), III 12.

19. Friedrich Nietzsche, *The Gay Science,* trans. Walter Kaufmann (New York: Vintage, 1974), 375.

20. Friedrich Nietzsche, *Human All Too Human,* part 1, trans. Helen Zimmern (New York: Gordon Press, 1974), 270.

21. Friedrich Nietzsche, *The Wanderer and His Shadow,* in *Human All Too Human,* part 2, trans. Paul V. Cohn (New York: Gordon Press, 1974), 17.

22. Friedrich Nietzsche, *The Antichrist,* in *The Portable Nietzsche,* trans. Walter Kaufmann (New York: Viking Penguin, 1982), 52.

23. Henry Sidgwick, "The Historical Method," *Mind* 11.42 (1886): 213.

24. Walter Pater, *Studies in the History of the Renaissance* (London: Macmillan, 1873), 22.

25. W. H. Mallock, *The New Republic: Culture, Faith, and Philosophy in an English Country House* (New York: Scribner and Welford, 1878), 107.

26. See F. M. Turner, *Greek Heritage in Victorian Britain* (New Haven: Yale University Press, 1981) for discussion of historical approaches in classics. See also Christopher

Stray's comprehensive study *Classics Transformed: Schools, Universities, and Society in England, 1830–1960* (Oxford: Clarendon Press, 1998).

27. Alexander Grant, *The "Ethics" of Aristotle, Illustrated with Essays and Notes* (Oxford: Parker, 1858), 2:xi.

28. For considerations of the study of language and philology in the Victorian period, see Hans Aarsleff's fine book *The Study of Language in England, 1780–1860* (Princeton: Princeton University Press, 1967); Aarsleff, *From Locke to Saussure: Essays on the Study of Language and Intellectual History* (Minneapolis: University of Minnesota Press, 1982); J. W. Burrow, "The Use of Philology in Victorian England," in *Ideas and Institutions of England,* ed. Robert Robson (London: G. Bell and Sons, 1967), 180–204; Linda Dowling, "Victorian Oxford and the Science of Language," *PMLA* 97.2 (March 1982): 160–78; and Cary H. Plotkin, *The Tenth Muse: Victorian Philology and the Genesis of the Poetic Language of Gerard Manley Hopkins* (Carbondale: Southern Illinois University Press, 1989).

29. Richard Trench, *On the Study of Words* (New York: Macmillan, 1892), 89.

30. Mueller agreed: "If we can but find an entrance into the ancient workshop of language, we can still listen there to the earliest thoughts of man." F. Max Mueller, *Natural Religion* (London: Longmans, Green, 1889), 281.

31. W. F. Cannon, "The Impact of Uniformitarianism: Two Letters from John Herschel to Charles Lyell, 1836–1837," *Proceedings of the American Philosophical Society* 105 (1961): 308.

32. F. Max Mueller, *Lectures on the Science of Language,* 2 vols. (London: Longmans, Green, 1899), 2:70.

33. Lewis Carroll, *Alice in Wonderland,* in *The Annotated Alice* (New York: Forum, 1963), 121.

34. Jean-Jacques Lecercle argues that there is "a close link between the practice of literary nonsense and the tradition of hermeneutics. Nonsense is the reflective image of our practice of interpretation, as philosophers or literary critics it is interpretation gone wild, but also lucid." *Philosophy of Nonsense: The Intuitions of Victorian Nonsense Literature* (New York: Routledge, 1994), 3.

35. See, for instance, George Pitcher, "Wittgenstein, Nonsense, and Lewis Carroll," *Massachusetts Review* 6: 591–611.

36. Lewis Carroll, *Through the Looking Glass,* in *The Annotated Alice,* 268–69.

37. "The judicial interpretation by the King is an emblem of all interpretation; and it is constructed not through cooperation, but along the principles of *agon,* by the manipulation of affects of violence and desire, a manipulation that the structure of language fully allows." Lecercle, *Philosophy of Nonsense,* 98.

38. See Carolyn Williams on Pater and interpretation in "Walter Pater's Impressionism," in *Knowing the Past,* ed. Suzy Anger, (Ithaca: Cornell University Press, 2001), 77–99.

39. See Herbert Tucker, "Arnold and the Authorization of Criticism" on *Empedocles* and interpretation in *Knowing the Past,* 100–120.

40. *The Complete Prose Works of Matthew Arnold,* ed. R. H. Super, 8 vols. (Ann Arbor: University of Michigan Press, 1960–72), 1:22.

41. Benjamin Jowett, "On the Interpretation of Scripture," in *Essays and Reviews: The 1860 Text and Its Reading,* ed. Victor Shea and William Whitla (Charlottesville: University of Virginia Press, 2000), 520.

42. George P. Landow argues that Ruskin pervasively uses typological interpretation in his art criticism and elsewhere in *The Aesthetic and Critical Theories of John Ruskin* (Princeton: Princeton University Press, 1971).

43. See Richard L. Stein for a discussion of Ruskin's art interpretation; Stein refers to Ruskin's art interpretation as "ritual" "to indicate the almost religious value he assigns to the act of interpretation itself." *The Ritual of Interpretation: The Fine Arts as Literature in Ruskin, Rossetti, and Pater* (Cambridge: Harvard University Press, 1975), 17.

See also Jeffrey L. Spear, "Ruskin as Prejudiced Reader," *ELH* 49.1 (Spring 1982). Spear argues that "Ruskin tried to expand his defense of Turner into a more general interpretive theory that would demonstrate the participation of both the physical world and the perceptive and creative faculties of man in the overarching unity of God" (73).

44. John Ruskin, "Of Kings' Treasuries," in *Sesames and Lilies* (New York: Chelsea, 1983), 14–16.

45. See Elinor Shaffer, *Kubla Khan and the Fall of Jerusalem: The Mythological School in Biblical Criticism and Secular Literature 1770–1880* (Cambridge: Cambridge University Press, 1972), and W. David Shaw, *The Lucid Veil: Poetic Truth in the Victorian Age* (London: Athlone, 1987). See also Shaw, *The Victorians and Mystery: Crises of Representation* (Ithaca: Cornell University Press, 1990) for further consideration of the Victorians and hermeneutics.

46. Thomas Hardy, *Far from the Madding Crowd* (New York: Penguin, 1978), 64.

47. Wilkie Collins, *The Moonstone* (New York: Oxford University Press, 1999), 42.

48. J. A. Froude, "History: Its Use and Meaning," *Westminster Review* 62 (October 1854): 423.

49. James Sully, *Illusions: A Psychological Study* (New York: DaCapo Press, 1982), 44.

50. Christopher Herbert reads Frazer's anthropology as interpretive in "*The Golden Bough* and the Unknowable," in *Knowing the Past*, 32–51.

51. Edward B. Tylor, "Mr. Spencer's 'Principles of Sociology,'" *Mind* 2:6 (1877): 144.

52. Herbert Spencer, *The Study of Sociology* (Ann Arbor: University of Michigan Press, 1961), 103–4.

53. Max Weber, *Economy and Society: An Outline of Interpretive Sociology*, ed. G. Roth and C. Wittich (Berkeley: University of California Press, 1978), 4.

54. Robert Browning, "A Pillar at Sebzevar," in *Robert Browning's Works*, Centenary ed., 10 vols. (New York: Barnes and Noble, 1966), 10:113. Browning's larger point in the poem is, of course, that love is ultimately more important than our always circumscribed knowledge, but also, in a sense, that love provides a knowledge that rationality can't quite get at.

1. Victorian Scriptural Hermeneutics

1. Walter Pater, *Appreciations* (Evanston, IL: Northwestern University Press, 1987), 202.

2. Useful studies of Victorian exegesis include John Rogerson, *Old Testament Criticism in the Nineteenth Century: England and Germany* (London: Society for Promoting Christian Knowledge, 1984); L. E. Elliott-Binns, *English Thought, 1860–1900: The Theological Aspect* (Greenwich, CT: Seabury Press, 1956); Richard Allan Riesen, *Criticism and Faith in Late Victorian Scotland* (Lanham, MD: University Press of America,

1985); A. O. J. Cockshut, ed., *Religious Controversies of the Nineteenth Century* (Lincoln: University of Nebraska Press, 1966).

3. Typological criticism, a prominent form of biblical hermeneutics through the early eighteenth century, is based on the idea that an earlier occurrence in the Bible prefigures a later event or person. Moses is a type of Christ, and the Old Testament anticipates and is fulfilled in the New Testament. Everything is part of a divine plan pointing toward a single event.

George P. Landow in his *Victorian Types, Victorian Shadows: Biblical Typology in Victorian Literature, Art, and Thought* (Boston: Routledge & Kegan Paul, 1980) demonstrates that typology is incorporated into Victorian literary works. He argues that typology remained an important interpretive mode for Victorians throughout the century. See also Linda H. Peterson, who argues that typological design is pervasively used as a structuring device in Victorian spiritual autobiography: "The genre depended upon—perhaps originated in— a particular system of biblical hermeneutics known as typology." *Victorian Autobiography: The Tradition of Self-Interpretation* (New Haven: Yale University Press, 1986), 6. Herbert L. Sussman examines the use of typology in Carlyle, Ruskin, and the Pre-Raphaelites in *Fact into Figure* (Columbus: Ohio State University Press, 1979).

4. Hans Frei's fine study *The Eclipse of Biblical Narrative: A Study in Eighteenth- and Nineteenth-Century Hermeneutics* (New Haven: Yale University Press, 1974) examines the collapse of realistic and figural approaches in the eighteenth century. He argues that as this occurred, the narrative aspects of the Bible were increasingly ignored. See also Robert M. Grant and David Tracy, *A Short History of the Interpretation of the Bible*, 2nd ed. (Philadelphia: Fortress, 1984), especially chapters 11 and 12, and John Drury's excellent introductory essays in *Critics of the Bible, 1724–1873* (Cambridge: Cambridge University Press, 1989). Nigel M. de S. Cameron's *Biblical Higher Criticism and the Defense of Infallibilism in 19th-Century Britain* (Lewiston, N.Y.: Edwin Mellen Press, 1987) makes available obscure primary source material.

5. The German Higher Critics believed that the Bible should be seen as a collection of myths that told spiritual and ethical truths. Like the rationalists, they dismissed the supernatural belief in miracles. D. F. Strauss, the most prominent of the Higher Critics (whose *Life of Jesus* was first translated into English by George Eliot), argued that the meaning of the text was not to be found in the facts about the historical figure of Christ. Historical analysis revealed that the meaning was discovered through an understanding of the historically conditioned consciousness of the writers. The stories were not to be seen either as intentionally misleading or as simply demonstrating an inaccurate understanding of the world, as the rationalists argued. (Rationalists attempted to explain supernatural events as being either erroneous accounts or deliberate misrepresentations of natural events; for instance, sightings of angels are accounted for by what we now know to be phosphorescence.) Rather, they were to be understood as expressions of the mythical consciousness of the period in which they were written. Elinor Shaffer traces the impact of the Higher Criticism on English writers from Coleridge through Eliot in *Kubla Khan and the Fall of Jerusalem: The Mythological School in Biblical Criticism and Secular Literature, 1770–1880* (Cambridge: Cambridge University Press, 1972).

6. The contributors to *Essays and Reviews* were often denounced for being Germanists. In Germany, biblical study was secularized earlier, with the advent of the historical-critical methods. Critics argued that, apart from questions of belief, the Bible must be examined as a historical document.

7. Ieuan Ellis examines the influence of German theology on the contributors in *Seven against Christ: A Study of Essays and Reviews* (Leiden: E. J. Brill, 1980). See also the introduction to *Essays and Reviews: The 1860 Text and Its Reading*, ed. Victor Shea and William Whitla (Charlottesville: University of Virginia Press, 2000).

8. Frederick Temple, "The Education of the World," in *Essays and Reviews,* 162.

9. Peter Hinchcliffe provides a good account of Jowett's thought in *Benjamin Jowett and the Christian Religion* (Oxford: Clarendon Press, 1987).

Jowett was to become a close friend of George Eliot's, and at the same period, headmaster of Balliol, Wilde's college at Oxford. Carlyle was very unsympathetic toward *Essays and Reviews,* denouncing the authors as atheists and dishonest.

10. Benjamin Jowett, "On the Interpretation of Scripture," in *Essays and Reviews,* 505. This essay hereafter cited in text by page number.

11. *The Letters of Matthew Arnold,* ed. Cecil Y. Lang, 6 vols. (Charlottesville: University of Virginia Press, 1996–), 3:404.

12. John Tulloch, D. D., *Leaders of the Reformation* (Edinburgh: William Blackwood and Sons, 1859), 170.

13. See Nicholas Lash, *Newman on Development* (Shepardstown, WV: Patmos Press, 1975). John Coulsen, *Newman and the Common Tradition: A Study in the Language of Church and Society* (Oxford: Clarendon Press, 1970) and Mark Pattison, *The Great Dissent* (Oxford: Oxford University Press, 1991) are good general studies of Newman's thought. Pattison, a literary critic, focuses on Newman's theories of language and truth; Lash and Coulsen are theologians with an interest in Newman's hermeneutic. Peter Jost's *Rhetorical Thought in John Henry Newman* (Columbia: University of South Carolina Press, 1989) connects Newman's rhetorical theory to contemporary literary theory. See also David Nicholls and Fergus Kerr, eds., *John Henry Newman: Reason, Rhetoric, and Romanticism* (Carbondale: Southern Illinois University Press, 1991), and Frank M. Turner, *John Henry Newman* (New Haven: Yale University Press, 2002).

14. Like many of the other writers discussed in this book, Newman does not confine his interest in hermeneutics to textual exegesis, and his skepticism about understanding is echoed in his theories of knowledge and belief. His epistemology is fundamentally interpretive, a version of the hermeneutic circle; we move back and forth between beliefs and the reasoning that we use to test those beliefs.

15. Valentine Cunningham, "Dangerous Conceits or Confirmations Strong?" in *Reason, Rhetoric, and Romanticism,* 233.

16. Charles Kingsley, "Review of Froude's *History of England,*" *Macmillans's Magazine,* vii–viii (Jan. 1864), reprinted in "Supplementary Material" to John Henry Newman, *Apologia Pro Vita Sua* (New York: Longmans, Green, 1947), 358. This edition, including supplementary material, hereafter cited as *Apologia.*

17. John Henry Newman, "Lying and Equivocation," in *Apologia,* 314–15.

18. John Henry Cardinal Newman, *An Essay on the Development of Christian Doctrine,* in *Conscience, Consensus, and the Development of Doctrine,* ed. James Gaffney (1878; New York: Doubleday, 1992), 395. Hereafter cited as *Essay on Development.*

19. Peterson argues that the exegetical mode Newman applies to his life in the *Apologia* is derived from ecclesiastical history (*Victorian Autobiography,* 93–119). In consciously departing from the commonly used typological structuring of spiritual autobiography, Newman acknowledges the hermeneutical nature of the enterprise of biography.

20. Paul G. Crowley connects Newman with Gadamer's theory of interpretation in "Catholicity, Inculturation, and Newman's *Sensus Fidelium,*" *Heythrop Journal* 33:2 (1992): 161–74, as does Jost in *Rhetorical Thought in John Henry Newman.* See also Thomas K. Carr, *Newman and Gadamer: Toward a Hermeneutics of Religious Knowledge* (Lanham, MD: American Academy of Religion, 1996).

21. John Henry Newman, "Apostolical Tradition," in *Essays Critical and Historical* (London: Longmans, Green, 1880), 1:110.

22. John Henry Newman, *Fifteen Sermons Preached before the University of Oxford* (London: Rivingtons, 1880), 191.

23. Sometimes Newman suggests that development is teleological; an idea may over time reach its complete expression. There is some confusion in his thought on this point, however, for elsewhere he suggests that such completion is impossible, given the nature of the human mind and its inability to see from other than limited points of view.

24. *Fifteen Sermons,* 84–85.

25. In *The Idea of a University* (London: Oxford University Press, 1976), however, discussing an individual writer's style, Newman contradicts himself: "I have exposed the unphilosophical notion, that the language was an extra which could be dispensed with, and provided to order according to demand" (239). Newman here argues that "thought and speech are inseparable from each other. Matter and expression are parts of one: style is a thinking out into language" (232).

26. John Henry Newman, *An Essay in Aid of a Grammar of Assent* (Oxford: Clarendon Press, 1985), 28.

27. In his discussion of literature in *The Idea,* however, he describes readers gaining access neither to underlying ideas nor to their own experiences. He instead suggests that we receive the author's subjective view, "the faithful expression of his intense personality" (232). This vacillation between impressionist and expressionist theories of meaning will play a central role in Wilde's thought as well.

28. Walter Pater, *Plato and Platonism* (New York: Macmillan, 1907), 151.

29. A. P. Stanley, in his 1865 article "Theology of the Nineteenth Century," points to the significance of "the whole principle of the *development* of doctrine, whether in or out of the Bible." "But of what importance has it become in every field of religious and philosophical thought," he writes. "Condemn or approve Dr. Newman's Essay on that subject, it is a proof how deeply the idea has penetrated into spheres apparently the most jealously guarded from the intrusion of novelty" (258). *Fraser's Magazine* 71 (Feb. 1865), 258.

30. Oscar Wilde, "The Critic as Artist," in *Complete Works of Oscar Wilde* (New York: Harper and Row, 1989), 1058.

31. Ian G. Barbour surveys various modes of reconciling theology and evolution in his excellent chapter on "Biology and Theology in the Nineteenth Century" in *Issues in Science and Religion* (Englewood Cliffs, NJ: Prentice-Hall, 1966). John Kent, *From Darwin to Blatchford: The Role of Darwinism in Christian Apologetic 1875–1910* (London: Dr. Williams's Trust, 1966) provides a good overview of the acceptance of evolution by Christians in Britain at the end of the century. Other useful accounts include Frederick Gregory, "The Impact of Darwinian Evolution on Protestant Theology in the Nineteenth Century," in *God and Nature,* ed. Donald C. Lindberg and Ronald L. Numbers (Berkeley: University of California Press, 1986); James R. Moore, *The Post-Darwinian Controversies: A Study of the Protestant Struggles to Come to Terms with Darwin in*

Great Britain and America, 1870–1900 (Cambridge: Cambridge University Press, 1979); Gregory Parviz Elder, *Chronic Vigour: Evolution, Biblical Criticism, and English Theology* (Lanham, MD: University Press of America, 1996); and David N. Livingston, *Darwin's Forgotten Defenders: The Encounter between Evangelical Theology and Evolutionary Thought* (Grand Rapids, MI: W. B. Eerdmans, 1987). For pre-Darwinian attempts to reconcile the scriptural accounts of creation with scientific findings see Charles Coulston Gillispie, *Genesis and Geology* (Cambridge: Harvard University Press, 1951).

32. Thomas Arnold, "On the Right Interpretation and Understanding of the Scriptures," in Drury, *Critics of the Bible,* 127–28.

33. F. D. Maurice, *The Epistle to the Hebrews* (London: John W. Parker, 1846), xliii.

34. H. P. Liddon, *Some Elements of Religion* (London: Longmans, Green, 1872).

35. A. F. Kirkpatrick, "The Claims of Criticism upon the Clergy and Laity" in *The Higher Criticism: Four Papers by S. R. Driver and A. F. Kirkpatrick,* new ed. (London: Hodey and Stoughton, 1912), 11.

36. W. Robertson Smith, *The Old Testament in the Jewish Church* (London: Adam and Charles Black, 1892), 99.

37. F. H. Johnson, "Reason and Revelation," *Andover Review* 5, no. 27 (March 1886): 240.

38. W. J. Mewman Williams, *Pascal, Loisy, and the Catholic Church* (London: Francis Griffiths, 1906), 198.

39. Frank Hugh Foster, "Evolution and the Evangelical System of Doctrine," *Biblio Sacra* 50 (July 1893): 420–21.

40. The Bampton lectures were given yearly throughout the century. They are now considered to be a good indication of the tendencies of religious thought at the time. Farrar was a friend of Jowett's and it is likely that his lectures were a response to Jowett's call for a history of interpretation in "On the Interpretation of Scripture."

41. Frederic W. Farrar, *History of Interpretation* (New York: E. P. Dutton, 1886), xxvi.

42. Henry Morton, "The Cosmogony of Genesis," *Biblio Sacra* 54 (April 1897), 285.

43. Friedrich Nietzsche, *The Dawn,* in *The Portable Nietzsche,* trans. and ed. Walter Kaufmann (New York: Viking Penguin, 1982), 84.

44. Ludwig Feuerbach, *The Essence of Christianity,* trans. George Eliot (New York: Harper & Brothers, 1957), 212.

45. Quoted in Cameron, *Biblical Higher Criticism,* 299.

46. George Eliot, *Middlemarch* (Boston: Houghton Mifflin, 1956), 18.

47. James Bannerham, quoted in Nicholas R. Needham, *Scripture in the Free Church Fathers* (Edinburgh: Rutherford House Books, 1991), 577.

48. W. Robertson Smith, *Lectures and Essays* (London: Adam and Charles Black, 1912), 157.

49. J. A. Biddle, "The New Theology," *Bibliotecha Sacra* 54 (Jan. 1897): 104, 100.

50. Milton S. Terry, *Biblical Hermeneutics* (1883; Grand Rapids, MI: Zondervan, 1979), 545–46.

51. Although Arnold read much German theology, he argued that his influences were primarily English theologians, foremost his father; he also greatly admired Spinoza. Arnold commented: "It makes me rather angry to be affiliated to German Biblical critics; I have had to read masses of them, and they would have drowned me if it had not been for the corks I had brought from the study of Spinoza." Matthew Arnold, *Literature and Dogma,* in *The Complete Prose Works of Matthew Arnold,* ed. R. H. Super (Ann Arbor: University of Michigan Press, 1960–72), 6:455. Hereafter cited as *CPW.*

52. Donald David Stone sees affinities between Arnold's and Gadamer's views on tradition and interpretation in *Communications with the Future: Matthew Arnold in Dialogue* (Ann Arbor: University of Michigan Press, 1997). See also James Livingston, *Matthew Arnold and Christianity* (Columbia: University of South Carolina Press, 1986).

53. Ruth apRoberts, in her excellent *Arnold and God* (Berkeley: University of California Press, 1983), argues that Arnold's biblical criticism is his finest and most fully developed literary criticism.

54. Philip Appleman argues that Pater's criticism was importantly shaped by Darwin's thought. "Darwin, Pater, and a Crisis in Criticism," in *1859: Entering an Age of Crisis*, ed. Philip Appleman, William A. Madden, and Michael Wolff (Bloomington: Indiana University Press, 1961), 81–95.

55. Oscar Wilde, *Complete Works of Oscar Wilde* (New York: Harper and Row, 1989), 1031.

56. Jacques Derrida, *Of Grammatology*, trans. Gayatri Spivak (Baltimore: Johns Hopkins University Press, 1976), 15.

57. Oscar Wilde, *Complete Works*, 1200.

Intertext 1. Victorian Legal Interpretation

1. Charles Dickens, *Bleak House* (New York: Penguin Books, 1996), 78.

2. See James A. Colaiaco, *James Fitzjames Stephen and the Crisis of Victorian Thought* (New York: St. Martin's Press, 1983) for a general discussion of Stephen.

3. James Fitzjames Stephen, *The Defense of the Reverend Rowland Williams, D.D., in the Arches Court of Canterbury* (London: Smith, Elder, 1862), 37. The book includes Stephen's account of his defense along with a transcript of the case. Hereafter cited in the text.

4. The *Cardoza Law Review* 16.6 (April 1995) is devoted to Lieber's work. See also John Catalano, *Francis Lieber: Hermeneutics and Practical Reason* (Lanham, MD: University Press of America, 2000).

5. Francis Lieber, *Legal and Political Hermeneutics; or, Principles of Interpretation and Construction in Law and Politics* (Boston: Charles C. Little and James Brown, 1839), 1. Further citations to this work are given in the text.

6. "Acts of Parliament are venerable; but if they correspond not with the writing on the 'Adamant Tablet,' what are they?" Thomas Carlyle, *Works*, Centenary Edition, ed. H. D. Traill, 30 vols. (London: Chapman and Hall, 1896–99), 10:9.

7. See H. L. A. Hart's overview of legal positivism in "Positivism, Law, and Morals," in *Essays in Jurisprudence and Philosophy* (Oxford: Oxford University Press, 1983): 49–87.

8. John Austin, *Lectures on Jurisprudence or The Philosophy of Positive Law*, 4th ed., rev. and ed. Robert Campbell (London: John Murray, 1879), 2:1026.

9. Sir Peter Benson Maxwell, *On the Interpretation of Statutes* (London: William Maxwell and Son, 1875), 3.

10. Sir Frederick Pollock, *A First Book of Jurisprudence for Students of the Common Law*, 6th ed. (1896; London: Macmillan, 1929), 240.

11. Sheldon Amos, *The Science of Law* (New York: D. Appleton, 1875; reprint, Littleton: Fred B. Rothman, 1982), 60.

12. John Salmond, *Jurisprudence*, 7th ed. (London: Sweet and Maxwell, 1924), 182.

13. See Sanford Levinson and Steven Mailloux, *Interpreting Law and Literature: A Hermeneutic Reader* (Evanston, IL: Northwestern University Press, 1988), and Richard A. Posner, *The Problems of Jurisprudence* (Cambridge: Harvard University Press, 1990).

14. Hans-Georg Gadamer, *Truth and Method,* 2nd ed., trans Joel Weinsheimer and Donald G. Marshall (New York: Crossroad, 1990), 324–30.

2. Carlyle

1. Wilhelm Dilthey, "*Sartor Resartus:* Philosophical Conflict, Positive and Negative Eras, and Personal Resolution," trans. Murray Baumgarten and Evelyn Kanes, *CLIO* 1.3 (1972): 59. Dilthey's main point in his essay is to place Carlyle in the transcendental movement; he argues that a detailed study of Carlyle's connection to German idealism is needed. Interestingly, Dilthey's criticisms of James Froude's biography sound surprisingly like the Editor's complaints about Teufelsdroeckh's autobiographical fragments in *Sartor.*

2. There are a number of studies that trace out the details of influence. The three general ones are C. F. Harrold, *Carlyle and German Thought: 1819–1834* (New Haven: Yale University Press, 1934); Rosemary Ashton, *The German Idea 1800–1860* (Cambridge: Cambridge University Press, 1980); and Elizabeth M. Vida, *Romantic Affinities: German Authors and Carlyle* (Toronto: University of Toronto Press, 1993). Studies concentrating on the connections between Carlyle and a single author include J. Douglas Rabb, who argues that Carlyle's primary influence is Fichte in "The Silence of Thomas Carlyle," *English Language Notes* 26.3 (March 1989): 70–81, and Richard W. Hannah, "Novalis, Carlyle and the Metaphysics of Semiosis," *Houston German Studies* 5 (1984): 27–41.

3. Although virtually every critic concedes the importance of his Calvinism, there has been only a single article devoted to establishing specific Calvinist influences in Carlyle's thought, this by C. F. Harrold in 1936. "The Nature of Carlyle's Calvinism," *Studies in Philology* 33 (July 1936): 475–86.

4. Thomas Carlyle, *Works,* Centenary Edition, ed. H. D. Traill, 30 vols. (London: Chapman and Hall, 1896–99), 27:25. Further references cited by volume and page in the text.

5. Thomas Carlyle, *Two Notebooks of Thomas Carlyle,* ed. Charles Eliot Norton (New York: Grolier Club, 1898), 211. Further references cited in the text as *Notebooks.*

6. Harrold writes: "In his handling of German ideas Carlyle touched nothing that he did not alter. From first to last, he was the born Calvinist, seeking to reconstruct, largely from German thought, a belief in the transcendent sovereignty of Right and in a world of immanent divine law." *Carlyle and German Thought,* 235.

Several critics have argued that to see Carlyle as reconciling German thought with the still potent influences of his Calvinist upbringing is unnecessarily reductionist. Eloise M. Behnken believes that Carlyle makes a radical break from Calvinism in *Thomas Carlyle: "Calvinist without the Theology"* (Columbia: University of Missouri Press, 1978). Froude does stress Carlyle's Calvinist roots, famously claiming that Carlyle "was a Calvinist without the theology." James Anthony Froude, *Life of Carlyle,* ed. John Clubbe (1882; Columbus: Ohio State University Press, 1979), 220. Carlyle himself acknowledged the potency of his Calvinism, even at the height of his German period.

7. Friedrich Schleiermacher, selections from *Hermeneutics: The Handwritten Manuscripts by F. D. E. Schleiermacher,* ed. Heinz Kimmerle, trans. James Duke and Jack Forstman (Missoula, MT: Scholars Press, 1977).

8. There is no definitive evidence that Carlyle read Calvin, although he would have encountered his writing in some form in the Burgher meetings of his youth and found his ideas expressed in the *Confession of Faith,* the Catechisms, and in John Knox's works. See Fred Kaplan, *Thomas Carlyle: A Biography* (Ithaca: Cornell University Press, 1983) on the Carlyle family's religious reading.

9. Richard C. Gamble, ed., *Calvin and Hermeneutics* (New York: Garland, 1992) gathers a number of essays on Calvin's exegetical views.

10. John Calvin, *Institutes of the Christian Religion,* trans. Ford Lewis Battles, in *The Library of Christian Classics,* ed. John T. McNeill (Philadelphia: Westminster Press, 1960), I.xvii.1. Hereafter cited as *Institutes.*

11. Quoted in Rev. T. H. L. Parker, "Calvin's Concept of Revelation," in *Calvin and Hermeneutics,* 342.

12. Quoted in Richard C. Gamble, "Exposition and Method in Calvin," in *Calvin and Hermeneutics,* 61.

13. Calvin vehemently insists that the Bible is the only means of understanding the divine: "Those who, having forsaken Scripture, imagine some way or other of reaching God, ought to be thought of as not so much gripped by error as carried away with frenzy" (*Institutes* I.ix.1).

14. *The Collected Letters of Thomas and Jane Welsh Carlyle,* ed. C. R. Sanders (Durham, NC: Duke University Press, 1970–), 12:165.

15. Useful approaches to Carlyle's views on language include Wayne C. Anderson, "The Rhetoric of Silence in the Discourse of Coleridge and Carlyle," *South Atlantic Review* 49, no. 1 (Jan. 1984): 72–90; Chris R. Vanden Bossche, "Revolution and Authority: The Metaphors of Language and Carlyle's Style," *Prose Studies* 6.3 (1983): 274–89; Christine Persak, "Rhetoric in Praise of Silence: The Ideology of Carlyle's Paradox," *Rhetoric Society Quarterly* 21 (Winter 1991): 38–52; John Holloway, *The Victorian Sage: Studies in Argument* (New York: St. Martin's Press, 1953); and G. B. Tennyson, *Sartor Called Resartus: The Genesis, Structure, and Style of Thomas Carlyle's First Major Work* (Princeton: Princeton University Press, 1965).

16. Paul Ricoeur also argues that human action can be interpreted in accordance with the model of textual exegesis. See "The Model of the Text: Meaningful Action Considered as Text," in *From Text to Action,* trans. Kathleen Blamey and John B. Thompson (Evanston: Northwestern University Press, 1991), 144–67.

17. Calvin refers to God as the author of the world, although he maintains we are unable to read his signs. In one sense, Carlyle elaborates on an idea suggested in Calvinism, but he also overturns the basic tenet that because God can be known only through the Bible, the study of Scripture should be the central activity in life.

Carlyle would have encountered similar ideas in Augustine, and Sir Thomas Browne, whom Carlyle admired, speaks of nature as "that universal and public manuscript that lies expansed unto the eyes of all." *Religio Medici* (Oxford: Clarendon Press, 1972), 16–17.

18. Carlyle's fragments from 1852 included in Froude's *Life of Carlyle,* 224. Froude claims that the fragments from which this quote is taken "are the key to Carlyle's mind" (226).

19. John P. McGowan argues that Carlyle, like many Victorian thinkers, "oscillates between his strong desire for direct, unmediated, and intuitive knowledge of the real

and his understanding that such revelation is impossible." For Carlyle, representations change, but not reality. *Representation and Revelation: Victorian Realism from Carlyle to Yeats* (Columbia: University of Missouri Press, 1986), 51.

20. Peter Allan Dale discusses "the pressures toward a complete historicism in which one dispenses with the saving notion of a permanent Idea behind the flux of changing beliefs" in Carlyle's work. *The Victorian Critic and the Idea of History* (Cambridge: Harvard University Press, 1977), 58.

21. See Marc Cumming's thorough discussion of Carlyle's views on reading in *A Disimprisoned Epic: Form and Vision in Carlyle's French Revolution* (Philadelphia: University of Pennsylvania Press, 1988).

22. See Gerald Bruns's comments on *Sartor Resartus* in his fine article "The Formal Nature of Victorian Thinking," *PMLA* 90 (1975): 904–18.

23. Schleiermacher says the same, writing of the divinatory aspect of interpretation: "The goal of technical interpretation can only be approximated." *Hermeneutics: The Handwritten Manuscripts*, 149.

24. Peter Allan Dale concludes that Carlyle's interest, despite his alleged belief in the absolute, really lies in changing cultural phenomena. "*Sartor Resartus* and the Inverse Sublime," in Morton W. Bloomfield, ed. *Allegory, Myth, and Symbol* (Cambridge: Harvard University Press, 1981): 293–312. Like Dale, Janice L. Haney believes that ultimately the historical and social take precedence over the absolute in Carlyle's thought. "'Shadow-Hunting': Romantic Irony, *Sartor Resartus*, and Victorian Romanticism," *Studies in Romanticism* 17 (Summer 1978): 307–33.

For other treatments of *Sartor* and interpretation, see Jonathan Loesberg, *Fictions of Consciousness: Mill, Newman, and the Reading of Victorian Prose* (New Brunswick, NJ: Rutgers University Press, 1986); J. Hillis Miller, "'Hieroglyphic Truth' in *Sartor Resartus:* Carlyle and the Language of Parable," in *Victorian Perspectives*, ed. John Clubbe and Jerome Meckier (Newark: University of Delaware Press, 1989), 1–20; and Anne K. Mellor, "Carlyle's *Sartor Resartus:* A Self-Consuming Artifact," in *English Romantic Irony* (Cambridge: Harvard University Press, 1980), 109–34.

25. Thomas Carlyle, *Reminiscences*, ed. James Anthony Froude (New York: Charles Scribner's Sons, 1881), 125. Compare *Santor*, where Carlyle writes of jottings "in indelible sympathetic-ink by an invisible interior penman" (I:61).

26. On Carlyle's historical methods, see Lee C. R. Baker, "The Diamond Necklace and the Golden Ring: Historical Imagination in Carlyle and Browning," *Victorian Poetry* 21.1 (Spring 1986): 31–36; Beverly Taylor, "Carlyle's Historical Imagination: Untrue Facts and Unfactual Truths," *Victorian Newsletter* 81 (Spring 1982): 29–31; Clyde de L. Ryals, "Carlyle's *The French Revolution:* A 'True Fiction,'" *ELH* 54:4 (Winter 1987): 925–40; G. Robert Stange, "Refractions of *Past and Present*" in *Carlyle Past and Present*, ed. K. J. Fielding and Roger L. Tarr (New York: Barnes and Noble, 1976), 98–111; and John M. Ulrich, *Signs of Their Times* (Athens: Ohio University Press, 2002). Several critics have seen Carlyle's histories, particularly *The French Revolution*, as relying on typology. See especially John D. Rosenberg, *Carlyle and the Burden of History* (Oxford: Clarendon Press, 1985). See A. Dwight Culler, *The Victorian Mirror of History* (New Haven: Yale University Press, 1985), 39–73, and Rosemary Jann, *The Art and Science of Victorian History* (Columbus: Ohio State University Press, 1985), 33–65, for general accounts of Carlyle's historiography and its relation to nineteenth-century history.

27. Gordon Hirsch argues that Carlyle believes we can understand the past only in its relation to the present in "History Writing in Carlyle's *Past and Present*," *Prose Studies* 7.3 (1984): 225–31.

28. Joseph W. Childers links Carlyle's views with "our modern concept of philosophical hermeneutics" (249), comparing his thought to Gadamer's and Ricoeur's. "Carlyle's *Past and Present*, History, and a Question of Hermeneutics," *CLIO* 13.3 (1984): 247–58. Childers's comparison is persuasive insofar as Carlyle believes that we cannot escape our historical viewpoints to know history as it actually occurred; in this he is in agreement with Gadamer and quite opposed to some of the main currents of nineteenth-century historiography. But for Gadamer tradition is an actual part of an event's meaning, not a way of pointing to an objective underlying meaning.

29. Dilthey notes a similarity between some of Carlyle's ideas and Humboldt's and claims that "through Novalis, Schleiermacher exerted a considerable influence on" Carlyle's concept of symbols. "*Sartor Resartus:* Philosophical Conflict," 56.

30. Hayden White has been among the most influential historians in arguing against the epistemological authority of historiography. See *The Content of the Form* (Baltimore: Johns Hopkins University Press, 1987), 74.

31. Roland Barthes, "The Reality Effect," in *The Rustle of Language*, trans. Richard Howard (New York: Hill and Wang, 1986), 140.

32. See Ann Rigney's fine discussion of Carlyle on the representation of the past in "The Untenanted Places of the Past: Carlyle and the Varieties of Historical Ignorance," *History and Theory* 35.3 (1990): 338–57.

33. John Rosenberg claims that "the historian's art for Carlyle consists in making the vanished past visibly present by evoking its absence." *Carlyle and the Burden*, 127.

34. Walter Pater, *Studies in the History of the Renaissance* (London: MacMillan, 1873), 22.

35. See, for instance, F. R. Ankersmit's poststructuralist historiography in *History and Tropology* (Berkeley: University of California Press, 1994)

36. Wilhelm von Humboldt, "On the Task of the Historian" in Kurt Mueller Vollmer, ed. *The Hermeneutics Reader: Texts of the German Tradition from the Enlightenment to the Present* (New York: Continuum, 1988), 115.

37. Johann Gustav Droysen, "History and the Historical Method," in *The Hermeneutics Reader*, 120.

38. René Wellek criticizes Carlyle for interpreting according to a set of predetermined moral principles "which are not derived from history itself and which prevent him from judging the individuality of a man or time by its own inherent criteria." He protests that when Carlyle "seems to apply a metaphysical criterion of reality versus illusion, he is also applying a thinly disguised ethical judgment." "Carlyle and the Philosophy of History," *Philological Quarterly* 23.1 (1944): 70.

INTERTEXT 2. VICTORIAN SCIENCE AND HERMENEUTICS

1. Thomas Carlyle, *Works*, Centenary Edition, ed. H. D. Traill, 30 vols. (London: Chapman and Hall, 1896–99), 5:82.

2. Frank Turner suggests that the views of later scientific naturalists, for instance, Spencer's doctrine of the Unknowable and Tyndall's ideas on mystery, are influenced

by Carlyle's Natural Supernaturalism in "Victorian Scientific Naturalism and Thomas Carlyle," *Victorian Studies* 18:2 (1975): 325–43.

3. Lorraine Daston and Peter Galison, "The Image of Objectivity," *Representations* 40 (Fall 1992): 84. Daston and Galison limit their analysis to scientific image making in anatomical atlases, rather than present a general account of science in the Victorian age, although they assert that "mechanical objectivity can be found in almost every scientific endeavor" (84). They are careful to emphasize that they are treating only one conception of scientific objectivity. See also Peter Galison, "Judgment against Objectivity," in *Picturing Science, Producing Art,* ed. Peter Galison and Caroline Jones (New York: Routledge, 1998), 327–59.

4. Christopher Herbert warns against taking this view as a monolithic account of Victorian science in *Victorian Relativity* (Chicago: University of Chicago Press, 2001). Herbert argues that the recognition of the conditioned nature of knowledge by the Victorians resulted in a Victorian relativity movement linked with antiauthoritarian politics.

5. George Levine traces the ideal of self-annihilation in Victorian epistemology in *Dying to Know: Scientific Epistemology and Narrative in Victorian England* (Chicago: University of Chicago Press, 2002).

6. Richard Bernstein maintains that the claims that Kuhn made about science (primarily related to the rejection of the dichotomy between observation and theory) are "consonant with those that have been at the very heart of hermeneutics" since the nineteenth century. *Beyond Objectivism and Relativism: Science, Hermeneutics, and Praxis* (Philadelphia: University of Pennsylvania Press, 1991), 31. Dimitri Ginev identifies a number of topics in current hermeneutic approaches to science, ranging from the theory ladenness of observation to the social and cultural organization of knowledge in *A Passage to the Hermeneutic Philosophy of Science* (Amsterdam: Rodopi, 1997).

7. A number of historians of science have suggested that that tradition was less common, at least in practice, than it has been taken to be. Susan Cannon, for example, writes: "Far from being a period of 'Baconian' influence, the second quarter of the 19th century was the period when Idealism had its strongest impact on British science." *Science in Culture* (New York: Science History Publications, 1978), 229.

8. Benjamin Jowett, "On the Interpretation of Scripture," *Essays and Reviews: The 1860 Text and Its Reading,* ed. Victor Shea and William Whitla (Charlottesville: University of Virginia Press, 2000), 484.

9. Henry Jones, *Browning as Philosophical Thinker* (New York: Macmillan, 1891), 40.

10. Benson examines Victorian science that dissented from the Baconian view that the scientist gathered mind-independent, objective facts through observation, and that instead acknowledged that the mind and imagination played essential roles in constructing scientific knowledge. Donald R. Benson, "Facts and Constructs: Victorian Humanists and Scientific Theorists on Scientific Knowledge," in *Victorian Science and Victorian Values: Literary Perspectives,* ed. James Paradis and Thomas Postlewait (New Brunswick, NJ: Rutgers University Press, 1985): 299–318. Jonathan Smith discusses the movement away from Baconian inductive method to the hypothetico-deductive method in the Victorian period, arguing that "'the scientific use of the imagination'" "brings scientific method into close accord with the methods of the literary imagination." *Fact and Feeling* (Madison: University of Wisconsin Press, 1994), 8. See also Maurice Mandelbaum, who says that by the end of the century scientists came to stress "the creative, constructive aspects of scientific imagination in the formulation of hypotheses

and models." *History, Man, & Reason: A Study in Nineteenth-Century Thought* (Baltimore: Johns Hopkins University Press, 1971), 19.

11. Helmholtz conceives of visual perception as comparable to the "signs of language" (314). Often, he says, "there is no correspondence at all between sensations and their object" (316). We are within a "system of signs," and "search after the meaning of sensible Images and Signs" (316). "The Recent Progress of the Theory of Vision," in *Popular Lectures on Scientific Subjects* (London: Longmans, Green, 1873), 197–316. Herbert Spencer similarly argues that visual perceptions are "merely symbols" and that we "conceive as objects what are only signs of objects." *First Principles* (1862; New York: A. L. Burt, 1880), 137.

12. See Richard Yeo's excellent account of Whewell in the context of Victorian debates on science in *Defining Science: William Whewell, Natural Knowledge, and Public Debate in Early Victorian Britain* (Cambridge: Cambridge University Press, 1993). See also E. W. Strong, "William Whewell and John Stuart Mill: Their Controversy about Scientific Knowledge," *Journal of the History of Ideas* 16.2 (April 1995): 209–31.

13. Robert E. Butts, "Whewell's Logic of Induction," in *Foundations of Scientific Method: The Nineteenth Century*, ed. Ronald N. Giere and Richard S. Westfall (Bloomington: Indiana University Press, 1973), 55.

14. William Whewell, *The Philosophy of the Inductive Sciences, Founded upon Their History*, 2 vols. (London: John W. Parker, 1847), 1:54. Hereafter cited as PI in the text.

15. William Whewell, *History of the Inductive Sciences: From the Earliest to the Present Time*, 3rd ed., 2 vols. (New York: D. Appleton, 1858), 1:43.

16. F. H. Bradley, *The Presuppositions of Critical History* (Don Mills, ON: J. M. Dent, 1968).

17. Friedrich Nietzsche, *The Will to Power*, trans. Walter Kaufmann and R. J. Hollingdale (New York: Viking Penguin, 1982), 481.

18. William B. Carpenter, "Man the Interpreter of Nature," in *Victorian Science: A Self Portrait from the Presidential Addresses of the British Association of the Advancement of Science*, ed. George Basalla, William Coleman, and Robert Kargon (New York: Anchor Books, 1970), 417.

19. J. C. Shairp, *The Poetic Interpretation of Nature* (Boston: H. O. Houghton, 1877).

20. See Peter Allan Dale's account of positivism's relation to aesthetics in *In Pursuit of a Scientific Culture* (Madison: University of Wisconsin Press, 1989).

21. Karl Pearson, *The Grammar of Science*, part 1, 3rd ed. (1892; London: Adam and Charles Black, 1911), 35.

22. Laurens Lauden argues that the view that science offers not certain knowledge, but instead approximations that progressively move closer to truth, was pervasive in the nineteenth century. "Peirce and the Trivialization of the Self-Correcting Thesis," in *Foundations of Scientific Method*, 275–306.

23. J. H. Tufts, "Can Epistemology Be Based on Mental States?" *Philosophical Review* 6.6 (Nov. 1897), 580.

24. George Henry Lewes, *Problems of Life and Mind: The Foundations of a Creed*, 1st series (Boston: James R. Osgood, 1874), 1:83.

3. GEORGE ELIOT'S HERMENEUTICS OF SYMPATHY

1. George Eliot, *Middlemarch* (New York: Oxford, 1996), 261.

2. J. Hillis Miller, "Optic and Semiotic in *Middlemarch*," in *The Worlds of Victorian Fiction, Harvard English Studies* 6 (Cambridge: Harvard University Press, 1975), 143.

3. See also "Narrative and History" in which Miller argues that for Eliot, "the only origin is an act of interpretation, that is, an act of the will to power imposed on a prior 'text.'" J. Hillis Miller, "Narrative and History," *ELH* 41 (1974): 468.

4. Daniel Cottom, *Social Figures* (Minneapolis: University of Minnesota Press, 1987), 112. See also K. M. Newton who sees Eliot moving toward "Nietzschean subversive thought." *George Eliot: Romantic Humanist* (Totowa, NJ: Barnes and Noble, 1981), 144.

5. It is not any surprise to see that Eliot puts great emphasis on sympathetic responsiveness to others. But I am trying to win this ground back from recent critics who argue that Eliot's emphasis on sympathy is undermined by other aspects of her text. An earlier account of Eliot's views on sympathy is found in Bernard Paris' *Experiments in Life* (Detroit: Wayne State University Press, 1965). Paris sees the thrust of Eliot's novels to be away from an innate illusory subjectivity toward objectivity via sympathy with others.

6. George Eliot, *Silas Marner* (New York: Penguin, 1967), 101.

7. Friedrich Schleiermacher, *Hermeneutics and Criticism, and Other Writings*, trans. Andrew Bowie (Cambridge: Cambridge University Press, 1998), 92.

8. F. D. E. Schleiermacher, *Confidential Letters on Friedrich Schlegel's Lucinde*, trans. Julie Ellison, in *Delicate Subjects: Romanticism, Gender, and the Ethics of Understanding* (Ithaca, NY: Cornell University Press, 1990), 41.

9. David Carroll, in *George Eliot and the Conflicts of Interpretation* (Cambridge: Cambridge University Press, 1992), asserts that "George Eliot is firmly within the context of mid-nineteenth-century hermeneutics" (xi). The book does not so much situate Eliot within nineteenth-century hermeneutics as ascribe to her a more contemporary view.

10. David Friedrich Strauss, *The Life of Jesus Critically Examined*, 5th ed., trans. George Eliot (London: Swan Sonnenschein, 1906).

11. We know from her letters that Eliot was translating the *Tractatus* in 1849, while she was still in Hennell's circle. It is uncertain whether she completed the translation. Eliot finished her translation of Spinoza's *Ethics* in 1856.

12. Benedict de Spinoza, *Tractatus Theologico-Politicus*, trans. R. H. M. Elwes (1670; London: George Routledge & Sons, 1895), 99.

13. See Berel Lang's analysis of Spinoza's hermeneutic. Lang writes: "It is not only that what now appears as a largely conservative theory of interpretation and meaning was in its original appearance radical—but that certain aspects of what made it radical at the time, beyond its critique of the tradition of Biblical reading, continue to claim that role for it now as well." *The Anatomy of Philosophical Style: Literary Philosophy and the Philosophy of Literature* (Oxford: Blackwell, 1990).

14. Ludwig Feuerbach, *The Essence of Christianity*, trans. George Eliot (New York: Harper & Brothers, 1957), 293. Further citations will appear in the text as *EC*.

15. George Eliot, *Essays of George Eliot*, ed. Thomas Pinney (London: Routledge and Kegan Paul, 1963), 39. Further references cited in the text as *Essays*.

16. George Eliot, *Felix Holt, The Radical* (New York: Penguin, 1972), 573–74.

17. George Levine's "George Eliot's Hypothesis of Reality" (*Nineteenth-Century Fiction* 3.5 [1980]: 1–28) is among the best accounts of Eliot's views on knowledge. A number of critics claim that Eliot rejects the notion of objective truth; see, for instance, Peter K. Garrett, *The Victorian Multiplot Novel: Studies in Dialogical Form* (New Haven: Yale University Press, 1980).

18. Elinor Shaffer argues that "fact" is shown to be only a fiction for Feuerbach, a making objective what we desire to regard as objective, and that Eliot is in agreement with Feuerbach on this. *Kubla Khan and the Fall of Jerusalem: The Mythological School in Biblical Criticism and Secular Literature, 1770–1880* (Cambridge: Cambridge University Press, 1972), 252.

19. *The George Eliot Letters,* ed. Gordon S. Haight, 7 vols. (New Haven: Yale University Press, 1954–55), 2:362. Further references will be cited in the text as *GEL.*

Eliot also concurs with Feuerbach's grounding of morality in the capacity for sympathy. His theory of knowledge is connected to his moral theory. In Feuerbach's view, we must be able to see from others' perspectives in order to verify and correct our own; thus the central importance of the I/thou relationship for Feuerbach. For further discussion of Feuerbach's philosophy see Van Harvey, *Feuerbach and the Interpretation of Religion* (Cambridge: Cambridge University Press, 1995), and Max W. Wartofsky, *Feuerbach* (Cambridge: Cambridge University Press, 1977).

20. For discussion of Lewes see Diana Postlethwaite, *Making it Whole: A Victorian Circle and the Shape of Their World* (Columbus: Ohio State University Press, 1984), and Hock Guan Tjoa, *George Henry Lewes. A Victorian Mind* (Cambridge: Harvard University Press, 1977).

21. G. H. Lewes, *The History of Philosophy from Thales to Comte,* 4th ed., vol. 1 (London: Longmans, Green, 1871), lxv.

22. G. H. Lewes, *Problems of Life and Mind. First series. The Foundation of a Creed* (Boston: Houghton, Osgood, 1874), 68.

23. See T. R. Wright, *The Religion of Humanity: The Impact of Comtean Positivism on Victorian England* (Cambridge: Cambridge University Press, 1986).

24. George Eliot, *Daniel Deronda* (New York: Oxford University Press, 1988), 194. All further references will be cited in the text as *DD.*

25. On Eliot and language see Jonathan Arac, who in "Rhetoric and Realism in Nineteenth-Century Fiction: Hyperbole in *The Mill on the Floss*" argues that the novel stages "an active clash between the hope of a fitting language and the recognition that language is never at one with reality" (80). Colin McCabe in "The End of Metalanguage: From George Eliot to *Dubliners,*" on the other hand, claims that Eliot fails to "problematize the relation between language and reality" (156). Both essays are in K. M. Newton, ed., *George Eliot* (London: Longman, 1991).

26. Sally Shuttleworth, for example, argues that Comte influences the realist position, "with its naive view of truth" (1), of *Adam Bede.* By *Daniel Deronda,* Eliot is "attempting to transcend" this "naive theory of signification" (197). *George Eliot and Nineteenth-Century Science* (Cambridge: Cambridge University Press, 1984).

27. Auguste Comte, *System of Positive Polity,* trans. Frederick Harrison (Paris: Carilian-Goery & Vor. Dalman, 1852), 7:214. All further references cited in the text as *System.*

28. George Eliot in K. K. Collins, "Questions of Method: Some Unpublished Late Essays," *Nineteenth-Century Fiction* 35.3 (December 1980): 385–405.

29. See, for example, Felicia Bonaparte, *Will and Destiny* (New York: New York University Press, 1975). In contrast, see K. K. Collins' account in "G. H. Lewes Revised: George Eliot and the Moral Sense," *Victorian Studies* 32 (1978): 465–92. Collins argues that the posthumous revisions Eliot makes to Lewes's manuscript of the third part of *Problems of Life and Mind* reveal that she departs from his historical and empiricist account of ethics in order to argue against moral relativism. Needing to establish a more solid ground to support her moral principles, Eliot moves toward an intuitionist account.

30. George Eliot, *Essays and Leaves from a Notebook* (New York: Harper and Brothers, 1884), 275.

31. See Peter Allan Dale's insightful discussions of Comte's and Lewes's moral theories in *In Pursuit of a Scientific Culture: Science, Art, and Society in the Victorian Age* (Madison: University of Wisconsin Press, 1989).

32. George Henry Lewes, *Problems of Life and Mind*, third series (Boston: Houghton, Osgood, 1879), 166.

33. George Eliot, *The Mill on the Floss* (New York: Oxford University Press, 1998), 498

34. Adam Smith, *The Theory of Moral Sentiments* (Indianapolis: Liberty Classics, 1969), 258. There is no evidence, however, that Eliot's theory of sympathy is connected with Smith's in its details. Eliot does not mention Smith anywhere and his views differ markedly from hers, particularly in his emphasis on sympathy's connection to approval. According to Smith, we judge the appropriateness of another's feelings by seeing whether we are able to sympathize with what the person does or feels. Sympathy, then, becomes a mode of judgment.

35. Matthew Arnold, *Last Essays on Church and Religion* (London: Smith, Elder, 1903), 75; G. H. Lewes, *Comte's Philosophy of Science* (London: H. G. Bohn, 1853), 216–17.

36. Stefan Collini examines the widespread use of a conceptual split between altruism and egoism in Victorian intellectual thought after 1850. *Public Moralists: Political Thought and Intellectual Life in Britain, 1850–1930* (Oxford: Oxford University Press, 1993).

37. James Martineau, *Types of Ethical Theory*, 2nd ed. (Oxford: Clarendon Press, 1886), 2:245. By 1916, in fact, these views had become so entrenched that the *New International Encyclopedia* would present them not as theory but as fact: "Later in the development of the human organism, the primitive instinct is reinforced by acquired tendencies which result from continued propinquity, from the entertainment of similar ideals and aspirations, from community of language, customs, etc. . . . Finally, alongside of the fundamental tendency to feel with or for, there develops a particular tendency to feel in the place of another person or thing." *New International Encyclopedia* (Cambridge: Cambridge University Press, 1916), 21:760.

38. *The Works of John Ruskin*, ed. E. T. Cook and Alexander Wedderburn (London: G. Allen, 1903–12), 27:627.

39. Walter Pater, *Appreciations* (Evanston: Northwestern University Press, 1987), 183.

40. *Complete Works of Oscar Wilde* (New York: Harper and Row, 1989), 931.

41. See Friedrich Nietzsche, "Expeditions of an Untimely Man," in *Twilight of the Idols*, trans. R. J. Hollingdale (New York: Penguin, 1968), 35.

42. Thomas Hobbes, *The Elements of Law: Natural and Politic* (New York: Barnes and Noble, 1969), 40.

43. Neil Hertz claims that it becomes impossible to distinguish between understanding and narcissism in *Middlemarch*. "Recognizing Casaubon," *Glyph* 6 (1979): 24–41.

44. Laura Hinton's *Perverse Gaze of Sympathy* (Albany: State University of New York Press, 1999) is representative of this view. She claims that sympathy is a "voyeuristic fetishistic medium" (23) and "that sadomasochistic desire underlies the experience of sympathy" (3).

45. Marc Redfield, *Phantom Formations : Aesthetic Ideology and the Bildungsroman* (Ithaca: Cornell University Press, 1996), 137.

46. Ann Cvetkovich, *Mixed Feelings: Feminism, Mass Culture, and Victorian Sensationalism* (New Brunswick, NJ: Rutgers University Press, 1992), 143.

47. Michael Heyns, *Expulsion and the Nineteenth-century Novel* (Oxford: Clarendon Press, 1999), 181. See also Elizabeth During, who writes that "sympathy acts as an incentive to egoism, rather than its corrective." "The Concept of Dread: Sympathy and Ethics in *Daniel Deronda*," in *Renegotiating Ethics in Literature, Philosophy, and Theory*, ed. Jane Adamson, Richard Freadman, and David Parker (Cambridge: Cambridge University Press, 1998), 77.

48. David Marshall, *The Figure of Theater: Shaftesbury, Defoe, Adam Smith, and George Eliot* (New York: Columbia University Press, 1985), 171. Marshall argues that Smith conceives of sympathy as demanding "a theatrical structure"; that is, it requires a spectacle and a spectator.

49. J. Jeffrey Franklin, *Serious Play* (Philadelphia: University of Pennsylvania Press, 1999), 123.

50. Audre Jaffe, *Scenes of Sympathy* (Ithaca: Cornell University Press, 2000), 11, 7.

51. Leslie Stephen, *The Science of Ethics* (New York: G. P. Putnam's Sons, 1882), 229.

52. Donald Davidson has argued for a Stephen-like form of epistemological triangulation as necessary for knowledge: "Third person knowledge—knowledge of other minds—is . . . essential to all other knowledge" (xvii). See "The Irreducibility of the Concept of the Self," in *Subjective, Intersubjective, Objective* (Oxford: Clarendon Press, 2001), 85–91.

53. Eliot's beliefs on sympathy anticipate recent developments in cognitive science, which also suggests that sympathy may be innate and, significantly, that the human mind has a unique capacity to shift between third- and first-person perspectives. Cognitive scientists John Barresi and Chris Moore argue that humans possess the ability to see their own activities from a third-person perspective and can translate a third-person perception of another into something close to a first-person representation of the other's point of view. John Barresi and Chris Moore, "Intentional Relations and Social Understanding," *Behavioral and Brain Science* 19 (1996): 107–54.

Psychological experiments also suggest that consciously trying to adopt another person's perspective does indeed lead to increased sympathy. See Alvin I. Goldman, "Ethics and Cognitive Science," *Ethics* 103:2 (1993): 337–60; Ezra Stotland, "Exploratory Studies in Empathy," in *Advances in Experimental Social Psychology*, vol. 4, ed. L. Berkowitz (New York: Academic Press, 1969); and Lauren Wispe, *The Psychology of Sympathy* (New York: Plenum, 1991).

54. George Eliot, *Adam Bede* (New York: Signet, 1961), 200.

55. Marshall suggests that the novel demonstrates a fear that the loss of otherness might entail the permanent effacement of self. *The Figure of Theater.*

56. George Eliot, *The Lifted Veil/Brother Jacob* (New York: Oxford University Press, 1999), 17.

57. Terry Eagleton, "Power and Knowledge in 'The Lifted Veil,'" *Literature and History* 9 (1983): 52–61, 56.

58. Max Scheler, *The Nature of Sympathy*, trans. Peter Heath (New Haven: Yale University Press, 1954). Scheler's views on sympathy are remarkably similar to Eliot's. He writes that "it is through fellow-feeling, in both its mutual and unreciprocated forms, that 'other minds in general' . . . are brought home to us, in individual cases as having *a reality equal to our own*. . . . It is precisely *in the act* of fellow-feeling that self-love, self-centered choice, solipsism and egoism are first wholly overcome" (98).

59. George Henry Lewes, *Problems of Life and Mind*, Third series, *The Study of Psychology: Its Object, Scope, and Method* (Boston: Houghton, Osgood, 1879), 492.

60. *Essays and Leaves from a Notebook,* 275.

61. John Stuart Mill, *Utilitarianism* (New York: Oxford University Press, 1998), 64. Mill tempers his view later in the book, writing, in a section that qualifies the demands of impartiality, "no one thinks it unjust to seek one person in preference to another as a friend, connection, or companion" (90).

62. See During, "The Concept of Dread," 82, and Jaffe, *Scenes of Sympathy,* 141.

INTERTEXT 3. VICTORIAN LITERARY CRITICISM

1. See Stanley Rosen, who argues that "we should not be misled by the numerous contemporary references to pagan rhetoric, dialectic, and jurisprudence into supposing that, in the Greco-Roman world, there was a hermeneutical problem analogous to the one that perplexes the heirs to the Judaeo-Christian tradition." "The Limits of Interpretation," in *Literature and the Question of Philosophy,* ed. Anthony J. Cascardi (Baltimore: Johns Hopkins University Press, 1987), 228.

2. Thomas Carlyle, *Works,* Centenary Edition, ed. H. D. Traill, 30 vols. (London: Chapman and Hall, 1896–99), 28:5.

3. George Henry Lewes, "Augustus Wilhelm Schlegel," *Foreign Quarterly Review* 32, no. 9 (1843): 164–79. Reprinted in *Literary Criticism of George Henry Lewes,* ed. Alice R. Kaminsky (Lincoln: University of Nebraska Press, 1964), 28.

4. See Harrison Ross Steeves, *Learned Societies and English Literary Scholarship in Great Britain and the United States* (New York: Columbia University Press, 1913) for a survey of literary societies from the sixteenth through the nineteenth centuries.

5. Victorian Shakespeare studies put forth many eccentric interpretations, some of which received strong support in the second half of the century. Good accounts include Aron Y. Stavisky, *Shakespeare and the Victorians* (Norman: University of Oklahoma Press, 1969); F. E. Halliday, *The Cult of Shakespeare* (London: Gerald Duckworth, 1957); S. Schoenbaum, *Shakespeare's Lives* (Oxford: Clarendon, 1991); and William Benzie, *Dr. F. J. Furnivall: A Victorian Scholar Adventurer* (Norman: Pilgrim Books, 1983).

6. See *The Succession of Shakspere's Works and the Use of Metrical Tests in Settling It* (London: Smith, Elder, 1874). Much of the book consists of passages such as the following: "Note that all the above *Love's Labours Lost* lines have only five measures, or ten syllables, each, and not one weak ending. . . . while in *The Winter's Tale* extract there are four lines with extra syllables (240 having one also before the central pause and three with weak endings, 234, 237, 242)" (xxiv).

7. F. J. Furnivall, *Browning Society Papers,* 3 vols. (London: Trubner, 1881–92), 1884:2. Further citations will be made in the text as *BSP* by year and page number.

8. Quoted in Stavisky, *Shakespeare,* 4.

9. Algernon Swinburne, *A Study of Shakespeare,* in *Prose Works, The Complete Works of Algernon Charles Swinburne,* Bonchurch Ed., ed. Edmund Gosse and Thomas James Wise, 11 vols. (London: William Heinemann, 1925–27), 1:6.

10. F. J. Furnivall, quoted in William S. Peterson, *Interpreting the Oracle: A History of the London Browning Society* (Athens: Ohio University Press, 1969), 10–11.

11. F. J. Furnivall, quoted in Benzie, *Dr. F. J. Furnivall,* 223.

12. Edward Dowden, "The Interpretation of Literature," *Contemporary Review* 49 (May 1886): 701; William Henry Hudson, *Studies in Interpretation* (London: G. P. Putnam's Sons, 1896).

13. John Addington Symonds, *Essays Speculative and Suggestive*, 3rd ed. (1890; London: Smith, Elder, 1907), 69.

14. John Ruskin, "Of King's Treasures." In *Sesames and Lilies* (1864; New York: Chelsea Press, 1983), 30.

15. Odin Dekkers discusses Victorian attempts to formulate scientific principles of criticism in *J. M. Robertson: Rationalist and Literary Critic* (Brookfield, VT: Ashgate, 1998). Dekkers contends that "the fact that literary criticism was and always had been a subjective affair was precisely the reason why these critics of the second half of the nineteenth century concluded that here there was a tremendous task for science to work upon" (95).

16. For accounts of the struggles over English studies in the universities see Stephen Potter, *The Muse in Chains* (London: Jonathan Cape, 1937); D. J. Palmer, *The Rise of English Studies* (London: Oxford University Press, 1965); and John Gross, *The Rise and Fall of the Man of Letters* (New York: Macmillan, 1969). Gross points out that the first professor appointed to fill the English chair was A. S. Napier, "a deeply obscure specialist in German philology" (174). Potter notes that the Oxford opponents of English studies argued that the study of English literature was clearly only a hobby for one's spare time. See also Ian Small's sociologically oriented study of the professionalization and institutionalization of criticism and the concomitant changes in the role of authority in literary studies in the last part of the nineteenth century. *Conditions for Criticism* (Oxford: Oxford University Press, 1991). See also Robert G. McPherson, *Theory of Higher Education in Nineteenth-Century England* (Athens: University of Georgia Press, 1959), and Franklin E. Court, *Institutionalizing English Literature: The Culture and Politics of Literary Study 1750–1900* (Stanford, CA: Stanford University Press, 1992).

17. Referring to I. A. Richards, Michael Hancher writes that "The first sustained efforts in English to formulate a disciplined approach to literary criticism and interpretation arose in reaction to the rhapsodic, impressionistic criticism that many thought had too long survived the end of the nineteenth century" (791). In fact, Moulton was attempting this already in the latter part of the Victorian period. Michael Hancher, "The Science of Interpretation and the Art of Interpretation," *MLN* 85.6 (1970): 791–802.

18. Richard G. Moulton, *Shakespeare as a Dramatic Artist: A Popular Illustration of the Principles of Scientific Criticism*, 3rd ed. (1885; Oxford: Clarendon, 1893), 3.

19. Richard G. Moulton, *The Modern Study of Literature: An Introduction to Literary Theory and Interpretation* (Chicago: University of Chicago Press, 1915), 226.

4. Subjectivism, Intersubjectivity, and Intention

1. *The Complete Letters of Oscar Wilde*, ed. Merlin Holland and Rupert Hart Davis (New York: Henry Holt, 2000), 102. This edition henceforth cited in the text as *Letters*.

2. *The Complete Prose Works of Matthew Arnold*, ed. R. H. Super, 8 vols. (Ann Arbor: University of Michigan Press, 1960–72): 3:261.

3. Walter Pater, *The Renaissance: Studies in Art and Poetry* (London: Macmillan, 1922), viii.

4. Oscar Wilde, "The Critic as Artist," in *Complete Works of Oscar Wilde* (New York: Harper and Row, 1989), 1028. All citations of Wilde's works are from this edition.

5. Wendell V. Harris discusses the influence of Arnold and Pater on Wilde, arguing that Wilde's subjectivist claims about interpretation are (implicitly) founded on a

perspectivist metaphysics. "Arnold, Pater, Wilde, and the Object as in Themselves They See It," *Studies in English Literature, 1500–1900* 11 (1971): 733–47.

6. René Wellek, for example, sees Wilde's theory as inviting "irresponsible subjectivity." *A History of Modern Criticism, 1750–1950: The Later Nineteenth Century* (New Haven: Yale University Press, 1965), 4:414. Bruce Bashford sees Wilde as a precursor of postmodernist criticism. He claims that "Wilde holds a strong or extreme version of [subjectivism]; that is, he does not merely believe that different people see things slightly differently—a weak version: he believes that forms have no existence independent of the individuals who create or perceive them" (218). Bruce Bashford, "Oscar Wilde and Subjectivist Criticism," *ELT* 21.4 (1978): 218.

7. Recent criticism has sometimes read the inconsistencies as an undermining of the values of unity and consistency. Critics who align Wilde's strategies with deconstruction include Jonathan Dollimore, "Different Desires: Subjectivity and Transgression in Wilde and Gide," *Textual Practice* 1:1 (Spring 1987): 46–67, and Christopher Craft, "Alias Bunbury: Desire and Termination in *The Importance of Being Earnest*," *Representations* 31 (Summer 1990): 19–46. Josephine M. Guy and Ian Small believe that the contradictions are in part due to publishing exigencies: simply put, Wilde needed more words and wasn't concerned with setting out a consistent or unified position. *Oscar Wilde's Profession: Writing and the Culture Industry in the Late Nineteenth Century* (Oxford: Oxford University Press), 2000.

8. Julia Prewitt Brown argues that while "Vivian's exaggerations invite correction," Wilde's sympathies are with Vivian. *Cosmopolitan Criticism: Oscar Wilde's Philosophy of Art* (Charlottesville: University Press of Virginia, 1997), 69. Lawrence Danson suggests that Gilbert and Vivian are the characters who introduce Wilde's positions in the dialogues, though Danson is attentive to the many inconsistencies. *Wilde's Intentions: The Artist in his Criticism* (Oxford: Clarendon Press, 1997). Other critics maintain that neither speaker should be seen as a mouthpiece for Wilde. Herbert Sussman argues that both speakers in the dialogues represent aspects of Wilde's views and cautions that it is a mistake to attempt to extract "Wilde's critical principles from the varied ways in which they are expressed." Herbert Sussman, "Criticism as Art: Form in Oscar Wilde's Critical Writing," *Studies in Philology* 70 (1973): 112.

9. We know that Wilde's "Decay of Lying" had its origins in an essay that became Vivian's speeches in the dialogue, so Wilde chose not to present the views as straightforward exposition.

10. Paul Ricoeur and Hans-Georg Gadamer, among others in recent hermeneutics, make comparable claims. Ricoeur writes: "What the text means now matters more than what the author meant when he wrote it." *Interpretation Theory: Discourse and the Surplus of Meaning* (Fort Worth: Texas Christian University Press, 1976), 30. Gadamer says: "What is fixed in writing has detached itself from the contingency of its origin and its author and made itself free for new relationships." *Truth and Method*, 2nd ed., trans. Joel Weinsheimer and Donald G. Marshall (New York: Crossroad, 1990), 357.

11. Amanda Anderson argues that Wilde's view is "a radicalization of Arnold's ideal of disinterestedness." *The Powers of Distance: Cosmopolitanism and the Cultivation of Detachment* (Princeton: Princeton University Press, 2001), 152.

12. Wilde's arguments on the personal nature of interpretation have something in common with Norman N. Holland's "transactive" model of interpretation. Holland also argues that what appear to be objective readings are in fact personal responses

triggered by the text, and he sees reading as a form of self-analysis and self-actualization. See *The Dynamics of Literary Response* (Oxford: Oxford University Press, 1968).

13. Gilbert's formulation of impressionism is noticeably similar to Anatole France's, who writes in 1887: "As I understand criticism it is, like philosophy and history, a kind of novel for the use of discreet and curious minds. And every novel rightly understood is an autobiography. The good critic is he who relates the adventures of his soul among masterpieces. There is no such thing as objective criticism any more than there is objective art, and all who flatter themselves that they put ought but themselves into their work are dupes of the most fallacious illusion. The truth is that one never gets out of oneself. . . . The best we can do, it seems to me, is gracefully to recognize this terrible situation and to admit that we speak of ourselves every time that we have not the strength to be silent. To be quite frank, the critic ought to say: 'Gentlemen, I am going to talk about myself on the subject of Shakespeare.'" "The Adventures of the Soul," *The Literary Life*, trans. Ludwig Lewisohn, in *A Modern Book of Criticism* (New York: Modern Library, 1919), 1.

14. E. D. Hirsch, "Objective Interpretation," *PMLA* 75 (1960): 470–79.

15. *Literary Criticism of Oscar Wilde*, ed. Stanley Weintraub (Lincoln: University of Nebraska Press, 1968), 244–45. Henceforth cited in the text as *Reviews*.

16. For a discussion of Wilde's belief in "organic memory" see *Oscar Wilde's Oxford Notebooks: A Portrait of Mind in the Making*, ed. Philip Smith and Michael Helfand (New York: Oxford University Press, 1989).

17. Many critics have noted that a strong ethical element runs throughout Wilde's work. See, for instance, Phillip K. Cohen, *The Moral Vision of Oscar Wilde* (Rutherford, NJ: Fairleigh Dickinson University Press, 1978), and John Quintus Allen, "The Moral Implications of Oscar Wilde's Aestheticism," *Texas Studies in Literature and Language* 22.4 (1980): 559–74.

18. See, for instance, Regenia Gagnier, Introduction to *Critical Essays on Oscar Wilde* (New York: Macmillan, 1991), 8, and Jonathan Dollimore, "Different Desires."

19. The short version of "The Portrait of Mr. W. H." was published in 1889; the long version, which I treat here, was written sometime between 1889 and 1893. Wilde greatly expands the narrator's analysis of the sonnets in the longer version.

20. Bruce Bashford argues in "Hermeneutics in Oscar Wilde's 'The Portrait of Mr. W. H.'" that Wilde puts forth an inspiration theory of interpretation at this time, which he later rejects in "The Critic as Artist." Bashford's presentation of Dilthey's hermeneutic as an inspirational hermeneutic on the model of that discussed in Plato's *Ion* is puzzling. *Papers on Language and Literature* 24.4 (1998): 413–22. Other treatments of interpretation in the story include Regenia Gagnier, *Idylls of the Marketplace: Oscar Wilde and the Victorian Public* (Stanford, CA: Stanford University Press, 1986), 39–36, and Louis J. Poteet, "Romantic Aesthetics in Oscar Wilde's 'Mr. W. H.,'" *Studies in Short Fiction* 7 (1970): 458–64.

21. A comparison of the narrator's interpretation with one presented by the Shakespearean scholar F. G. Fleay shows how closely Wilde engaged contemporary analysis. Fleay's essay seems to be written to defend Shakespeare against charges of homosexuality, although the topic is never more than alluded to in equivocal ways. His methods are strikingly similar to the narrator's; he uses like forms of argument, also reconstructing a largely imaginary narrative from the sonnets. "On the Motive of Shakspere's Sonnets (1–125): A Defense of his Morality," *Macmillan's Magazine*, (March 1875): 433–45.

22. Horst Schroeder, *Annotations to Oscar Wilde, The Portrait of Mr. W. H.* (Braunschweig, Ger.: privately printed, 1986). Schroeder demonstrates that a number of lines are taken verbatim or almost verbatim from the works of Victorian Shakespeare critics.

23. See Christopher Stray, *Classics Transformed: Schools, Universities, and Society in England, 1830–1960* (Oxford: Clarendon Press, 1998) for a discussion of changes in the approach to classics in the period.

24. See Horst Schroeder's reception study, *Oscar Wilde, The Portrait of Mr. W. H.—Its Composition, Publication, and Reception* (Braunschweig: Braunschweiger Anglistische Arbeiten 9, 1984). Schroeder points out that the story was treated as Shakespearean criticism when it first appeared, with the majority of the reviewers ignoring the fictional aspects altogether. Alfred Douglas was later to argue that Wilde was entirely serious about the interpretation, writing that "it is a thousand pities that he did not write it and put it forth as a theory and nothing else," rather than leaving "his readers in doubt as to whether he is really advancing a serious theory or simply indulging in a clever piece of 'leg-pulling'" (quoted in Schroeder, 54).

25. See Lawrence Danson, "Oscar Wilde, W. H., and the Unspoken Name of Love," *ELH* 59.4 (1991): 979–1000.

26. Gerhard Joseph, "Framing Wilde," *Victorian Newsletter* (Fall 1987): 61–63.

27. Wilde said to Robbie Ross on completion of "Mr. W. H.," "My next Shakespeare book will be a discussion as to whether the commentators on Hamlet are mad or only pretending to be." Richard Ellman, *Oscar Wilde* (New York: Vintage, 1984), 299.

28. Robert Ross claimed that the story demonstrates "Wilde's favorite theory that when you convert someone to an idea, you lose your faith in it." See his Introduction to *Miscellanies* in *The First Collected Edition of the Works of Oscar Wilde*, 15 vols. (London: Dawsons, 1969), 14:xiii.

29. Ed Cohen argues that Wilde "encodes traces of male homoerotic desire" in *Dorian Gray*, sublimating them in the discussion of aesthetic concerns. See "Writing Gone Wilde: Homoerotic Desire in the Closet of Representation," *PMLA* 102 (1987): 801–13.

30. F. J. Furnivall, *Great Thoughts from Master Minds* (1910), 8:90, quoted in William Benzie, *Dr. F. J. Furnivall: A Victorian Scholar Adventurer* (Norman, OK: Pilgrim Books, 1983), 191.

31. Gerhard Joseph notes in his fine short essay "Framing Wilde" that Wilde becomes Arnoldian in wanting this letter to be seen "as in itself it really is."

32. A notable exception is Julia Prewitt Brown, who in *Cosmopolitan Criticism* sees *De Profundis* as "the culmination of the Wildean aesthetic speculations" (xiii).

33. W. B. Yeats, quoted in *The Letters of Oscar Wilde*, ed. Rupert Hart-Davis (New York: Harcourt, Brace, and World, 1962), 270 n. 1.

Epilogue

1. George Henry Lewes, *Problems of Life and Mind*, 3rd series, *The Study of Psychology* (Boston: Houghton, Osgood, 1879), 85.
George Trumball Ladd, author of the epigraph that begins this epilogue, was a nineteenth-century psychologist. The quotation is from his "Contribution to the Psychology of Visual Dreams," *Mind* 1:2 (April 1892): 299–304.

2. Sigmund Freud, *The Interpretation of Dreams*, trans. James Strachey (1900; New York: Basic Books, 1955), 48.

3. James Sully, "The Dream as a Revelation," *Fortnightly Review* 59 (March 1893): 364.

4. Ian Hacking argues that these sciences of memory were born in the nineteenth century as a way of secularizing the soul, giving science control over the last sphere from which it had been excluded. *Rewriting the Soul: Multiple Personality and the Sciences of Memory* (Princeton: Princeton University Press, 1995).

5. W. H. Burnham, "Memory, Historically and Experimentally Considered," *American Journal of Psychology* 2 (1882): 39–90, 225–70, 431–64, 566–622.

6. See Jenny Bourne Taylor and Sally Shuttleworth, *Embodied Selves: An Anthology of Psychological Texts, 1830–1890* (Oxford: Clarendon Press, 1998) for an excellent selection of primary texts on memory.

7. Nicholas Dames argues that the nineteenth-century novel from Jane Austen onward depends on "nostalgic forgetting" and "the construction of an 'amnesiac self.'" *Amnesiac Selves* (New York: Oxford University Press, 2001), 7.

8. James Sully, "Illusions of Memory," in *Illusions: A Psychological Study* (New York: DaCapo Press, 1982), 232. Hereafter cited in text by page number.

9. R. Verdon, "Forgetfulness," *Mind* 2.8 (1877): 439.

10. James Mill, *Analysis of the Phenomena of the Human Mind*, ed. John Stuart Mill (London: Longmans, 1869), 2:174.

11. Frances Power Cobbe, "The Fallacies of Memory," in *Hours of Work and Play* (Philadelphia: J. B. Lippincott, 1867), 87.

12. Jacques Derrida, *Mémoires: For Paul de Man*, trans. Cecile Lindsay, Jonathan Culler, and Eduardo Cadava (New York: Columbia University Press, 1986), 57–58.

13. Friedrich Nietzsche, *On the Genealogy of Morals*, in *On the Genealogy of Morals and Ecce Homo*, trans. Walter Kaufmann and R. J. Hollingdale (New York: Vintage, 1967), III 12.

Index